ONE-PIECE FLOW

Cell Design for Transforming
the Production Process

ONE-PIECE FLOW

Cell Design for Transforming the Production Process

by Kenichi Sekine

Translated by Bruce Talbot

Originally published as *Ikko nagashi* by the Nikkan Kogyo Shimbun, Ltd., Tokyo © 1990.

Productivity Press
444 Park Avenue South, Suite 604
New York, NY 10016
United States of America
Telephone: 212-686-5900
Fax: 212-686-5411
Email: info@productivitypress.com

Printed and bound by BookCrafters
Printed in the United States of America

91-23723
CIP

02 01 00 99 98   12 11 10 9

Contents

Illustrations

Publisher's Message

Something has happened to manufacturing in the last decade. In a word, *revolution*. No longer can we daydream about reconfiguring our traditional large-lot manufacturing operations into a flow production system based on making one, or only a few, items at a time. If we don't do it now, we will perish.

This masterful book, *One-Piece Flow: Cell Design for Transforming the Production Process* tells why and how to restructure the traditional Ford-type assembly production plant into a one-piece flow operation based on the demands of the marketplace — not the planning department. The author, Kenichi Sekine, is a phenomenon among Japan's leading consultants. He is experienced, friendly to his readers, and a good writer. He studied with the late great Shigeo Shingo and applies the latest advances in the deployment of the Toyota Production System.

Sekine prepared this extraordinary book for the Western manufacturer. Consisting of chapters taken from two books originally published in Japan (*Cutting Assembly Personnel in Half*, 1988, and *Practical Process Razing*, 1986), it presents the basic background and application methods necessary to understand and implement one-piece production and manpower reduction. "Process razing" is Sekine's term for improving the design of manufacturing cells and plant floor layouts in industry.

In Chapter 1, Sekine explains the concept of one-piece flow production beginning with the Ford Production System. He discusses its evolution into market-oriented one-piece production, its rules and conditions, and how to achieve it.

Chapter 2 presents fourteen four-part (THEME, PLAN, ACTION, RESULT) improvement case studies on how to cut assembly personnel by half.

Sekine covers a variety of industries including electronic component assembly, a printing plant, transformer coils, fishing rod assembly, power supply assembly, and an assembly conveyor line.

In Chapter 3, the topics are changeover improvement versus process razing in building a wide-variety small-lot production line. Sekine discusses product-quantity (P-Q) analysis, process route analysis, equipment-specific layouts, vertical layouts, circular layouts, and others. A "Test Your Skills" section leads the reader through changing a three-worker line into one requiring a single operator.

Chapter 4 looks at "overstaffing" waste and how it can be eliminated by applying the process-razing method. Sekine discusses three approaches: (1) reducing in-process inventory waste, (2) reducing standby waste, and (3) reducing operation waste by changing human operation time into machine operation time.

Chapter 5 defines eight process-razing steps and provides examples of their application on a gear processing line and a welding process, among others.

In Chapter 6, the author tells how and why to eliminate conveyors from assembly lines. He discusses the avoidance of circular layout designs that are often used as alternatives. Emphasis is placed on learning process-razing techniques, and examples show how to begin.

Chapter 7 carefully examines the basic principles of building U-shaped cells for assembly — tearing down the lot production system and implementing U-shaped cells that promote both one-piece flow production and one-piece inspection. The case studied is a garment factory whose actions are juxtaposed with a motor assembly operation.

Chapter 8 establishes U-shaped cells for assembly lines regardless of product type. Each step is examined in the process of change and improving operations (such as dealing with missing items and preventing rework). Topics covered include *kanban*, the tickler system, zero changeover, and preventive maintenance. "Test Your Skills" leads the reader through what is wrong in a specific U-shaped cell design.

Chapter 9 looks at U-shaped cells for electronic component assembly. Sekine begins with the mammoth assembly lines first encountered in such an operation and follows by applying process-razing techniques. The case study is of a maker of power supply switches and the reader is asked to come up with a manpower reduction plan and examine waste elimination methods.

Chapter 10 presents an overall discussion of removing waste from factories — the basis of process razing. Looking at the classic Gilbreth study of bricklaying operations, Sekine does a motion study for assembly lines. "Test Your Skills" asks the reader to eliminate walking waste from an assembly process.

The final four chapters are specific — and fascinating — case studies that apply Sekine's methods. Chapter 11 studies changeover improvements in Japan's largest plastic molding factory, Starlight Industries in Osaka. Sekine looks at linking the assembly line with the plastic molding equipment, a large mold changeover, and achieving single changeover for color changes in six months. "Test Your Skills" has the reader determine optimal free shot conditions and the minimum number of injection shots needed (the measure of this particular industry's success in changeover tests).

While many studies have looked at Toyota Production System's success in large-lot production, few show similar successes at factories producing small lots on a customer-order basis. Chapter 12 does just that with Oriental Motor's establishment of one-piece production for its immense array of 60,000 product models.

Chapter 13 studies how MYNAC, a ready-to-wear apparel manufacturer, achieved "single delivery." With a previous lead time of fifteen to thirty days from receipt of bolts of cloth, MYNAC workers challenged themselves to reduce their production period to a "single" nine-day period.

Chapter 14 is a case study of Kumamoto Electronics. While the electronics industry works with various high-tech materials and components, it is amazing how low-tech some of its factories are. Assembly operations often rely on large batches of workers seated along assembly lines. Using the example of mounting components on printed circuit boards (PCBs), Sekine discusses how companies can reduce their PCB mounting personnel by half by adopting new production methods.

Sekine's expertise lies in the specific areas of implementing TPS, JIT, zero setup, innovative Total Productive Maintenance (TPM), and inventory reduction as well as cutting assembly/processing personnel and the design period and personnel in half. Although he has produced numerous books and videos in Japan, this is his first book published in English. It will be followed shortly by a companion video training set.

Kenichi Sekine attended Kurume Industrial Special School and joined Bridgestone in 1948 where, as chief quality control inspector, he introduced TQC and promoted Deming Prize activities. From 1968 to 1972, he worked for a Toyota affiliate promoting the Toyota Production System. He founded the TPS Consulting Group in 1973 and the Value-added Management Institute (TPS Consulting Company, Ltd.) in 1985. Its accomplishments include providing consulting on worksite IE to Toyota-affiliated companies, building U-shaped lines and load-load lines with minimum personnel in the assembly departments of a number of Japanese companies, and providing consulting on the JIT production system and on the wide-variety (or high-diversified) small-lot production systems.

There is an urgent need today for those in manufacturing to reduce (to under ten minutes) — or even eliminate (by incorporating it totally within the cycle time) — changeover time. The demand for wide-variety small-lot production has brought changeover loss to 20 percent or more of a company's overall losses. I recommend Mr. Sekine and his methods to you unabashedly. He has proved their value again and again.

Many people made this book possible. I sincerely thank Kenichi Sekine for choosing us as his American publisher. I also am grateful to Hajime Kitamura, director of publication for Nikkan Kogyo Shimbun, Ltd., Mr. Sekine's Japanese publisher, for allowing us to produce this material in the United States. Lastly, I wish to acknowledge the efforts of Bruce Talbot, translator; Steven Ott, vice president of Productivity Press; Cheryl Rosen, series/acquisition editor, and Dorothy Lohmann, managing editor; Bill Berling, freelance copyeditor; Jennifer Cross, indexer; the production team of David Lennon, Kathlin Sweeney, Gayle Joyce, Caroline Kutil, and Karla Tolbert; Joyce C. Weston, cover design; and Maple-Vail Book Manufacturing Group, printing and binding.

Norman Bodek

Preface

You must tear down the old to build the new.
— K. Sekine

The just-in-time (JIT) concept was invented by Toyota Motor Company executive Taiichi Ohno one day in 1954 as he was taking a tour of an American supermarket. He noticed how shoppers pushed their carts up and down the rows of shelves, selecting only the types and amounts of products that they needed right then. This type of shopping, in which the end user (the shopper) is able to "pull" exactly the types and amounts of products needed from a wide variety of shelved stock, was still a dream to the average shopper in Japan.

It occurred to this Toyota executive that enabling the shopper (the downstream process) to freely select and purchase just what he or she needs from the next upstream process (generally, the assembly process) would naturally tend to eliminate assembly-related problems such as standby due to missing parts, overproduction, overpurchasing, and inventory waste.

Thus was born the first principle of JIT production, namely that downstream processes "pull" products from upstream processes. In this sense, we can say that the United States provided the inspiration for the birth of the Toyota production system.

The pioneer of one-piece flow — Henry Ford — was also American. There are two basic approaches to assembling automobiles. The first is to have assembly workers move among the various automobiles under assembly to attach parts. The automobiles stay in fixed positions and the assembly workers do the moving around.

Ford invented the second approach: he connected a rope to the automobiles under assembly and had them pulled along through the various assembly stages. In this way, the cars were moved, assembled, and inspected one at a time. Using this new one-piece-flow approach, the Ford assembly plant managed to cut assembly time by about half. And thus we have another American origin for part of what today is regarded as a Japanese approach to production.

Why did these JIT concepts take root and develop in Japan rather than in the United States? One reason is that Japanese industry was starting from scratch right after its defeat in World War II. Most of Japan's prewar industry had been razed to the ground, and there was precious little left. During the postwar recovery period, the idea was to catch up to and one day surpass America.

The Japanese knew they had a lot to learn in order to catch up, but they also knew that they could not surpass the United States merely by imitating it. One of Japan's original developments came when Japanese factory managers rejected the American idea of having specialized jobs for factory workers. Instead, they trained factory workers to handle several types of jobs, now referred to as multiprocess handling. This method was applied to machining lines in Japan. The development of U-shaped cells evolved from the application of multiprocess handling.

Even if the concepts of multiprocess handling and U-shaped cells had been invented in the United States, America's development of strong skill-specific (craft-based) trade unions would have made their implementation very difficult there. In Japan, however, where labor unions are company-based, the implementation of JIT concepts has been relatively easier.

As JIT production developed in Japan, the following three principles came to the fore as most essential:

- pull production
- one-piece flow
- multiprocess handling in U-shaped cells

I do not mean to suggest that the process of developing a production system based on the above three principles was problem-free. To the contrary, many hurdles had to be cleared, such as negotiations with labor unions over the introduction of multiprocess handling, problems in skills training, worker discipline, and so on.

Japanese companies found that the road to successful introduction of one-piece flow lay in making "process-building" improvements in the factory via the following seven steps:

1. Build an environment for multiprocess handling and develop worker discipline and training.

2. Build U-shaped cells and devise defect prevention measures.

3. Establish cycle-time production. Calculate the minimum required number of workers and the optimal work distribution.

4. Make changeover improvements and work toward zero changeover.

5. Establish pull production and its corresponding supply system and take measures to prevent missing items.

6. Introduce simple automation methods.

7. Gradually introduce the kanban system.

This book has a companion video presentation available through Productivity Press. It introduces the steps and case studies described in this book in a more easily understood audio-visual format. Consultants who have mastered these one-piece flow techniques and who lend their guidance to factories still unexposed to these techniques have been surprised to find that the factory staff hold them in awe, as if they possessed some magical means of achieving factory improvement.

Among the case studies of such factory improvement in Japan is the example of Company T, where in just two months the number of workers on an electronic component assembly line at Factory K was reduced from 27 to 15, and four months later it was further reduced to 12. In case after case, it has been shown that assembly lines can use these techniques to cut their personnel needs by half.

To cite a few more examples, Factory T cut its switch assembly line personnel from 11 to 4 persons and Factory S reduced staffing on each of its eight transformer coil winding lines from 6 to 3 workers, thereby freeing up 24 workers in all. Factory S also turned its 10-person converter line into a 7-person line. At Factory Y, the 13-person filter assembly line was improved to where it needed only 5 people. At Company O, small-motor assembly lines saw their required manpower shrink from 9 persons to 2 persons over a three-year period. Since Company O operates 40 small-motor assembly lines, the total manpower reduction came to 280 workers.

Among the most recent examples is Company M, where over a three-year period the manpower requirement for the assembly and processing lines at the company's automobile carburetor factory were cut from 10 workers per line to just 5 per line, and since there are 50 lines, that meant a manpower reduction of 250 workers.

But for lack of space, I would also list many similar examples of dramatic reductions in manpower needs that have been achieved in South Korea.

I hope I have cited enough examples to gain the reader's interest in what this book has to offer. Please read the material. Then begin dismantling your current production system to make room for a new improved one. There is no question but that you will succeed. This book and tape set is the product of a decade of experience-based know-how in factory improvement, garnered by myself and my colleagues.

If you are a manager or IE professional who does not know how to proceed in achieving sure-fire factory improvement, this is just what you need. If all U.S. manufacturers were to implement the lessons taught herein, the productivity of their industry would more than double and U.S.-Japan trade friction would subside.

If, for some reason, any of my American readers find these lessons either hard to understand or ineffective for making improvements, contact me through my publisher, Productivity Press. I will gladly fly to the United States and personally explain the meaning of "process-razing know-how." I guarantee the quality of this product.

Part I
Basics

1

The Basic Concept of One-Piece Production

At Company T, they call it "one-piece flow." At Company O, it is "one-piece production." Chairman K's engineering background taught him that his company's customers could be best served by switching from batch-style operations to one-piece operations that extend from one-piece ordering to one-piece flow, one-piece production, one-piece inspection, and one-piece delivery.

This chapter explains the basic concept of one-piece production.

HENRY FORD: FOUNDER OF ONE-PIECE PRODUCTION

Let us first look at Figure 1-1, which illustrates how Henry Ford created one-piece production.

There were two basic concepts for assembling automobiles. One was to keep the automobiles stationary while moving the assembly workers around; the other was to keep the assembly workers stationary while moving the automobiles around.

Recognizing how bulky and heavy the automobiles were, Ford initially thought it better to follow the first concept. However, one day, while looking for ways to eliminate waste from assembly processes, Ford noticed the following:

- waste in the scattered movements of workers
- waste in searching for, comparing, and finding objects
- waste in conveying objects

After noticing these types of waste, Ford thought long and hard about how he could eliminate them. Finally, he hit upon the idea of mounting cars on a

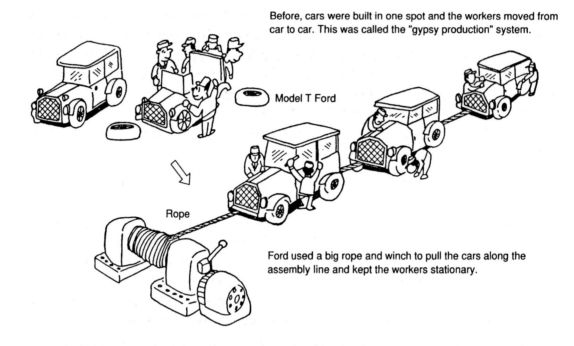

Before, cars were built in one spot and the workers moved from car to car. This was called the "gypsy production" system.

Model T Ford

Rope

Ford used a big rope and winch to pull the cars along the assembly line and kept the workers stationary.

Figure 1-1. Ford's Invention of One-Piece Production

row of carts that could be pulled along by a rope and winch. Right away, he issued the following instructions to his employees:

1. Set up a large winch and a long, thick rope to pull the automobiles along during assembly.
2. Since the factory was about 80 meters long, divide the assembly line into 15 one-hour processes. This would allow the rope to pull all of the automobiles to the next process once per hour.
3. Distribute the assembly parts to their corresponding processes before they are needed.
4. Assign three or four workers to each process and work out the balance of labor by observing the assembly line.

The experiment was a big success. It reduced the assembly time per vehicle from 13 hours to just five hours and 50 minutes. Later, Ford's assembly line bosses conducted their own little experiments to further eliminate waste and to improve the division of processes and the balance of labor. They found it particularly effective, for example, to assign the most experienced assembly workers to the final assembly processes. Pulling the automobiles forward from up-stream processes also helped the assembly workers improve their skills, so that in only three months the per-unit assembly time was reduced to just 2 hours and 38 minutes. The Ford Production System became famous for its flow-type assembly, in which units moved at a steady rhythm.

Although Ford had successfully established one-piece flow production for his automobile assembly operations, his machining operations were still done batch-by-batch for three reasons:

1. Maximizing the capacity utilization of the equipment was emphasized since the equipment was very expensive.
2. The craft-oriented labor unions taught workers to stick to certain skills and to not "invade the territory" of workers with other skills.
3. Conventional wisdom emphasized by Frederick Taylor and others said that things are always "cheaper by the dozen." (This point of view is still strong today in areas such as the process industry, where a "high operating rate" remains a chief selling point for products.)

Meanwhile, people at another automobile company that we shall call Company T were intent on keeping up with Ford. Cunningly, they managed to have a look at a Ford factory and studied up on whatever relevant literature they could find. They eventually reached the conclusion that the Ford Production System was based on the use of conveyors and one-piece flow.

It is hard to successfully make improvements if you rely simply on what you know. Those who proposed setting up a Ford-style production system at Company T decided they would apply the principle of one-piece flow not only to assembly processes but to machining processes as well. As a result, this meant that they had to reduce their machining changeover time to zero. Their attempts to do this resulted in what we now know as U-shaped cells for machining processes.

ONE-PIECE PRODUCTION MEANS MARKET-ORIENTED PRODUCTION

In a seller's market (product-out orientation) where just about whatever is made sells, materials requirement planning (the MRP approach) is all we need. First we draw up a sales plan, then we set up a standard production schedule to suit the plan. After that, we have a computer work out the parts lists, order lists, and goods to be procured for each day of production. Both processing and assembly become orderly, logical, and neat. If this results in the factory's output exceeding the current number of orders, products still can be shipped off to intermediaries and eventually be sold.

We have lived in an era of relative peace and prosperity in which people are not interested in run-of-the-mill products. Markets are diversifying and individual preferences determine buying patterns. Consumers no longer buy according to a scientific sales plan developed by market researchers. What does not sell gets warehoused. If it sits in the warehouse for over three months, it becomes dead inventory.

In times such as these, we cannot afford to have planning-oriented production. Although it may be an oversimplification, we should be encouraged to set sales targets and be discouraged from setting up detailed production schedules. In other words, we must adopt the concept of market-oriented production.

Figure 1-2 shows an outline of one-piece production. Notice that the processes that are closest to the market are the assembly processes.

At the assembly processes, workers assemble only what has been brought to the process (i.e., what has already been sold and awaits delivery). These processes use *kanban* to order parts from the machining processes to replace the parts used in the previous assembly order. Likewise, the machining processes send kanban to the materials storehouses to order new supplies of materials after each machining job.

As we see in Figure 1-2, this system includes the use of kanban. Accordingly, one can say that this kind of one-piece production system strongly emphasizes the assembly processes. Let us take a closer look at the rules and conditions governing one-piece production.

RULES AND CONDITIONS OF ONE-PIECE PRODUCTION

Rule 1: Base the cycle time (CT) on market requirements.

Figure 1-3 illustrates the basic approach to one-piece production. This approach starts by coordinating the timing of production with customer needs. In other words, we base the number of items to be produced on the number required by the customers.

Under this approach, the basic principle of cycle time is that the selling cycle time (S_C) should equal the manufacturing cycle time (S_M). This is shown in Figure 1-3 as the equation $S_C = S_M$. The S_C cycle time includes the whole-salers' speculative demand.

Rule 2: Base equipment capacity utilization on cycle time.

Figure 1-4 describes the quality, cost, delivery, and safety (QCDS) factors for equipment based on one-piece production.

Establishing one-piece production is most difficult when using large equipment and other devices that production engineers have designed for flexible manufacturing system (FMS) applications. Such equipment and devices are intended for batch production and are not at all easy to coordinate with one-piece production cycle times.

Rule 3: Center production on assembly processes.

While turning away from planning-centered production, we must also shun the traditional emphasis on processing (such as machining) of parts.

In one-piece production systems, the latest market information is passed exclusively to the assembly department, which also receives a weekly production plan based on that information. The information is not passed to any upstream processes. Instead, the upstream processes receive orders to replace the goods used up by the assembly processes. In other words, the factory follows the *pull production* principle.

Rule 4: Factory layout must be conducive to one-piece production.

Figure 1-5 shows the vertical nature of the factory layout that includes many U-shaped cells consisting of several machines operated by just one operator.

1. Make the factory layout conducive to the overall production flow.
2. The factory must include clear pathways.
3. The production line should clearly distinguish between material input and product output.
4. The production line should consist mainly of single-operator U-shaped cells.

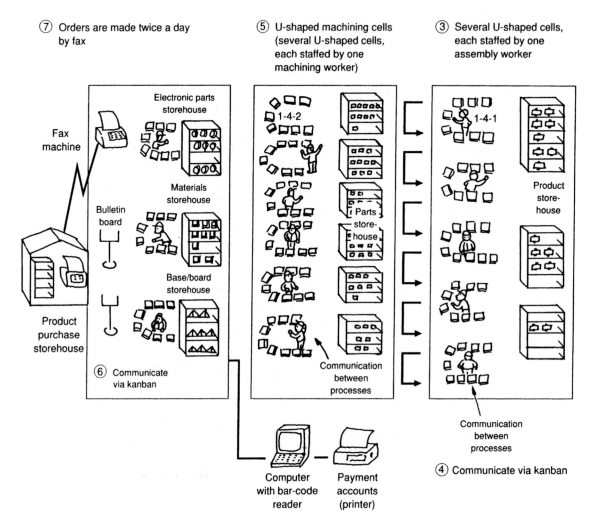

⑦ Orders are made twice a day by fax

⑤ U-shaped machining cells (several U-shaped cells, each staffed by one machining worker)

③ Several U-shaped cells, each staffed by one assembly worker

Fax machine

Electronic parts storehouse

1-4-2

1-4-1

Product store-house

Materials storehouse

Bulletin board

Parts store-house

Base/board storehouse

⑥ Communicate via kanban

Product purchase storehouse

Communication between processes

Communication between processes

④ Communicate via kanban

Computer with bar-code reader

Payment accounts (printer)

Figure 1-2. Market-oriented Just-in-Time Production

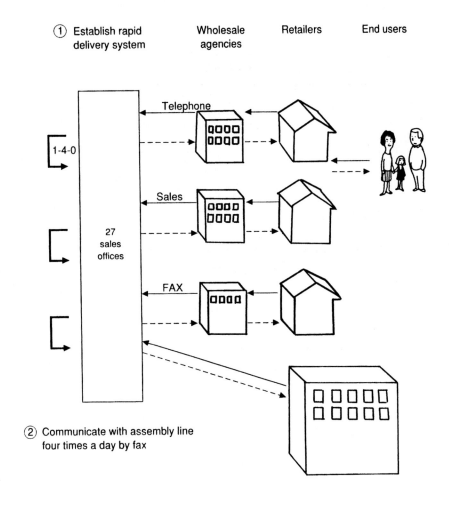

① Establish rapid delivery system

Wholesale agencies

Retailers

End users

1-4-0

27 sales offices

Telephone

Sales

FAX

② Communicate with assembly line four times a day by fax

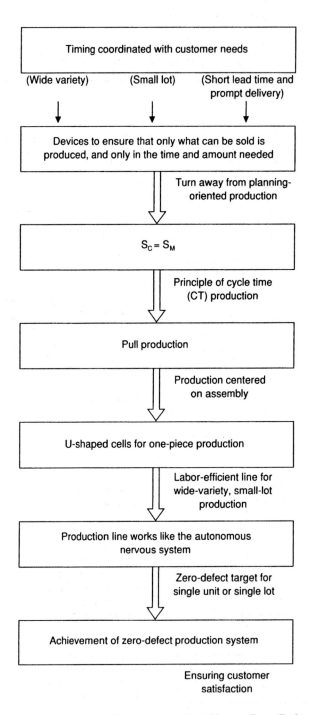

Figure 1-3. One-Piece Production Means Zero-Defect Production

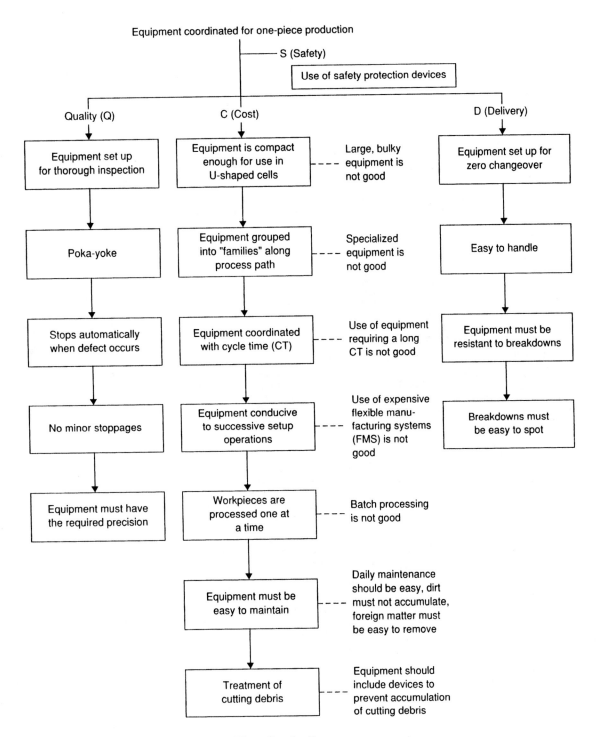

Figure 1-4. QCDS Factors for One-Piece Production

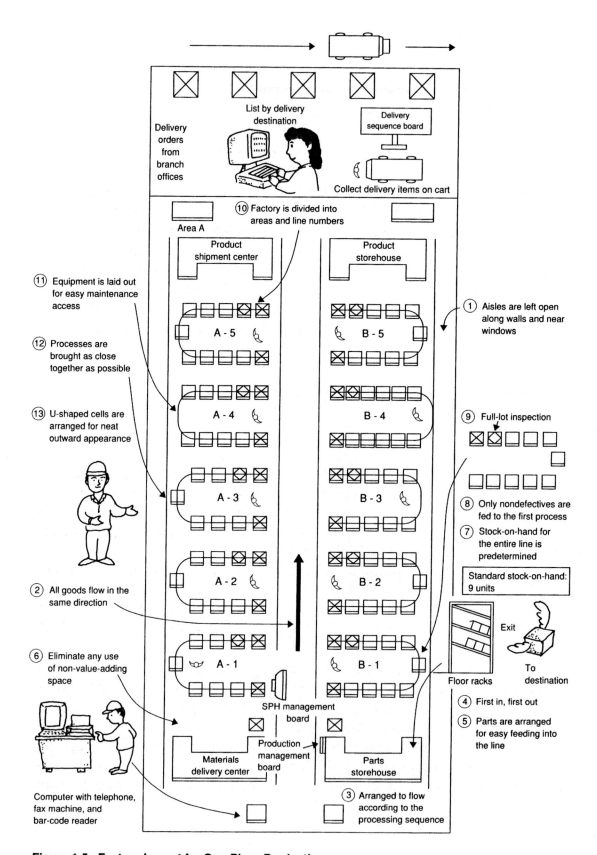

Figure 1-5. Factory Layout for One-Piece Production

5. Include thorough inspection in the layout.

6. Minimize in-process inventory.

Rule 5: Goods must be conducive to one-piece production.

Generally, very small workpieces are not conducive to one-piece production because of the waste involved in the setup, positioning, and removal of such small items. If their conveyance can be completely automated and the cycle time is not long, however, one-piece production is still possible.

It is also impossible to have one-piece production if changeover times are long. In such cases, we can pave the way for it by making improvements toward achieving zero changeover. When a wide variety of parts entails many time-consuming changeover operations, however, one-piece production is impossible.

HOW TO ACHIEVE ONE-PIECE PRODUCTION

Abolish planning-centered production.

The concept of one-piece production differs radically from that of materials requirement planning (MRP). Even when MRP is used in a system that supplies "just what is needed, just in the amount needed, and just when it is needed" to factories, it is still a system based on standard production planning and therefore does not really suit the just-in-time philosophy.

Standard production planning takes sales plans based on scientific market research or demand forecasts taken from statistical trends and tries to revise and fine-tune them to meet market needs. Such efforts do little good, however, and are analogous to an amateur golfer trying to score a hole-in-one on a short hole (see Figure 1-6).

This kind of planning-oriented production system ends up being a system that requires pushing for sales. The factory unloads its output onto the wholesalers, the wholesalers end up returning what they cannot sell, and the returned items end up as dead inventory.

By contrast, the one-piece production system outputs products based on the needs of the assembly processes, which are the closest processes to the market. Only when products have been shipped are more products ordered from

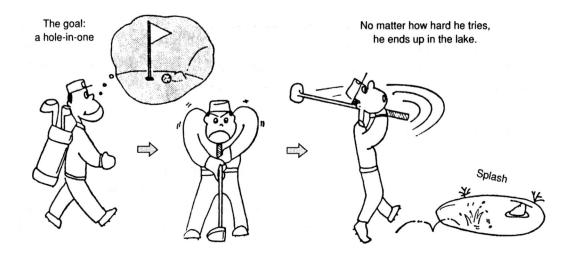

Figure 1-6. Perfection in Standard Production Planning Is Like a Hole-in-One in Golf

upstream. Because all parts and materials are pulled from downstream, there is no need for inventory.

Some people find the concept of pull production difficult to understand. Thus, many factory managers are more comfortable with planning-centered systems in which goods are developed, ordered, and procured according to MRP-based specifications.

Abandon the idea that batch production is the most efficient production method.

As Japanese manufacturing companies establish more and more production overseas while using domestic factories to produce the newest, most experimental products, fewer companies still subscribe to the notion of "cheaper by the dozen" batch production.

I recall a certain subcontractor factory that supplied automobile parts in which batch production led to a surplus of parts. A recent rise in the value of the yen hurt its client's automobile sales, and the parts supplier was in the red month after month. They ended up selling off truckloads of parts as scrap metal every month and had a truck come each month to haul away excess inventory.

The company president decided it was time to switch to small-lot production and one-piece flow production. The factory managers, who only understood batch production, tried to switch to small-lot, one-piece flow production while still using the same large equipment and horizontal layout that they had used for batch production. They did not know any better, nor did they know anything about having to shorten changeover times.

Should we stop using the word "system"?

Everybody likes to use — and abuse — the word "system." It is a magic word that can be used to charm people. It lends credence and significance to whatever it describes, such as a "production management system," "information system," "automated warehouse system," "MRP system," and so on, ad infinitum.

The word "system" generally implies an overarching idea that helps give shape to the structure and contents of the system components. If we accept this idea and do our work by interpreting factory conditions according to the overall "system" concept, we risk losing touch with reality due to the distortions and misunderstandings built into the system concept. In planning-centered production, we move from plan to plan to plan, and end up wasting a lot of time and energy (see Figure 1-7).

I failed to mention another kind of system; the kind where a wasteful set of components gets organized, waste and all, in a complex system that requires an increase in the number of indirect personnel.

What can we do about such systems? First, we can begin removing waste bit by bit, starting with the assembly processes that are closest to the market. Then we remove the causes of flow retention to build in a better production flow.

"Building in" implies changing the structure and design. It is in keeping with this sense of the word that we seek to remove waste and redesign the factory to build in a better production flow.

We must also abandon the idea of automated warehouses.

For factories attempting to establish one-piece production, automated warehouses present a hundred disadvantages and zero advantages. The biggest drawback of automated warehouses is that they tend to hide waste (see Figure 1-8).

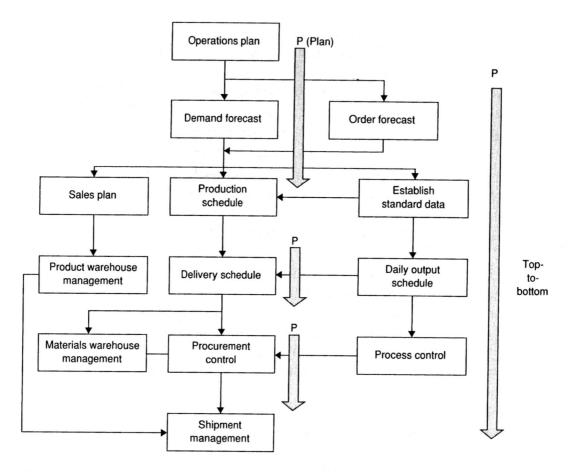

Figure 1-7. The "Plan-Plan-Plan" System

First, there is the standby waste that occurs when inventory is moved into and out of the warehouse.

Second, there are the warehouse supervisors who pride themselves on how much inventory they can handle.

Third, there is the labor expense involved in getting the warehouse computer system installed and running. The result is top-heavy management.

Fourth, the expensive automated warehousing equipment must be put to some kind of use to avoid an embarrassing waste of investment.

Fifth, the one-piece production approach simply goes against the grain of automated warehousing, which is invariably designed for batch production factories.

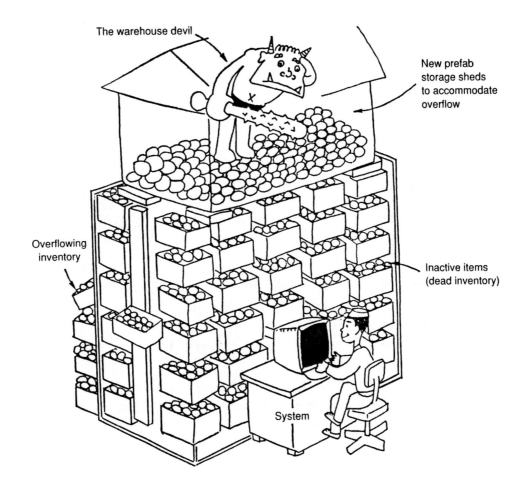

The warehouse devil

New prefab storage sheds to accommodate overflow

Overflowing inventory

Inactive items (dead inventory)

System

Figure 1-8. Abandon the Idea of Automated Warehousing

Abandon the idea of horizontal layout.

If we try to establish one-piece production while hanging onto the idea of horizontal layout, we are ruining our chances of success right from the start. Horizontal layout allows retention to occur all over the factory. Such retention includes not only retention in the flow of in-process inventory but also retention in the flow of information, making it doubly hard to establish smooth-flowing one-piece production.

We need to develop new methods for quality control.

In one-piece production, lots are reduced to the size of a single workpiece. In other words, lots no longer exist. This means that we can no longer think of quality control in terms of random inspection of lot samples or other lot-based statistical quality control methods. In particular, we can no longer think in terms of a calculated defect risk for the manufacturer or consumer. The only method worth considering is a thorough inspection that reduces the consumer's risk of defects to zero.

The only quality control method appropriate for one-piece production is described in the book *Zero Defect Production System* (Nikkan Kogyo Shimbun, 1987) that I coauthored with Sumio Iwasaki. This quality control method has the following characteristics:

- Thorough inspection is built into the production line. Workpieces are conveyed, processed, and inspected one at a time. The result is zero shipped defects.
- When a defect occurs, the line is stopped until the cause is found and eliminated.
- Mistake-proofing devices are built into the production line.
- Quality assurance (QA) managers avoid having to double-check products by building quality (and defect detection) into the processes.
- The inspection department is not independent of the production department.

The one-piece production system was only developed about ten years ago. Consequently, the system is still far from perfect. As I continue to work with people who are establishing one-piece production, I hope that we can put the finishing touches onto this system.

2

Cutting Assembly Personnel by Half: Case Studies

There are countless case studies of factories that have successfully used process razing to cut their assembly personnel needs by half. Such halving of personnel requirements via process razing has been realized not only for assembly lines but also for machining and sheet metal processing, the process industry, design processes, and many other fields.

The following case studies are generally presented as four-part, single-page summaries. First is the *THEME* section, stating the problem (object of improvement) identified through observation of current conditions. Next is the *PLAN* section, describing the improvement targets that must be eliminated to solve the problem named in the theme. After that, the *ACTION* section states what was actually done to make the improvement. Finally, the *RESULT* section sums up the effects of the improvement. A list of these figures follows.

Improvement Case Study

An electronic component assembly plant where, in one year, productivity rose 400 percent, inventory dropped 50 percent, and defects were reduced 90 percent.

The following is a step-by-step description of the successful process-razing campaign carried out by the personnel reduction team at Company A.

Step 1: Form a personnel reduction team centered on the production division chief.

Step 2: Select the target equipment models by applying a product-quantity (P-Q) analysis.

Step 3: Select the target processes.

Step 4: Prepare the data required for process razing beginning with assembly line charts.

Step 5: Carry out waste elimination measures for the assembly line. Although the team actually identified over 50 instances of waste in the assembly line, the *PLAN* section of the summary lists only the three principal types of waste. The group did not go as far as to implement a zero-defects production system for the assembly conveyor.

Step 6: Immediately implement process razing. Ideally, the team could have carried out conveyor razing. Instead, they started out with small improvements and divided the conveyor lengthwise to form two assembly lines staffed by seven people each, which jointly supplied the downstream process.

As a result, they were able to increase the standard production per day (SPD) from 700 units to 800 units while reducing personnel from 20 to 18 workers.

Step 7: Go back and eliminate waste at individual processes. Team efforts were aimed at (1) standby waste, (2) rework waste and defect production waste, and (3) defective board waste. They also switched to standing while working.

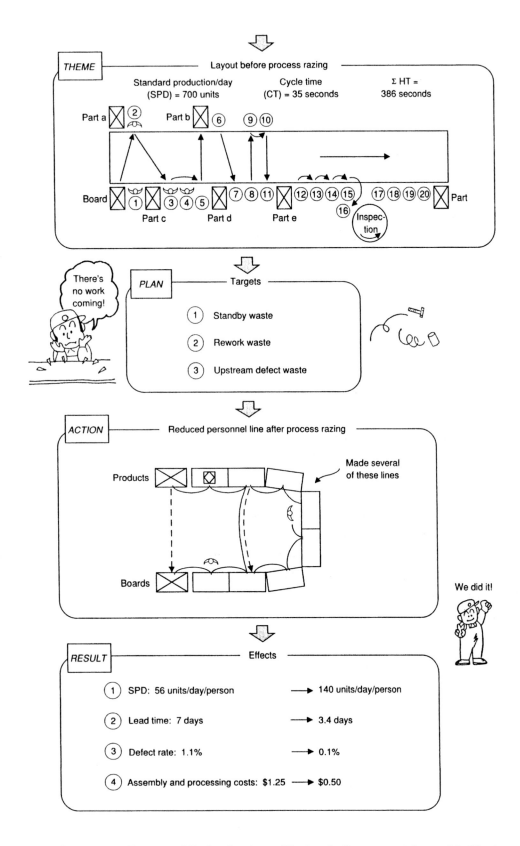

Figure 2-1. Personnel Reduction in an Electronic Component Assembly Plant

Step 8: Calculate the target number of personnel. They calculated the target number of personnel as seven workers per line, all standing while working at linear conveyor assembly operations.

Step 9: Go back once again to eliminate waste.

Step 10: Switch to U-shaped cells, each staffed by three workers.

Step 11: Switch from three-person U-shaped cells to two-person U-shaped cells. Since it was difficult to compare the results to a conveyor line with independent assembly workers, the comparison in the *RESULT* figures were made in relation to standing while working at a linear assembly line.

Improvement Case Study

Name plate manufacturing (from an improvement report issued by the Nagano Diversification Council).

Company F is primarily a metal printing company. It was founded in 1962, has 103 employees, and is currently capitalized at $400,000. In 1985, Company F built a factory in Chino as an integrated factory for plastic products. This factory was designed as a model factory using U-shaped manufacturing cells.

At first, production at the Chino plant revolved around alumite printing. Today, however, it is used mainly for screen printing and other operations that include offset printing and seal printing. Currently the plant is being pressured by its clients to reduce costs from 10 to 30 percent or more. Since the plant's printing operations are relatively labor intensive, management saw buying new, more automated equipment as the only way to meet client needs. Management was also discouraged because the plant's value-added-per-worker figures had improved little over the past three years and real productivity had declined.

Using the information contained in the factory improvement report issued by the Nagano Diversification Council, researchers at the FU Center, Company F's U-shaped cell research group, carried out the improvement campaign shown in Figure 2-8.

As shown in the *PLAN* section of Figure 2-8, while the FU Center found many other instances of minor waste, it focused its waste elimination efforts on the seven primary types. These efforts followed these steps:

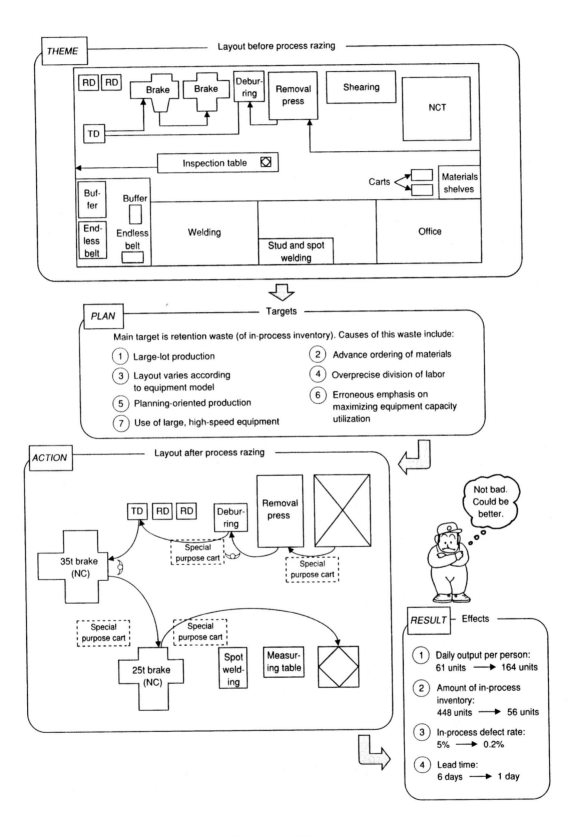

Figure 2-2. Personnel Reduction in a Sheet Metal Plant

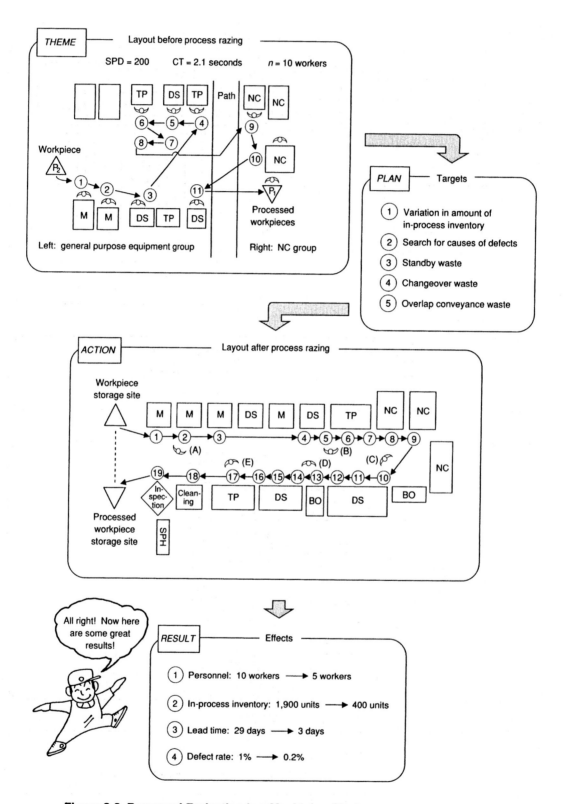

Figure 2-3. Personnel Reduction in a Machining Plant

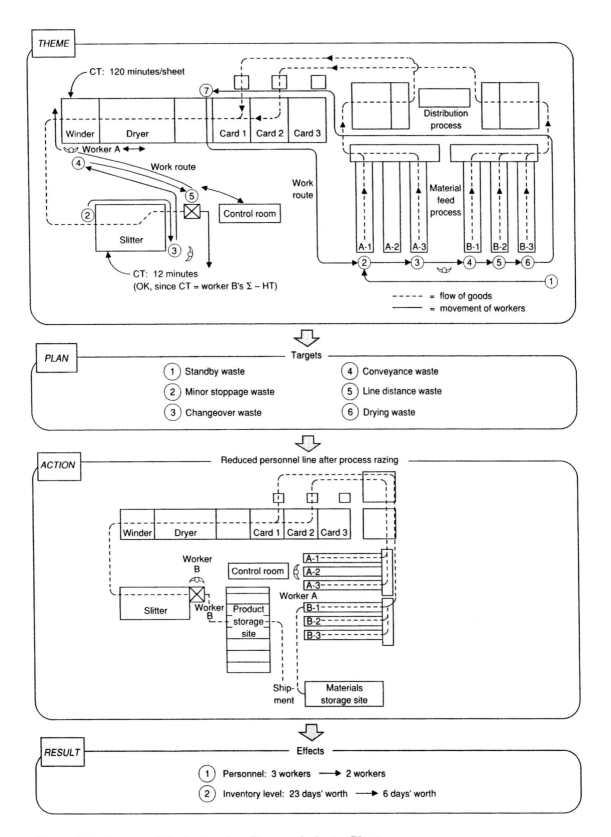

Figure 2-4. Personnel Reduction in a Process Industry Plant

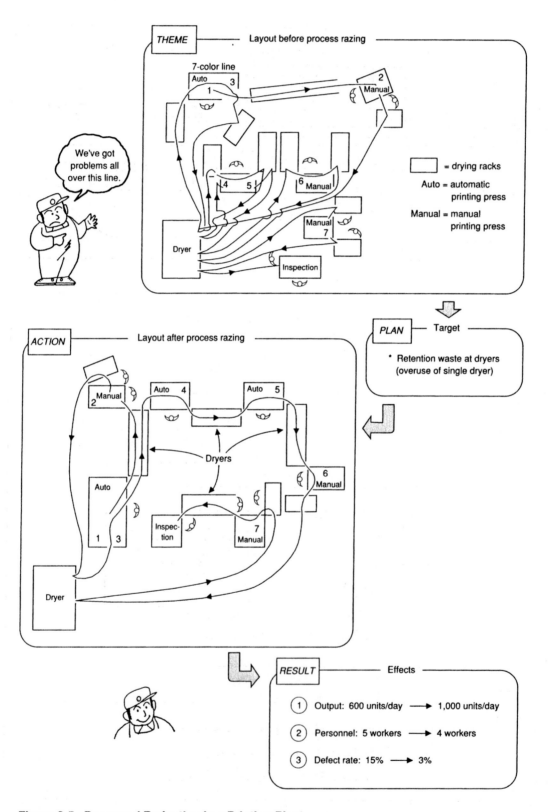

Figure 2-5. Personnel Reduction in a Printing Plant

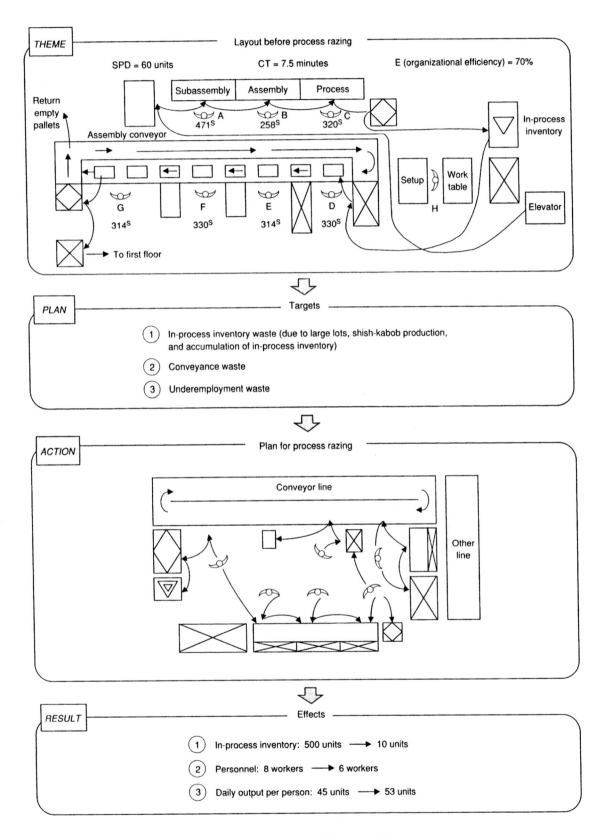

Figure 2-6. Personnel Reduction on an Assembly Conveyor Line

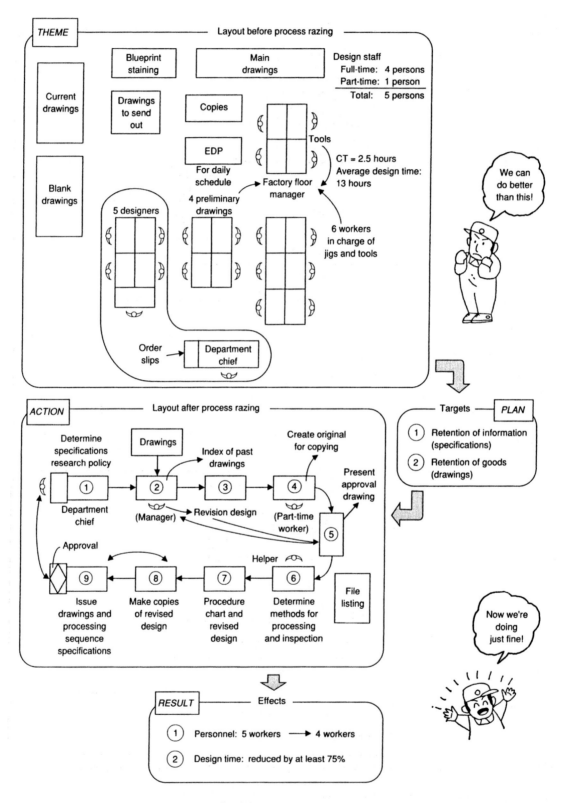

Figure 2-7. Personnel Reduction in Design Processes

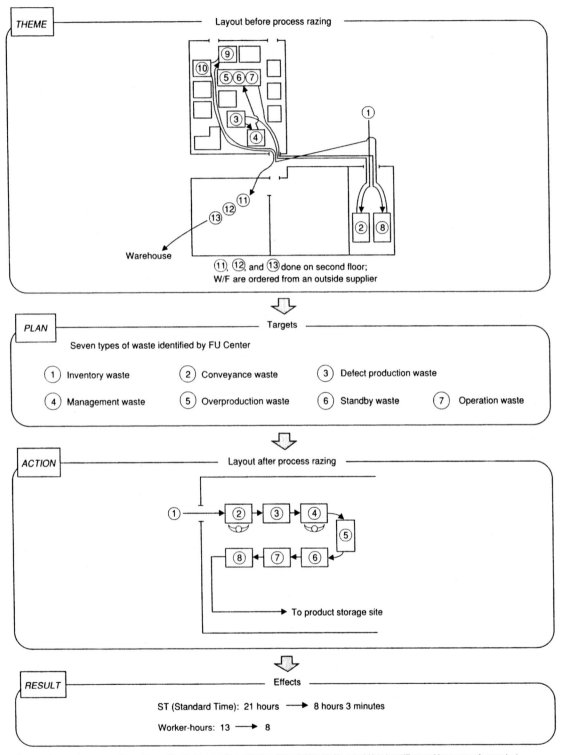

THEME — Layout before process razing

(11), (12), and (13) done on second floor;
W/F are ordered from an outside supplier

Warehouse

PLAN — Targets

Seven types of waste identified by FU Center

(1) Inventory waste   (2) Conveyance waste   (3) Defect production waste

(4) Management waste   (5) Overproduction waste   (6) Standby waste   (7) Operation waste

ACTION — Layout after process razing

To product storage site

RESULT — Effects

ST (Standard Time): 21 hours ➝ 8 hours 3 minutes

Worker-hours: 13 ➝ 8

Source: From an improvement report issued by the Nagano Diversification Council (Vol. 33, No. 11 of *Kojo kanri* [Factory Management] magazine)

Figure 2-8. U-shaped Cells for Name Plates

Step 1: Reach a consensus with managers.

Step 2: Hold brainstorming sessions to draft improvement plans.

Step 3: Set standards for line production. First, conduct an analysis using processing path diagrams. Then, select equipment models by using P-Q analysis. Conduct process analysis on the model product. Revise the layout. (See the *THEME*, *PLAN*, and *ACTION* sections of Figure 2-8.) Finally, measure the standard time (ST) after improvement. (See the *RESULT* section of Figure 2-8.)

By incorporating improvements into the layout revisions, the FU Center was able to reduce standard time to about one-third its previous level. Some of the improvements were:

- improved processing of reference holes and guide holes
- improving the method of attaching double-adhesive tape
- incorporating inspection into the line
- incorporating letter sheets from Company T into the line
- developing a positioning jig for print materials

Improvement Case Study

A fishing rod production line (from an improvement report issued by the Nagano Diversification Council)

Company T was founded in 1961, has 80 employees, and is currently capitalized at $1 million. The company's four divisions manufacture fishing rods, commercial fishing rods, plastic molding and processing, and sports equipment such as golf club shafts.

The main problem facing Company T was the maturation of the fishing rod market, which accounted for almost 40 percent of the company's total sales. To combat this difficult market situation, the company decided to develop and market new types of colored fishing rods. To build a smooth supply network for the new products, top management pointed out the following three requirements:

1. The new products must have higher added value.
2. They must be produced with short lead times.
3. The new products must help break the deadlock in overall sales expansion.

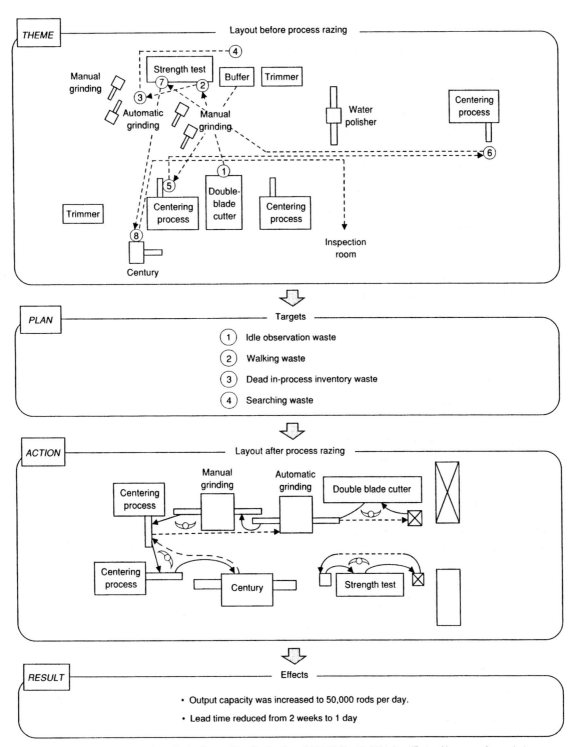

Figure 2-9. Layout of a Fishing Rod Production Line

Source: From an improvement report issued by the Nagano Diversification Council (Vol. 33, No. 11 of *Kojo kanri* [Factory Management] magazine)

Fortunately, Company T was one of twelve companies from various industries that belonged to the Nagano Diversification Council. Having joined the Council when it was established in 1983, Company T had garnered a lot of valuable experience in making improvements. In July and August of the previous year, member companies of the council representing various other industries made a waste-finding inspection visit to Company T. Company T studied the improvement suggestions that were made following the tour and put some of them to work to build an improved fishing rod production line.

The following is a step-by-step description of Company T's improvement project.

Step 1: Remove waste from the production line. The group reviewed the processing methods based on the targeted items pointed out in the *PLAN* section of Figure 2-9. Being particularly concerned with eliminating idle observation waste, members made improvements in the centering process and grinding machines.

Step 2: Directly link processes. As shown in the diagram of the layout before improvement (see the *THEME* section of Figure 2-9), piles of in-process inventory lie between each of the processes. This pile-up, called shish-kabob production, contributes to dead in-process inventory waste and searching waste. The group (1) performed a P-Q analysis, (2) drafted process route diagrams to group the processes into families, and then (3) revised the layout according to the sequence of processes.

Step 3: Improvement of layout. That weekend, everyone came in and changed the layout around. Initially, while trying to rearrange the equipment, they ran into several obstacles. They worked together, however, and found ways to clear them. Their first rearrangement failed to raise efficiency and ended up making the work more tiring. Therefore, the group carried out the process razing again, rearranging the layout as shown in the *ACTION* section of Figure 2-9. This time, as the *RESULT* section shows, they succeeded and went on to implement similar improvements throughout the factory.

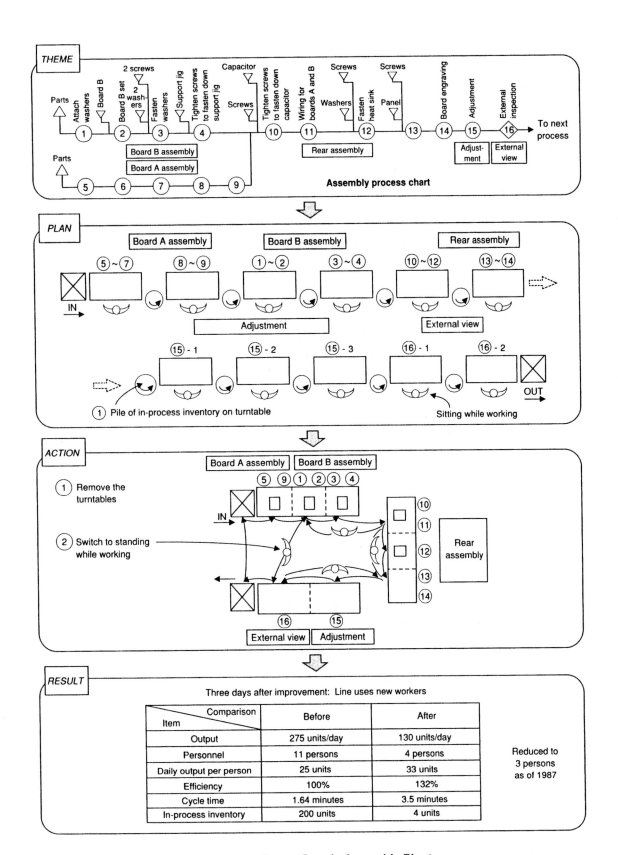

Figure 2-10. Personnel Reduction in a Power Supply Assembly Plant

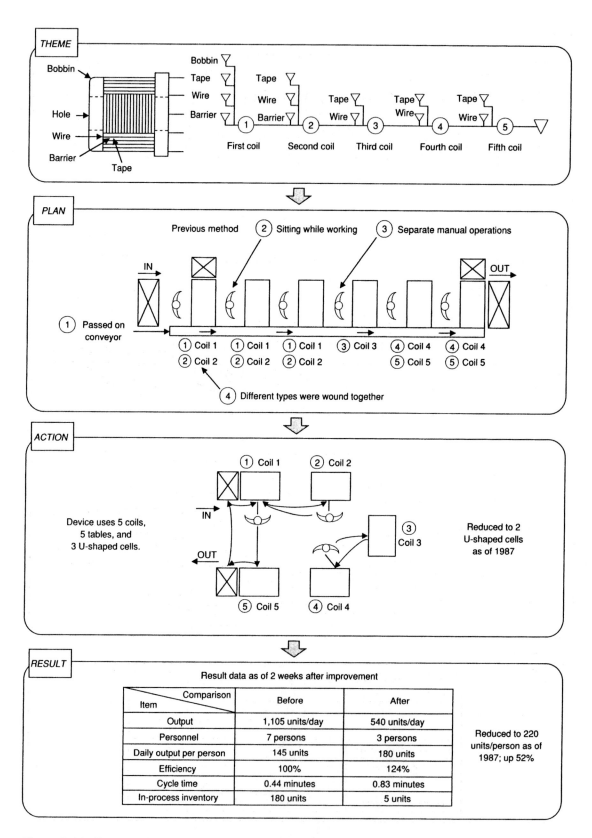

Figure 2-11. Personnel Reduction for Transformer Coils

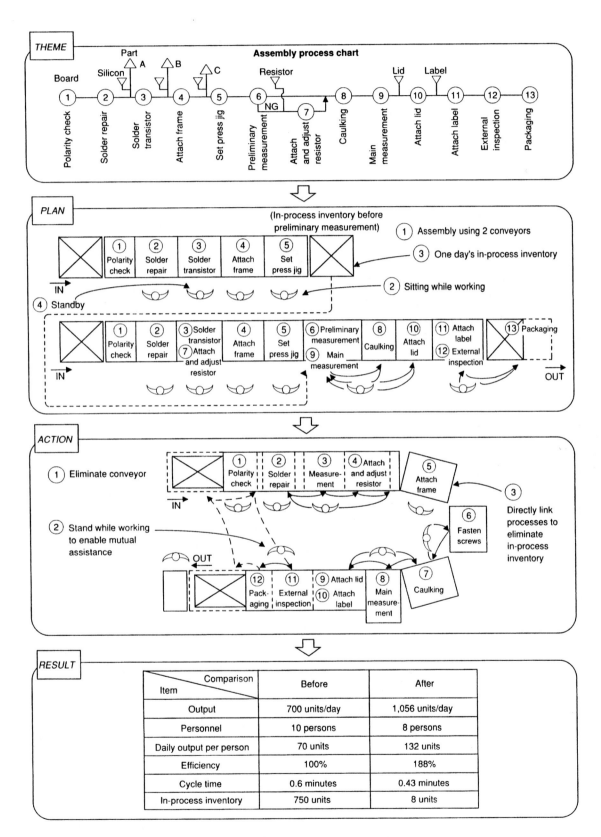

Figure 2-12. Personnel Reduction on a Converter Assembly Line

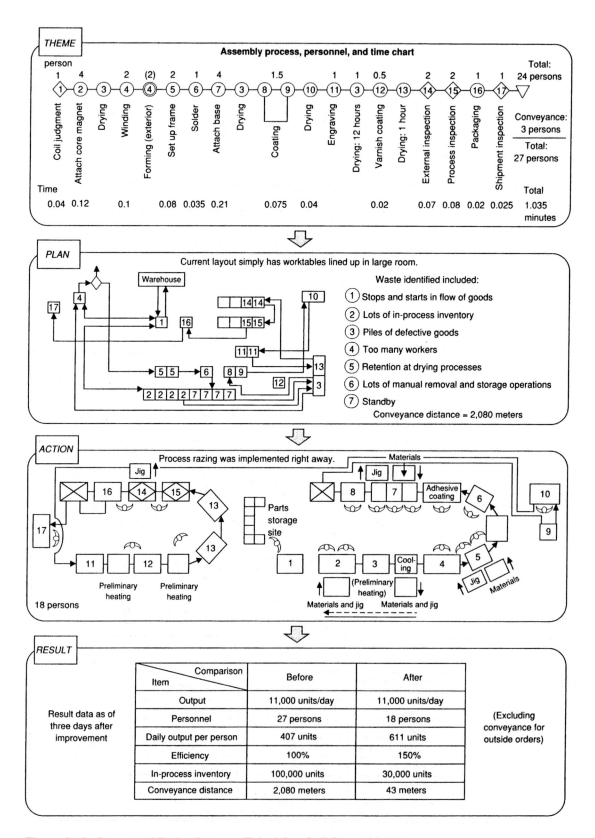

Figure 2-13. Personnel Reduction on a Television Coil Assembly Line

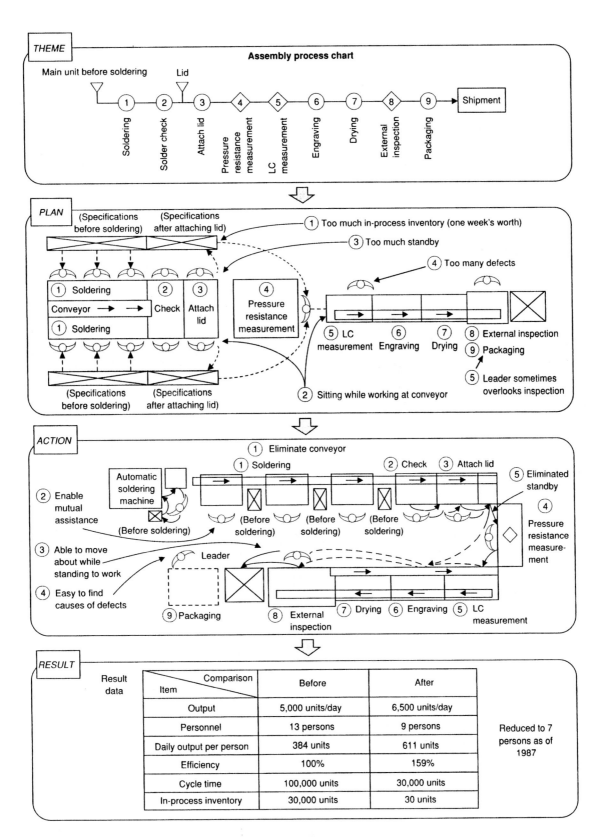

Figure 2-14. Personnel Reduction on a Noise Filter Assembly Line

3

Establishing a Wide-variety
Small-lot Production System

WHICH COMES FIRST: CHANGEOVER IMPROVEMENT OR PROCESS RAZING?

Finding myself increasingly in demand as a consultant in factory floor projects aimed at achieving either single-minute changeover (within nine minutes) or zero changeover (within the cycle time), I wonder about this sudden interest in changeover improvements. Factory managers are seeking help in achieving at least single-minute changeover because the advent of wide-variety small-lot production has increased the percentage of changeover loss to total loss. It is now 20 percent or more.

I ask these factory managers if they have conducted an analysis of sequential product quantities for each type of product (*P-Q analysis*) to gain an understanding of current conditions. Their answer is generally "No." While they usually have an abstract understanding of the situation, they seldom have a concrete and specific grasp of the current conditions.

Figure 3-1 shows an example of P-Q analysis.

As illustrated in the figure:

1. The quantities for all items are shown.
2. The figure enables us to immediately see what percentage group A, the most important product group, occupies in the total quantity of products.
3. We can determine the number of changeovers and the related loss time based on the average units produced per lot.
4. It also gives us a picture of the concept behind wide-variety small-lot production. For example, we can see which is more appropriate — a conveyor or a two-person assembly line.

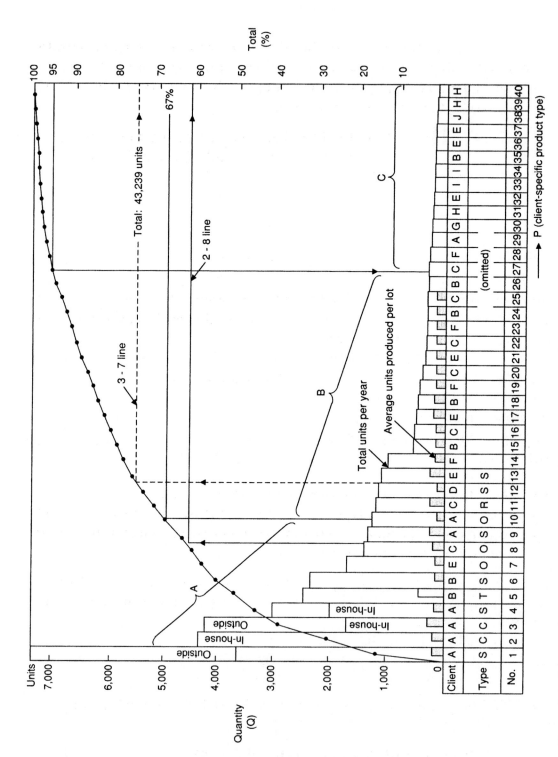

Figure 3-1. Product-Quantity (P-Q) Analysis

5. By comparing the line changing times, we can get a fairly accurate understanding of how many months' worth of goods are in the warehouse inventory, how many days' worth are in the in-process inventory, and the length of production periods.

Since there is some truth to the joke that once people become upper-level managers in a factory they forget how things are made, I will quickly note the steps for making a P-Q analysis.

Step 1: Confirm the definition of P-Q analysis.

"P" stands for product and "Q" for quantity. Accordingly, a P-Q analysis arranges the quantities of products according to their destinations (the clients). Although they often are confused with ABC analyses or Pareto analyses, P-Q analyses differ in the quantity values (shown along the vertical axis in Figure 3-1) and their lack of any monetary values.

Step 2: Draft a table listing client-specific product quantities.

If we include the number of lots, we can determine the average number of units per lot. This will enable us also to determine the number of changeovers (see Table 3-1).

- Compile statistics from the past six months to one year.
- In Table 3-1, the first category is "Client" and the second is "Product type." If a third category is needed, it should be one that helps show how product types differ from season to season.

It should take three or four days to manually prepare a table that includes about 100 product (P) items. A skilled word processor can do it in about 15 minutes on a computer.

Step 3: Make the table into a graph like the one shown in Figure 3-1.

This kind of graph can be easily drawn by hand, but a computer can print it out automatically in less time.

- Total share of product group A: 70 percent or less

Table 3-1. Sequential List of Product Quantities Categorized by Client

No.	Client	Product type	Lot size	Quantity	Average quantity	Total	Total share (%)
1	A	S	45	7,462	166	7,462	23.1
2	B	C	25	4,332	173	11,794	27.3
3	C	C	15	4,270	284	16,064	37.2
4	D	S	7	2,966	423	19,030	44.0
5	A	J	21	2,424	115	21,454	49.6
6	E	S	22	2,261	103	23,715	54.8
7	C	O	15	1,831	122	25,546	59.1
8	B	O	13	1,241	95	26,787	62.0
9	A	S	5	1,234	247	28,021	64.8
10	A	O	20	1,138	57	29,159	67.4
11	B	R	5	1,119	224	30,278	70.0
12	A	S	15	1,106	74	31,384	72.6
13	E	S	12	1,100	83	32,484	75.1
39	E	B	1	92	0.2	43,195	99.9
40	E	B	1	44	0.1	43,239	100.0

- Total share of product group B: 71-95 percent
- Total share of product group C: 96 percent or more

Step 4: Enter the 2-8 line and determine whether or not the factory has wide-variety small-lot production.

The 2-8 line tells us whether or not we can apply the Pareto principles. We start this line at the point that represents 20 percent of the P axis and 80 percent of the Q axis. Since Figure 3-1 shows 40 P items listed on the P axis, the 2-8 line begins at 40 × 0.20 = 8.

When we look at the total share axis at the right side of the figure, we see that the 2-8 line intersects at 63 percent, not 80 percent. Seeing this, we should next draw a 3-7 line and check the total share axis again. The 3-7 line starts at 12 percent on the P axis and intersects the total share axis at about 76 percent, showing a closer accuracy than that of the 2-8 line. Figure 3-1 thus appears to be conducive to the Pareto principles, which means that the production line should not be thought of as a wide-variety small-lot production line.

To enter the category of wide-variety small-lot production, the P-Q analysis needs to approximate the 4-to-6 ratio. Many of the Japanese factories that managers complain of as "difficult to manage because of their wide-variety small-lot production" are revealed by P-Q analysis to be typical Japanese factories rather than wide-variety small-lot production facilities.

The next step is to analyze the flow of goods in product group A in order to better understand current conditions in the factory. If possible, although by no means essential, we should use the process analysis technique at this point. While tracing the flow of goods in the factory, we need to (1) find out the changeover times for each equipment and device unit on each line, and then (2) draw up a table listing equipment-specific changeover time loss figures.

Quite often, as we walk around the factory gathering these data, we are surprised to discover that the loss due to changeover time pales in comparison to loss due to retention of goods at various points in the production flow. Figure 3-2 shows an example of this kind of factory.

According to sources at the factory illustrated in Figure 3-2, this factory was awarded a factory excellence prize ten years ago as a model of modern plant investment. Then, factories generally still handled large lots and fell under the 2-to-8 ratio category in the P-Q analysis shown in Figure 3-1. Consequently, the factory layout featured machining and assembly lines designed for mass production of major product models.

In the past decade, however, the variety of products has increased while production lots have shrunk, producing more complicated kinds of layouts such as the one shown in Figure 3-2. The result has been a rise in waste stemming from the factory managers' ignorance of the flow of goods. At first glance, almost all of this waste appears to be conveyance waste. A closer look, however, usually reveals plenty of "dead in-process inventory" and overflowing warehouse stock. When in-process inventory piles up at intermediate processes, the inability to pinpoint the causes of defects results in a lot of waste stemming from

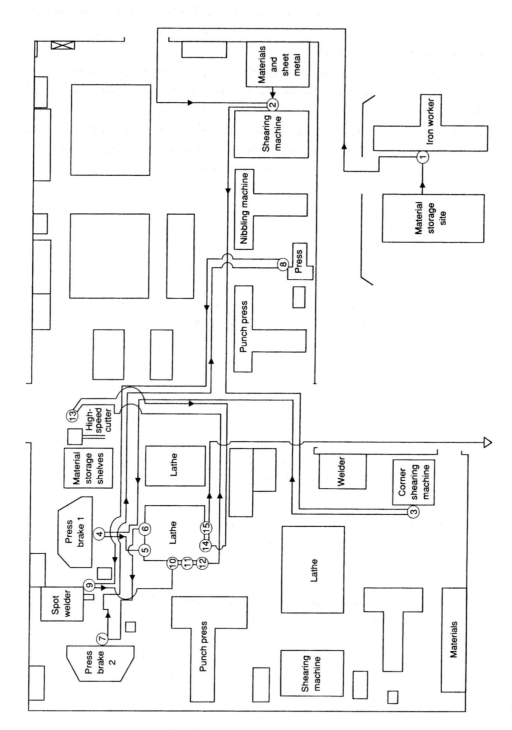

Figure 3-2. Flow Diagram of Current Conditions (Before Improvement)

rework, defects, and operational errors. When defective production waste occurs, workpieces with missing parts arrive at the assembly line and almost invariably lead to delayed shipments.

We all know that when a factory frequently fails to meet shipment deadlines, it loses the trust of its customers. When it lowers prices to remain competitive, what we might call "late delivery waste" or "red-ink loss" is created. Managers whose factories still belong in the large-lot production era should take note of Figure 3-3, which shows how red-ink loss is produced. One good way to avoid such loss is to thoroughly implement process razing while building a wide-variety small-lot production system.

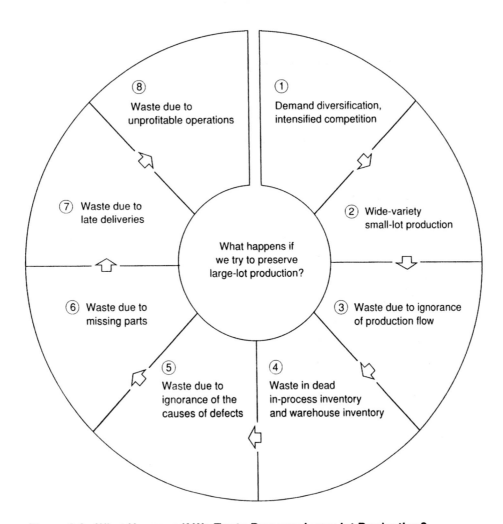

Figure 3-3. What Happens if We Try to Preserve Large-lot Production?

BUILDING A WIDE-VARIETY SMALL-LOT PRODUCTION LINE

What we have just discussed may lead us to conclude that changeover improvement is the best type of improvement in wide-variety small-lot production factories. However, this depends upon the purposes of improvement.

For example, in Chapter 12 I will discuss Company O, in which changeover loss time accounted for at least 20 percent of the total operating time. In this case study, the best type of improvement was process razing.

Changeover improvement is one type of operation improvement that results in reduced work-hours. It also helps raise the equipment capacity utilization rate as well as overall productivity. However, it does little toward improving management or making a difference in the amount of value added to products.

This is because changeover improvement does not reduce personnel requirements. Company O started with process razing, which made waste much more visible. The result was that zero changeover and successive line switching became much easier to achieve. For factories that are anxious to raise their added-value figures and ensure higher profits, it is probably best to begin with process razing.

Let us look at a simple example of how factories can lay the foundations for wide-variety small-lot production.

Step 1: Carry out a P-Q analysis with the "P" standing for process route rather than product.

To begin with, we need to draw up a part-specific process route analysis table (see Figure 3-4). After making an improvement to consolidate the processes and group them into families, the process route analysis table might appear as the one shown in Figure 3-5.

In any wide-variety small-lot production factory, we can generally group all of the processes (P) into five or fewer families. This is because the "wide variety" alluded to in wide-variety small-lot production usually means variety in dimensions and materials but not in manufacturing methods.

Let us look at an even simpler example. Figure 3-6 presents a simple P-Q analysis of different product (P) models, which will be used for process route analysis.

Machine name / Process name →	Cutter / Cutting	Auto lathe / Lathe cutting	Single-purpose lathe / Lathe cut 1	Single-purpose lathe / Lathe cut 2	Single-purpose lathe / Lathe cut 3	Single-purpose lathe / Lathe cut 4	Centerless grinder / Grinding	Multi-spindle drilling machine / Drilling	Drilling machine / Chamfering	Multi-spindle tapping machine / Screw cutting	Milling machine / Milling	Wash basin / Cleaning	Rolling machine / Rolling	Deburring	Gear hob / Gear teeth cutting	Milling machine / Milling	Milling machine / Milling	Bench lathe / Drilling
Part code	Part symbol																	
1 OBR-026	K																	
2 OBR-030	K																	
3 OSK-008	O																	
4 OKS-009	R																	
5 320147	S																	
6 320149	S																	
7 330033	R.S																	
8 330003	R.S																	
9 330030	R.S																	
10 330018	R.S																	
11 320148	S																	
12 320087	S																	
13 320088	S																	
14 320146	S																	
15 OBR-035	C																	
16 OBR-004	K																	

Figure 3-4. Process Route Analysis Table (Before Improvement)

		Machine name	NC	Bench lathe	Cleaning vat	Centerless grinder	Rolling machine	Gear hob
	Part code	Part symbol / Process name	Combined machining	Center lathe	Cleaning	Grinding	Rolling	Gear teeth cutting
1	OBR-026	K	O	O	O	O		
2	OBR-030	K	O	O	O	O		
3	OSK-008	O	O	O	O	O		
4	OKS-009	R	O	O	O	O		
5	320147	S	O		O	O	O	
6	320149	S	O		O	O	O	
7	330033	R.S	O		O	O	O	O
8	330003	R.S	O		O	O	O	
9	330030	R.S	O		O	O	O	
10	330018	R.S	O		O	O	O	
11	320148	S	O		O	O	O	
12	320087	S	O		O	O	O	
13	320088	S	O		O	O	O	
14	320146	S	O		O	O	O	
15	OBR-035	C	O		O	O		
16	OBR-004	K	O		O	O		

Figure 3-5. Process Route Analysis Table (After Improvement)

Figure 3-7 shows the corresponding process route analysis chart. Initially, we can see that the process routes differ for the four types of products. A closer look, however, shows that types I and IV and types II and III can be grouped together as two families.

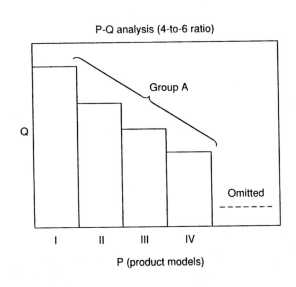

Figure 3-6. A Simple P-Q Analysis

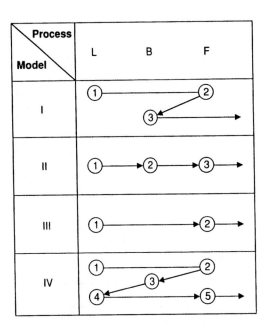

Figure 3-7. Process Route Analysis

Step 2: Diagram the current process layout, personnel layout, and walking routes.

For the time being, we first group together the different types of machines and processes as shown in Figure 3-8; the lathes and lathing processes, drilling machines and drilling processes, and milling machine and milling processes.

In wide-variety small-lot production, the equipment is usually laid out as shown in Figure 3-8 to promote versatility. The drawbacks of this equipment-specific layout include in-process inventory waste, waste due to ignorance about the causes of defects, waste due to long production lead times, and idle observation waste.

Step 3: Carry out process razing.

Figure 3-9 shows how this layout changes when we carry out process razing to create a horizontal arrangement of process cells each with multi-process handling. Figure 3-10 shows how we can take this one step further by creating a vertical arrangement of processes in which all processes are integrated into a single test production line.

The upper part of the line in Figure 3-10 includes equipment types II and III and the bottom part types I and IV.

Step 4: Establish synchronized (or cycle time-coordinated) production using one-piece flow, one-piece production, and one-piece inspection techniques

Follow this sequence:

1. Determine the cycle time (CT) based on the processing costs.
2. Before taking the previous steps, remodel the mechanical operations to include auto-feed devices.
3. Begin practicing multi-process handling at the start of the production line. It is okay to attempt multi-process handling without rehearsing it beforehand.
4. As we operate the test line, find ways to shorten the manual operations time.
5. To build enthusiasm, changeover improvements should also be done from the start of the line.
6. Blade replacement should occur consistently when the blades reach 70 percent of their estimated service life.
7. Since inspections will be made on all products, finding and promptly responding to the causes of defects should be relatively easy.
8. If production output must be increased, it should be done by switching to a two-worker line.

Implementing all of these process-razing measures beforehand will contribute to management improvements. Again, we should remember that changeover improvements alone do not directly contribute to profitability.

TEST YOUR SKILLS

Can You Change a Three-Person Line into a One-Person Line?

Currently, the factory has three production lines, shown as lines A, B, and C in Figure 3-11. Each line is operated by one person. The cycle times are 10 minutes for line A, 14 minutes for line B, and 8 minutes for line C.

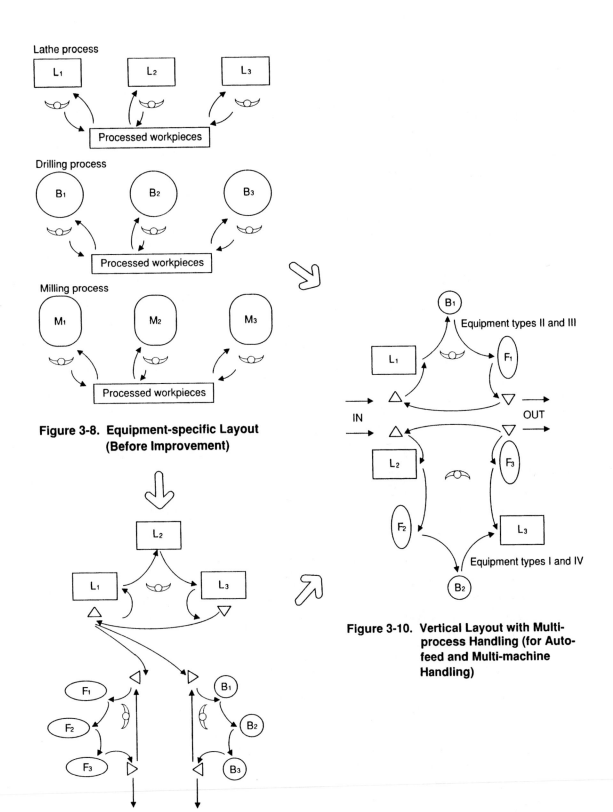

Figure 3-8. **Equipment-specific Layout (Before Improvement)**

Figure 3-9. **Horizontal Layout with Multi-process Handling (for Auto-feed and Three-machine Handling)**

Figure 3-10. **Vertical Layout with Multi-process Handling (for Auto-feed and Multi-machine Handling)**

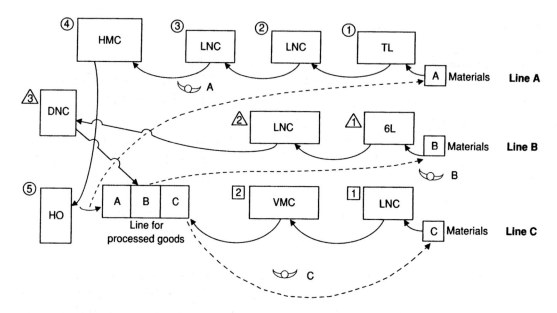

Figure 3-11. Linear Layout of Three Lines Operated by Three Workers

One day, you decide to categorize the three lines' operations into manual operations and auto-feed operations and perform a time analysis. The time analysis reveals that the three workers' manual operation times add up to nine minutes. If this total could be shortened by one minute, it would be possible to have all three lines handled by one person. After studying the matter from various angles, you determine the following:

1. The 6L process can be incorporated into the adjacent LNC process. This eliminates one equipment unit to give a new total of nine units.
2. To reduce the overall walking time, the equipment units can be moved closer together to keep walking time to 1.5 seconds or less between each adjacent pair.
3. The one-touch operation method used for numerical controlled (NC) machines can be used for some work setup operations to reduce the nine minutes of overall manual operations to eight minutes. However, an extra worker must sometimes be used for line A only to meet occasionally higher output requirements for its products. The question is what kind of process razing will produce a layout that enables two-worker flexibility for line A while keeping total walking time to nine minutes or less?

Solution

This test may be too difficult for beginners at factory improvement while readers who work in a different industry may find this production line layout confusing. However, the process-razing principles remain the same regardless of the type of factory.

As a hint, consider that we need to think of ways to link the three lines. We might consider, for example, putting line A in the middle and linking lines B and C on either side of it. Figure 3-12 illustrates how this kind of simple circular layout would work.

The chief drawback in this layout is that when a second worker is added to line A alone, he or she must walk empty-handed from the last process back to the first one at the end of each cycle.

One engineer with some experience in making factory improvements came up with the rather unusual layout plan shown in Figure 3-13, in which line A basically encircles lines B and C. Although this plan was original and had no major drawbacks, it received the following criticism.

- The wide entry and exit points between lines leave the operator empty-handed too much of the time.
- When line A switches to a two-worker schedule, the extra person makes it crowded.

People trained at the Nagano Diversification Center would recognize instantly that the best layout would be (1) to turn line A into a U-shaped cell and (2) to attach lines B and C at the two ends of the cell, as shown in Figure 3-14.

A single worker operating the three lines makes the full circle. A second worker added to line A makes a smaller circle via processes 3, 4, 5, 6, and 7 only. This layout is the best of the three ideas since it offers overall simplicity (with minimal walking waste) as well as flexibility for increased production on line A.

In the future, the trend will be toward U-shaped cells that can be easily adapted to meet changing personnel requirements.

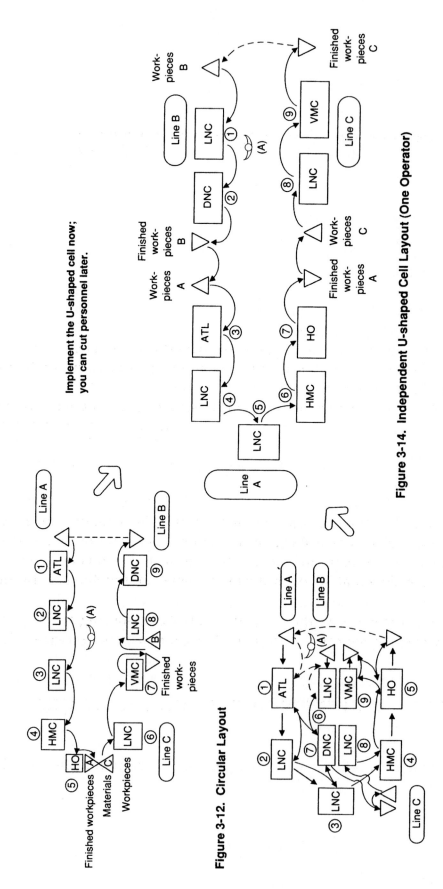

Implement the U-shaped cell now; you can cut personnel later.

Figure 3-12. Circular Layout

Figure 3-13. Double-layer U-shaped Cell Layout

Figure 3-14. Independent U-shaped Cell Layout (One Operator)

4

Examples of Process Razing

Toyota defines seven types of waste: (1) overproduction waste, (2) standby waste, (3) conveyance waste, (4) processing waste, (5) inventory waste, (6) motion waste, and (7) defect production waste.

Implementation of the Toyota Production System begins with overproduction waste — and materials requirement planning (MRP) for remote causes such as in-process inventory, bottleneck processes, and inventory. In the context of our present discussion, however, if we start with overproduction waste, we will probably fail.

This is because the real purpose of the Toyota Production System is not easily understood. For beginners, it is better to start with standby waste (i.e., manpower reduction), which is easier to understand. The most comprehendible method for reducing manpower on production lines is the process-razing method developed at Toyota's assembly plants. This method is also the most effective.

This chapter focuses on what we might call "overstaffing waste" and describes how such waste can be eliminated by applying the process-razing method.

REDUCING PRESS FACTORY MANPOWER FROM FOUR WORKERS TO ONE

Let us first look at Figure 4-1, which presents the steps implemented by Company A.

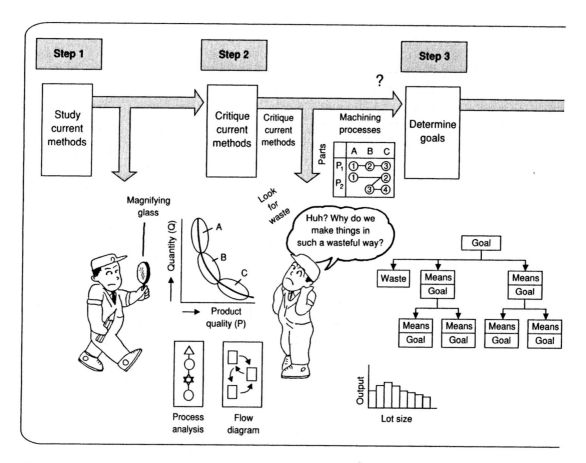

Figure 4-1. Illustrated Process Razing (Part 1)

Company A has a press factory that turns out a wide variety of parts in small lots. Of 98 employees, 52 operate 100 presses in the press division to produce 700 types of parts each month. In the wake of a sharp increase in the value of the yen, the parent company has begun pressuring Company A's management for hard-to-meet price reductions, shorter delivery times, smaller lots, and shorter product cycles. Although the following is not quite an example of necessity being the mother of invention, it shows how a determined company can overcome such challenges when its back is against the wall.

Figure 4-2 illustrates how a four-person line was changed into a U-shaped cell with a single operator. This change raised worker productivity on the line by a factor of 2.7 and reduced the line's in-process inventory from 6,000 units to 1,000 units while cutting the production period from three days to half a day. It also eliminated 90 percent of the previous defect rate.

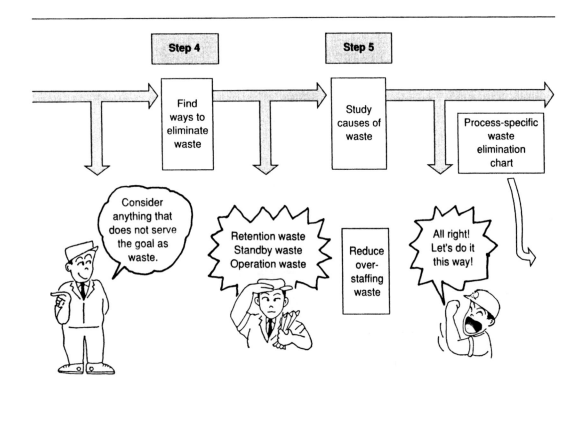

Figure 4-1. Illustrated Process Razing (Part 2)

THREE WAYS TO ELIMINATE OVERSTAFFING WASTE

When reducing manpower, it is best not to begin by directly removing wasteful worker actions. When Company A's president asked his managers to create a line that could maintain current output levels with only half the manpower, they approached the challenge from three angles.

1. Reduce in-process inventory waste.
2. Reduce standby waste.
3. Reduce operation waste.

Based on their understanding of the current conditions, they saw standby waste as the heart of the problem, operation waste as the starting point for waste reduction efforts, and in-process inventory waste as the final goal.

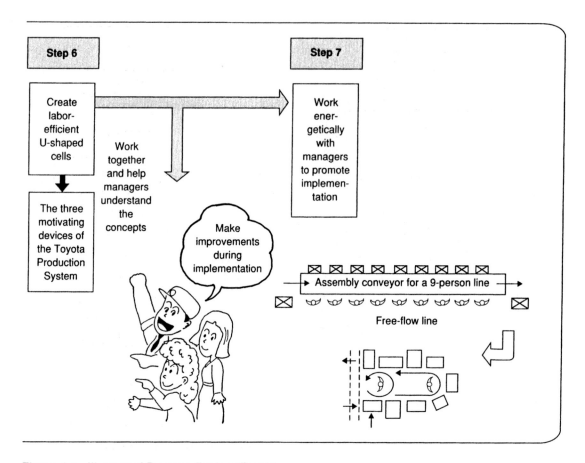

Figure 4-1. Illustrated Process Razing (Part 3)

Observe the Flow of Processes as Well as the Factory

When observing actual conditions in the factory, first watch the way goods move along the production line. Next, watch the movement of people.

Only one item should be processed at each machine (process). All items not being processed should be considered as retention (in-process inventory). In observing the factory, we should pay the most attention to the work-in-process. These goods are always in one of four stages: (1) retention, (2) conveyance, (3) processing, or (4) inspection. The processing stage should command the most attention, however, since it is the only stage that adds value (and thereby produces profit for the company).

Beside each press in the press factory there is a certain quantity of goods (the lot size minus one) at the retention stage, either awaiting processing at the

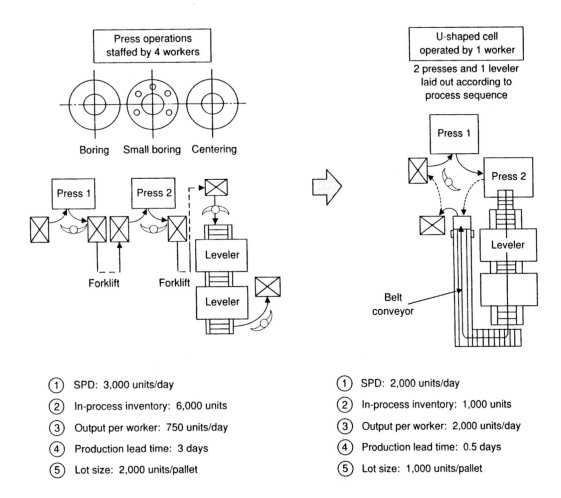

Figure 4-2. **Establishing a U-shaped Cell for Press Operations**

current process or conveyance to the next process. A lot size of 2,000 units, therefore, means that 1,999 units are in retention. In other words, at any given moment, only one two-thousandths of the lot is being used in a profitable way.

The simplest way to eliminate this in-process inventory or retention waste is the process linkage method. Instead of loading workpieces into a box after being processed at press 1, we should send them directly, one at a time, to press 2. Likewise, as each workpiece is processed at press 2, we should send it directly to the next machine. Individual workpieces are not loaded into a box until after the final process.

In the equipment layout shown on the right side of Figure 4-2, the machines are arranged as closely together as possible. Very little walking by the operator is required. Generally, we call this kind of equipment layout a *U-shaped cell*. When only two machines are involved, however, the shape is more L-shaped. When only three machines are involved, the "U" becomes sharp at the corners, like a square with one side missing.

Reduce Operation Waste

To reduce operation waste, we begin by studying standby waste.

Waste in having two workers.

First, we observe the workers at work and look for instances of standby. Whenever there are two workers at one process, there will inevitably be some standby. For example, there must be standby when two workers operate the leveler process shown in Figure 4-2. The time between the workpiece's insertion into the machine and its extraction is standby time. The cause of waste in having two workers may be a wasteful division of labor. If the leveler was simply equipped with a return conveyor, it could be handled by a single operator.

Waste in setting up and removing workpieces.

Table 4-1 lists work element analysis statistics for the two presses at the left "before-improvement" side of Figure 4-2.

As seen in Table 4-1, each worker spent seven seconds at each press. If we did a motion study by asking of each motion "Does this motion add value to the product?" we would discover that less than 10 percent of the motions are value-adding (or profit-making). In other words, over 90 percent of the motions were either setup, extraction, or other non-value-adding motions as far as the product was concerned. From Table 4-2's analysis statistics, we can calculate that the profit-making motions in each of these press operations account for 0.5 seconds of the 7-second total, or about 7 percent.

By bringing the percentage of profit-making motions to 14 percent, we can double productivity. By bringing it to 21 percent, we can triple productivity. The total elimination of workpiece setup and removal waste will require a layout similar to the illustration at the right in Figure 4-2. The machine's start switch should be a push button installed between the machine and the next

Table 4-1. Analysis of Press Operations Before Improvement (One-Piece Production)

Process / Work element	Press	
	# 1	# 2
Pick up	2	2
Set and position	2	2
Press switch	1	1
Remove and put down	2	2
Tact time	7	7
Human operation time (total)	14 seconds	

process, allowing the operator to press the switch as he or she walks to the next machine. All sitting work should be changed to standing work to enable one person to handle three processes. Table 4-2 lists analysis statistics for the improved layout.

Table 4-2. Analysis of Press Operations After Improvement

Process / Work element	Press		Leveler
	# 1	# 2	
Pick up	1	—	0.5
Set and position	2	1	
Press switch	0.5	0.5	
Remove and put down	1	0.5	1
Human operation time (per process)	4.5	2	1.5
Human operation time (total)	8 seconds		

As described, we have approached the reduction of overstaffing waste from other angles, namely by reducing retention waste (or in-process inventory), standby waste, and motion waste. In so doing, we have effectively reduced the manpower requirements from four workers to one. To be more precise, since the centering operations included two workers, we can say that we changed a three-worker line into a single-worker line.

CHANGING HUMAN OPERATION TIME INTO MACHINE TIME AT LOW EXPENSE

Machine operation time (MT) is the time required for a mechanical operation. Human operation time (HT) is the time required for a manual operation. We should substitute MT for HT whenever possible, such as by installing auto-feed mechanisms and/or mechanisms that automatically stop a machine after it processes each workpiece that the operator sets up. As such, MT differs from the kind of "workerless" operations that are sought by using sophisticated flexible manufacturing systems (FMS).

The implementation of MT has four levels (see Table 4-3).

Level 1 changes some manual operations into machine operations. We separate the work into that which people can do better and that which machines can do better.

Since machines are generally better at processing work, we mechanize processing whenever possible. After all, we usually need a press for processing such as bending, cutting, and squeezing. Even when these processes can be done by people, they usually require a lot of strength, cause fatigue, and therefore are better assigned to machines. In Figure 4-1's before-improvement layout, there is no division between human work and press work. If, for example, we use a press for processing, the press will not work unless we push two safety buttons. This requires some HT, ostensibly for safety's sake. However, safety can also be assured while changing HT into MT by simply installing a single start button to be pushed from the next process instead of the double-switch device at the press.

Level 2 of changing HT into MT utilizes the setup and removal method. The setup part of this method includes setting the workpiece into the machine and pressing the start button. Removal means removing the processed workpiece from the machine. At this second level, we have established a division

Table 4-3. The Four Levels of MT Implementation

Level	Name of method	Division	(1) Setup	(2) Processing	(3) Inspection	(4) Removal	Characteristics
0	100% manual method	Human work and machine work	○	○ ●	○	○	
1	Mechanization of processing	Human work and machine work	○	●	○	○	Only processing is done by machines and/or tools
2	Setup and removal method	Human work and machine work	○	●	○ ●	○	Machine is equipped with auto-start and auto-stop devices
3	Setup only method	Human work and machine work	○	●	●	●	Workpieces are picked up and set up automatically
4	Workerless method	Human work and machine work	●	●	●	●	All work (including conveyance) done by robots or other machines

○ : human operation time (HT)   ● : machine operation time (MT)

between the machine's processing work and the operator's setup and removal work. This method requires the following devices:

- a start button
- a device that automatically stops the machine after processing
- a device that automatically stops the machine when a defect or other abnormality occurs

By using simple electrical devices, such as push buttons, limit switches, and relays, we can change HT into second-level MT at a cost of $700 or less.

In the press example described, the question of safety precautions can be a difficult one, since regulations may not allow the replacement of a double-switch device with a more remote single-switch device. Stringent safety standards can still be met, although at somewhat greater expense, however, by attaching an electric-eye safety device to the press. This would assure the operator pressing the start button while walking to the next process that no one is near it.

Level 3 uses the setup method. The machines automatically remove processed workpieces. This rarely requires anything as sophisticated as a robot, and can usually be done by (1) jigs that expel workpieces one at a time and (2) rods or air jets that move the workpieces into position on the machine.

At level 4, everything is automatic. There is no need to describe such automatic time (AT) systems in this book. Suffice it to say that establishing zero changeover is a prerequisite for AT systems in wide-variety small-lot production.

TEST YOUR SKILLS

The goal is to change a three-person line into a one-person line. This problem was presented by Mr. Y at Company K. The solution to the problem involves a one-person line with single changeover (nine minutes or less). The process components are described next.

As shown in Figure 4-3, there are currently two shift teams — a one-person team and a two-person team — for a total of three persons.

The results of P-Q analysis show that with 100 products (P), the line's monthly output is 1,200 group A products, 100 group B products, and from two to five group C products.

The same processing route is used throughout. The time measurements are:

Processing Route and Times (in minutes)

Process / Type	①	②	③	④	⑤	⑥	Total
HT	1.0	0.5	0.5	0.5	0.5	0.5	3.5
MT	0.5	3.0	1.5	2.0	1.5	1.0	

- *Problem 1:* If the cycle time includes an operating time of 480 minutes and the SPD is 120 units, how many people are needed for this line?
- *Problem 2:* Show how process razing can be implemented.

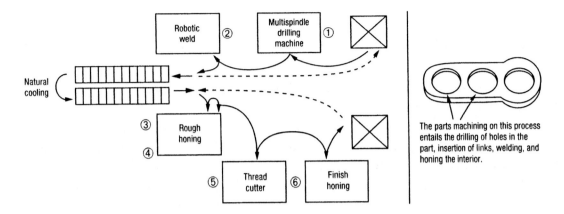

Figure 4-3. 2-Shift, 2-Operator Layout

Solutions

Answer 1

1. $CT = \dfrac{480 \text{ min.} \times 2 \text{ shifts}}{120 \text{ pieces}} = \dfrac{960 \text{ min.}}{120 \text{ pieces}} = 8$ min.

2. $\dfrac{\Sigma HT}{CT} = N^{people} \dots \dfrac{3.5 \text{ min.}}{8 \text{ min.}} = 0.4375^{people}$

This shows that one operator per shift is sufficient.

Answer 2

The result of process razing is as shown in Figure 4-4.

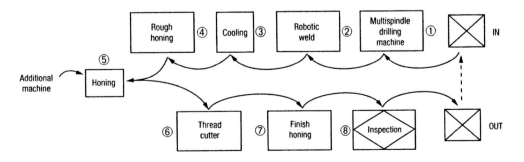

Figure 4-4. 1-Operator Layout

Hints

1. The layout is the major cause of waste because it separates the welding and honing process.
2. Bring in an additional honing machine, separate processes 3 and 4, and replace natural cooling with air cooling. Doing so will permit the use of one operator per shift.
3. As a result, you can operate with one operator instead of three, and the additional honing machine can be easily amortized.
4. Post improvement work standard combination sheets.

5

Process-razing Techniques

WHAT IS PROCESS RAZING?

Many factories in Japan are not successful in implementing layout improvement plans. Even though the layout becomes worse with each new addition to the factory's facilities and equipment, managers are well aware why no one bothers to make layout improvements.

At many Japanese mid-size companies, the factory layout has become a monument to Japan's rapid-growth era. I have noted the hastily tagged-on equipment arrangements at such factories and have made comments such as "Your factory's layout is pretty bad" or "Why don't you improve the factory layout?" My suggestions, however, almost always fall on deaf ears. Managers claim the problem is that the advantages of improving the layout do not make up for the high costs such improvements require.

This cost-effectiveness problem led to the development of the process-razing method as a new technique for layout improvement. In practical terms, process razing is aimed only at processes that contain a lot of waste or that contribute very little to profitability.

The steps in process razing are as follows:

1. Study current conditions at target processes.
2. Critique current conditions.
3. Define the purpose of each target process.
4. Determine the starting point for process razing.
5. Develop a flow concept.
6. Draft a new layout plan.

7. Estimation development.
8. Trial implementation.

Of these eight steps, steps 2 through 6 are collectively called the "process-razing techniques" and have been used successfully at many factories. Chapter 6 will describe these steps in more detail. At this time, we will examine how the techniques are used.

INDUSTRY-SPECIFIC PROCESS RAZING

Manpower Reduction in Pipe Drilling and Caulking Processes

Figure 5-1 illustrates the drilling and caulking processes at Company B.

At process 1, two boring machines drill holes through the pipes. To keep costs at a minimum, this process is handled by two part-time workers, A and B. At process 2, paired sets of pipes are positioned into the caulking machine by full-time worker C.

To achieve lower processing costs, we must change this simple set of processes from a three-person to a two-person operation.

The current processing time is eight seconds per pipe at the two boring machines, each handled by one worker, and eight seconds per two-pipe set at the caulking machine. This is a good balance between the processing times at the two processes. In planning our process razing, we first define our objective — to reduce the total number of workers from three to two. Here are some hints:

- Remove the in-process inventory table between the two processes.
- Establish vertical operations.
- Bring in another caulking machine.
- Install an auto-feed device to aid manual work at the boring machines.

We can approach this problem creatively by imagining layouts that enable the work to be done by just two workers. Figure 5-2 illustrates a vertical layout idea that includes the following points.

1. A worker picks up two pipes and sets them up at the boring machine, which is equipped with an auto-feed device.
2. The worker manually operates the caulking machine and sets down the caulked pipes on a stand.

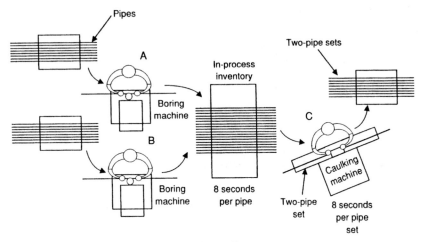

Figure 5-1. Pipe Drilling and Caulking Processes

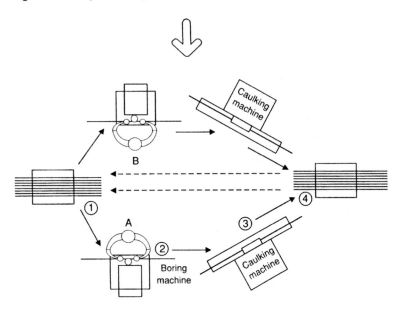

Figure 5-2. Pipe Drilling and Caulking Processes Using Fewer Workers

Once the two workers are accustomed to these changes, a table should be installed at the boring machines for the in-process inventory (i.e., standard inventory). The workers can remove workpieces from stations 3 to 4 to 2, then set up workpieces between stations 1 and 2, activate the auto-feed device, and then return to stations 3 and 4 (see Figure 5-2).

Process Razing at a Gear Processing Line

As shown in Figure 5-3, this line consists of three straight processing lines: lines A, B, and C with three workers, one for each line. Each line handles at least 20 product models and turns out about 3,000 product units per month.

The cycle times are 3.5 minutes for line A, 5.0 minutes for line B, and 4.0 minutes for line C. Since the current cycle times are sums of the manual operation times, the workers are always busy. In this particular case, we should take the following type of approaches to eliminate waste from processes.

Shorten changeover times.

We can universalize the cover replacement method, for example, and achieve zero changeover in that way. Or, when changing the ALT cutter, we can install a holder to make it a one-touch operation.

Improve processing methods.

Examples of this kind of improvement include changing T-shaped drills to V-shaped drills, simultaneous single-axle processing, increasing the machine feed rate by 20 percent, changing the gear hobbing from 1.5 mm to 2.0 mm, and so on.

Improve manual operations.

This can be done by eliminating the waste involved in picking up and setting down things, using an auto-clamp mechanism to simplify manual work-piece setup, using auto-feed mechanisms to simplify chamfering and deburring processes, and so on. Such a combination of improvements can reduce the total manual operation time to two minutes or less.

To reduce the line's manpower from three persons to two persons, we can use the formula: Cycle time (minimum) ÷ manual operation time = number of lines per worker.

In this case, the formula is: 3.5 minutes ÷ 2.0 minutes = 1.75 lines. This gives us an idea of how two workers can handle the three lines.

Now we come to the question of the layout for process razing. Since the available space usually consists of either rectangular areas or long, narrow areas, let us think of a layout plan A that is rectangular and a plan B that can be in any shape.

Without looking at the solution in this book, use your imagination to think of ways in which three lines can be handled by two workers. While there is only one goal, there are several ways to achieve it. The important thing is to be creative. If you are completely at a loss for ideas, clues are given in Figures 3-12, 3-13, and 3-14 in Chapter 3. It is better, however, to imagine layout patterns without resorting to those suggested patterns.

After you have done this, refer to Figure 5-4, which shows a possible plan A. Here, worker A handles line A and the first half of line B, while worker B handles the second half of line B and all of line C. Both workers walk a figure-eight pattern and return empty-handed to the start of the line.

Since the gear-hobbing (GH) process usually handles several workpiece units at a time (depending upon the machine design), we have arranged for several items to be handled here, in pace with the cycle time. Ideally, however, it is better to reduce the operating rate and preserve synchronized one-piece production.

Figure 5-5 is similar to the double-layer U-shaped cell layout shown in Figure 3-13. It features two types of U-shaped cells in which three lines are operated by two people.

A rather unusual idea would be to propose a concentric layout in which one U-shaped cell encircles the other. Such a layout, however, tends to take up a lot of space and requires a lot of walking waste. In addition, since the operator does not handle both the start and end points of the line for the same product run, waste is created due to the difficulty in spotting defects.

In line C, handling several workpiece units at the GH process could cause problems within an otherwise one-piece production system. It would also make standard operations more difficult to organize.

Plan B, shown in Figure 5-6, illustrates a layout that is similar to the independent U-shaped cell layout shown in Figure 3-14. In this case, the distance between machines has been drastically shortened to keep walking to a minimum. If possible, the GH process should also be made a one-piece production process (1) to avoid problems due to multiple-workpiece handling and (2) to facilitate standard operations using an orthodox walking pattern.

This arrangement also benefits from the flexibility to accommodate production output increases by adding an extra worker on line A only. This type of layout is also flexible enough to enable all three lines to be operated by just one worker when reduced output is required.

Which layout is better?

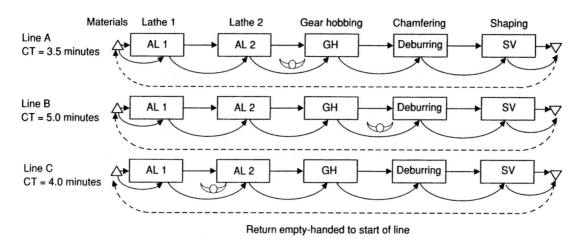

Figure 5-3. **Vertical Operations Using Three Straight Lines (One Worker per Line)**

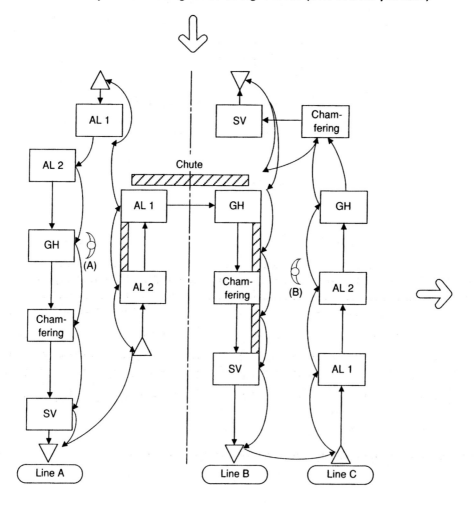

Figure 5-5. **Two U-shaped Cells Consisting of Three Lines and Two Operators**

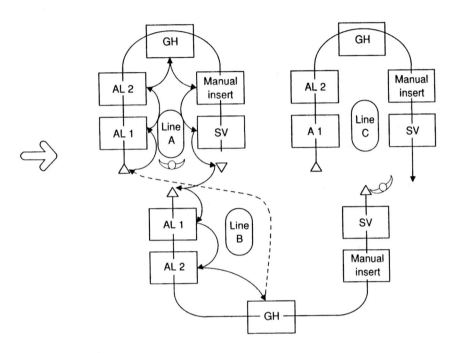

Figure 5-4. Three Lines Handled by Two Workers ("S" Pattern)

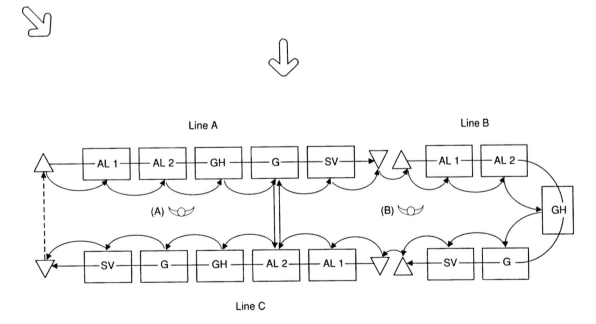

Figure 5-6. U-shaped Cell Layout for Three Lines and Two Operators

Process Razing of Welding Processes

The current layout divides the line into two parts: (1) the preliminary welding process and (2) the main welding process, as shown in Figure 5-7. The preliminary welding process is operated by two workers, A and B, who place two workpieces on the preliminary welding table and weld the top surface only. Next, they take the welded workpiece to the in-process inventory site for the main welding process, which is operated by four workers. Two of these four workers set the workpiece on the welding table and reweld the top surface, then turn it over and weld the back surface. The single weld made by the two workers at the preliminary welding process balances well with the timing of the double welds made by the four workers at the main welding process.

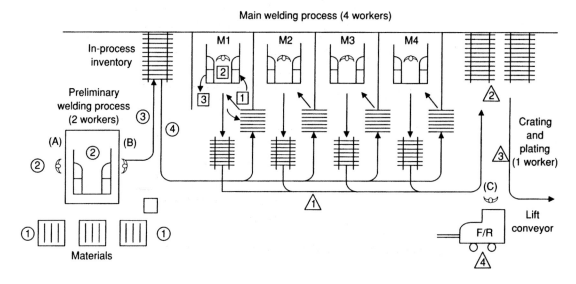

Figure 5-7. Layout with Preliminary and Main Welding Processes

TEST YOUR SKILLS

Because this line consists of a preliminary process and a main process, it includes the waste of picking up and setting down workpieces as well as that of in-process inventory. If possible, we should directly link or combine these two processes. How can process razing be implemented in this case?

Here is a hint: The solution involves making an inverter device at minimal expense.

Solution

This solution was developed by the K factory superintendent at Company S (see Figure 5-8). In this layout, the preliminary welding process has been placed in the middle to bring it closer to the main welding process and improve the flow. This layout was called a "distributed manual conveyance system." Although the line still includes a lot of in-process inventory, the workpieces flow in short, straight lines. I now ask the reader to identify the disadvantages of this layout.

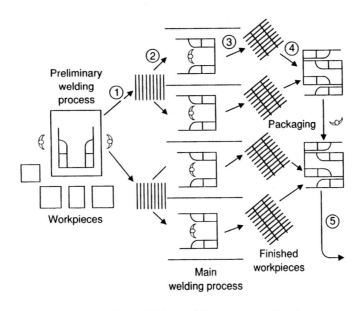

Figure 5-8. Distributed Manual Conveyance System

Now refer to Figure 5-9. Similar to the layout we have just studied, it eliminates conveyance waste by using roller conveyors. Remaining disadvantages are (1) that work is still divided into preliminary welding and main welding; (2) that in order to weld the rear surface of the workpieces, they must be turned over manually at point 2; and (3) that waste in picking up and setting down workpieces occurs at both points 3 and 4.

Looking at Figure 5-10, we find that the preliminary welding process has been integrated with the main welding process. The flow and line balance are maintained with the help of an assembly inverter device and a belt conveyor. In addition, the worker at point 2 handles both packaging and conveyance.

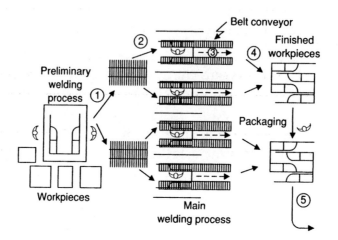

Figure 5-9. Distributed Belt Conveyor Method

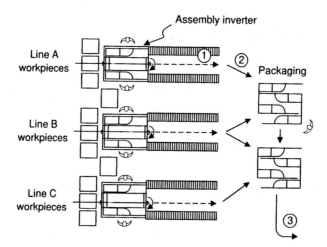

Figure 5-10. Integrated Welding Line

Although this layout plan is clearly the best of the three plans just described, we should note that the long belt conveyor leads to waste in the way the assembly workers and the packaging worker pick up and set down things.

TEST YOUR SKILLS

Something is strange about these sewing operations (an assembly process). The current work conditions are described on the left side of Figure 5-11.

Description	Pick up and align fabric pieces (parts) from left and right and sew them using the sewing machine.	
	Plan A (one worker)	Plan B (two workers)
Outline	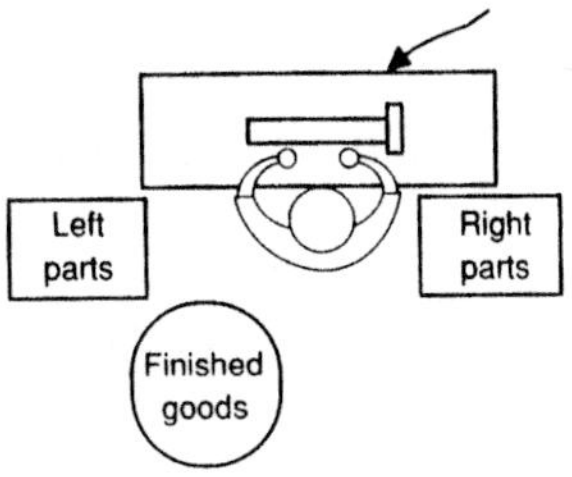 Worker picks up parts from right and left, checks the front and back surfaces, aligns the two parts, sets them on the sewing machine, aligns them, sews them together, and puts them on the pile of finished goods.	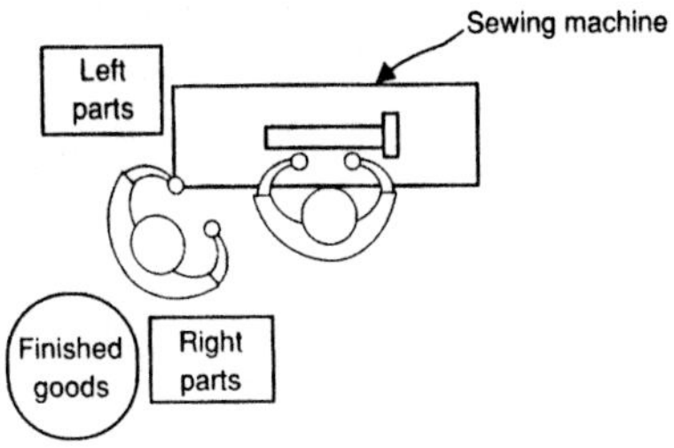 Worker guides cloths that have been set up and sews them in that position.
Workplace observations	It can be difficult to align the left and right parts and still keep up with the production pace.	Can continuously sew pre-aligned cloths while keeping up with the production pace without fatigue.
Quality	Good	Excellent
Time	69 seconds	25 seconds

Figure 5-11. What Is Strange about These Operations?

1. Under the current conditions, the parts are split up on the left and right sides of the operator. For example, one stack of parts (cloths) is kept in a red container on the operator's left while another stack is kept in a blue container on the operator's right.

2. The operator picks up one part (cloth) from each side, checks the fronts and backs, then aligns them to be sewn together.

3. The operator sets up the aligned cloths on the sewing machine and sews them together. When finished, an auto cutter cuts the thread and the operator puts the sewn cloths onto the finished goods stack. The overall operation time is 69 seconds.

One disadvantage of this one-worker method is that value-adding work (i.e., actual sewing) accounts for only 20 percent of the operation time while positioning accounts for more than 50 percent.

A second clue to consider is that one goal of our improvement should be to double the value-adding (sewing) operation's share in overall operation time by leaving all of the positioning work to another worker. Suppose, for example, that we hire a new employee or part-time worker to pick up and align the cloths. We could then try out a new layout plan for this operation, as shown in the right half of Figure 5-11.

1. While the main operator is sewing, the assistant can prepare the next set of cloths.
2. When finished sewing, the main operator can proceed directly to setting up the next set of cloths on the machine and sewing them. This reduces the overall operation time to 25 seconds.

Here we have an example of an improvement that more than doubles productivity, or value-adding operation time. However, there are some strange things about this improvement. What are they?

Solution

1. Manpower reduction is always a goal of process razing, such as by rationalizing labor-intensive operations or otherwise minimizing manhours. This example, which doubles the number of workers, makes the operations more labor-intensive than before.
2. One starting point for process razing is the reduction of standby waste. In this example, the assistant's job includes a lot of standby waste. Even if the processing time is shortened in some areas, the line's overall standard production per hour (SPH) will not increase.
3. Process razing improves the processing flow. This flow is based on the cycle time. It is important, therefore, to consider the overall flow and not just the operation time required by a single process.
4. While this solution incurs some expense, productivity could be raised by purchasing a similar used sewing machine and equipping both machines with auto-feed devices enabling a single operator to alternate between the two machines. Or we could equip the one sewing machine so that the operator can alternate between the sewing machine and another process, such as a press process.

6

Trial Elimination of Conveyors

WHAT HAPPENS IF WE REMOVE THE CONVEYOR?

This improvement case study first appeared in the Japanese journal *Factory Management*. It is included here as a helpful illustration of the concept of eliminating conveyors.

Figure 6-1 shows two parallel roller conveyors that serve two processing lines, a crank arm processing line and a rod processing line.

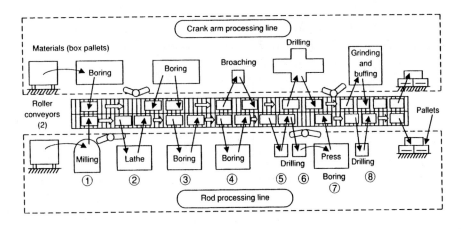

Figure 6-1. Belt Conveyor Lines (Before Improvement)

While this type of belt conveyor was often very useful for transporting heavy items, it suffered from the following disadvantages:

- A sort of invisible wall developed between the two lines linked by the conveyors.

79

- Once this happened, there was very little mutual assistance between the workers on the two lines, even though they all had the same supervisor.
- The belt conveyor tended to get used as a storage place for in-process inventory and thus interfered with one-piece flow production.
- Since the belt conveyors were in straight lines, half of the belt was always moving back to the start point without carrying anything.
- Since different workers were at the start and end of the lines, it was harder to prevent defects from being passed downstream.

Next, the improvement team eliminated waste from specific processes. These improvements enabled each of the two lines to be handled by one worker instead of two. The improvements were:

- eliminating standby waste and waste in picking up and setting down workpieces
- installing auto-clamp devices for positioning workpieces
- improving jigs
- installing auto-feed devices to implement one-piece flow

In other words, post-improvement handling time was reduced to a level more or less equivalent to the cycle time. Next, the team began to carry out process razing, which successfully reduced manpower requirements to one worker per line (see Figure 6-2).

However, the improvement team then considered the sort of layout shown in Figure 6-3 as a means of enabling both processing lines to be handled by just one worker.

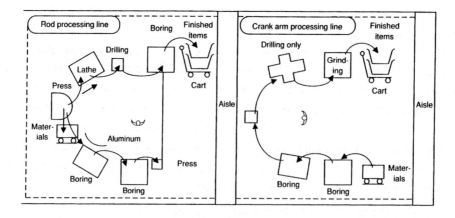

Figure 6-2. Two Lines Handled by Two Workers (After First Improvement)

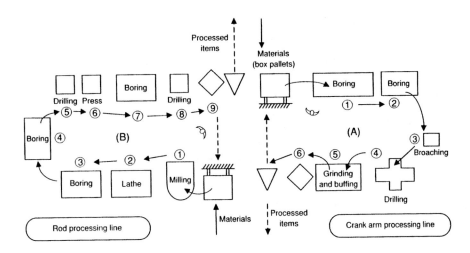

Figure 6-3. Two Lines Operated by One Worker (After Second Improvement)

At the moment, the two lines are still being handled with one worker on each line. The improvement team knows, however, that as soon as it can get the manual operation time of the two lines on par with their cycle times, it will be able to adopt the layout in Figure 6-3 that utilizes only one worker for both lines.

REMOVING THE CONVEYOR FROM AN ASSEMBLY LINE

In today's era of wide-variety small-lot production, many processes still employ conveyors that were designed for the days of small varieties and large lots. At Company O, the factory turns out 60,000 items with an average lot size of five items. Until 1978, it still used a conveyor line for the assembly of small motors (see Figure 6-4).

The flow of goods on the assembly line follows the zigzag pattern indicated by the arrows in Figure 6-4. Even when the assembly work can be done right on the main assembly line conveyor, it is instead done at work tables that have been attached to the side of the main conveyor. This requires unnecessary lifting and carrying. Of the eight processes on the assembly line, bottlenecks tend to occur at processes 1 and 8. Therefore, each are handled by two workers — bringing the number of line workers to ten. Figure 6-5 lists the time measurements and personnel assignments for each process on the line.

Marks were made on the conveyor to show the workers where they should sit to work. While the line appeared to be well organized, the improvement team made the following observations:

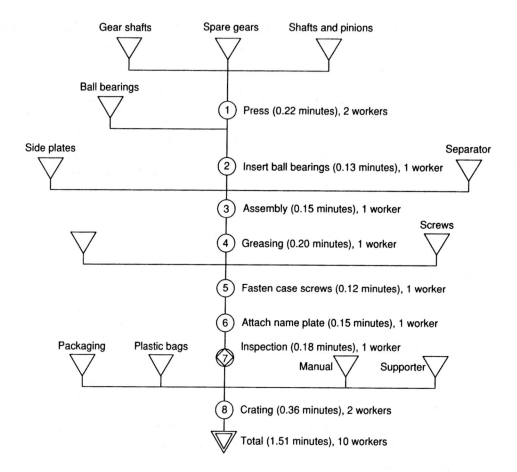

Figure 6-5. Motor Assembly Process Table

1. Because conveyors were tools designed for large-lot production, they tended to work better with larger lots. This caused an increase in the warehouse inventory, which usually stood at about two month's output.

2. Sitting while working made it difficult for workers to help each other. Since the line's cycle time is set according to the speed of the slowest worker, the result was a low line organization efficiency rate, as indicated by the data shown in Figure 6-5.

3. Keeping work in line with the marks on the conveyor resulted in standby waste.

4. All parts for product changeovers were changed at the same time, resulting in changeover loss.

5. Because different workers handled the line's start and end points, it was more difficult to discover the causes of defects. The result was that

entire lots of defective products tended to be produced. As a general observation, it is very difficult to achieve zero defects on a straight-line production line.

Of course, conveyors have certain advantages. One is their forcefulness. Under standard conditions, standard procedures and standard parts without variation are used. Conveyors compel all workers to work at the same pitch. Another advantage is that conveyors encourage workers to specialize, resulting in the development of strong skills. When work is divided into specialized jobs, even a part-time worker can become highly skilled at a particular job after only a week on the line. A third advantage of conveyors is that they encourage mechanization, tool development, and automation at each process on the line. Linear production lines make it easy to see which processes can profit from further mechanization or automation.

There are other advantages. The main point to consider, however, is that conveyor lines are generally at a disadvantage in wide-variety small-lot, or one-piece, production. They are really only suitable as tools for large-scale continuous production lines.

Today's diversifying markets require that more and more factories adopt wide-variety small-lot production systems. Over the past decade, many factories have seen the variety of their products increase tenfold. All factory managers should take the time to perform a P-Q analysis of their products to see how this diversification trend has affected their workplaces. Computerized P-Q analysis programs greatly simplify this task.

Intent on establishing one-piece production, after performing a P-Q analysis, the improvement team at Company O decided to try to remove the conveyors from its motor assembly line and implement process razing by creating a U-shaped cell handled by four workers (see Figure 6-6).

Since then, the improvement team has turned the four separate presses into four linked presses. It has also installed an auto-feed device to feed three screws at once. This allows the motor assembly line to be operated by only two workers (see Figure 6-7).

Without delving into too much detail, the following lists a few major results of these improvements:

1. The assembly line is now conducive to the implementation of a zero-defects campaign.
2. The line is conducive to small-lot production with an average lot size of ten units.

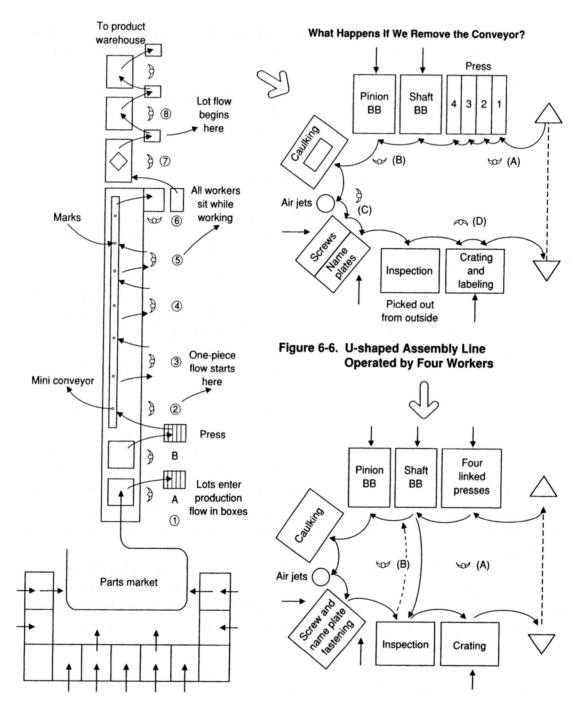

Figure 6-4. Conveyor Assembly Line for Small Motors

What Happens If We Remove the Conveyor?

Figure 6-6. U-shaped Assembly Line Operated by Four Workers

Figure 6-7. U-shaped Assembly Line Operated by Two Workers

3. Inventory reduction was proportionate to lot size reduction. For example, when the lot size dropped from 100 units to ten, inventory shrank 90 percent.
4. The line now allows for successive changeover, reducing changeover loss to 5 percent of its previous level.
5. A sharp reduction in manpower requirements was achieved.

AVOID ENCLOSED CIRCLE LAYOUT DESIGNS

When implementing process razing, we often think in terms of how things have always been done at the factory. We tend to think the best layout is that which brings the line into an enclosed circle that workers operate from the perimeter, like a group of people eating Chinese-style at a large round table with a lazy Susan in the middle. If we put the two ends of the line together in such a layout, the workers will be facing each other across the equipment, which is an invitation for "standing around the water cooler" conversations that interfere with work.

Figure 6-8 shows the small motor assembly line at Company S. The line contains nine conveyor-linked processes which are operated by four workers. Changeover is carried out four times a day and changeover loss has been calculated at about 20 percent of the total operating time. Faced with a need for more cost-efficient management, an improvement team was formed to establish small-lot production and reduce the warehouse and in-process inventory levels.

Figure 6-9 shows this "lazy Susan" kind of layout. In contrast to lazy Susans, in this case, it is the workers — not the equipment — who must move around in circles. This arrangement makes it difficult for workers to assist each other.

Now look at the layout shown in Figure 6-10. More experienced workers handle the first and last processes; part-time workers work on the inside of the U-shaped cell. This enables workers to help each other when necessary. For instance, an experienced worker can easily help a part-time worker who is behind or encounters a problem.

LEARNING PROCESS-RAZING TECHNIQUES

When I go to factories and teach process razing, people are often surprised by my techniques. They act as if I were a factory improvement sorcerer.

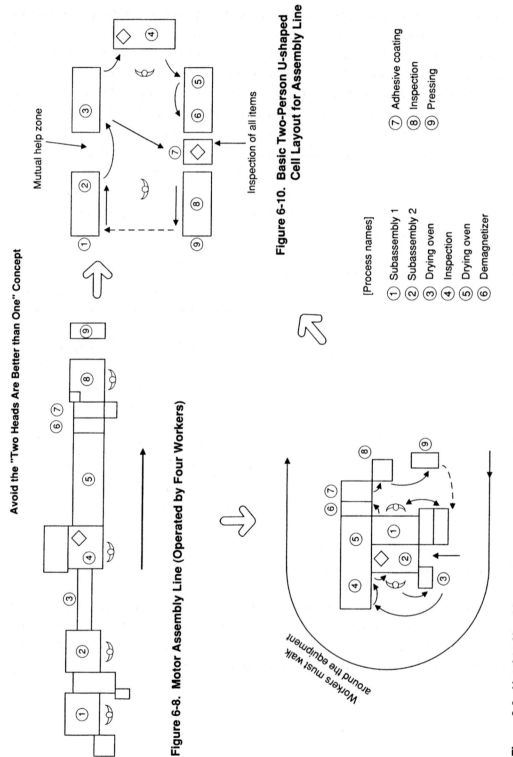

Avoid the "Two Heads Are Better than One" Concept

Mutual help zone

Inspection of all items

Figure 6-10. Basic Two-Person U-shaped Cell Layout for Assembly Line

[Process names]

① Subassembly 1
② Subassembly 2
③ Drying oven
④ Inspection
⑤ Drying oven
⑥ Demagnetizer

⑦ Adhesive coating
⑧ Inspection
⑨ Pressing

Figure 6-8. Motor Assembly Line (Operated by Four Workers)

Workers must walk around the equipment

Figure 6-9. Head-to-Head Layouts Are Disadvantageous

I know that many readers, after studying the layout changes shown in Figures 5-10 and 6-3 (that turn two-person lines into one-person lines) or in Figures 6-7 and 6-10 (that create two-person U-shaped assembly lines), will shake their heads and declare that their factories could never do that.

While it is true that Rome was not built in a day, it is amazing to see what people who are well-versed in process-razing techniques can do in a single day. To aid readers' initial efforts at process razing, I have outlined the major steps in Figure 6-11. From left to right, you will find a list of process-razing steps, corresponding checkpoints, and reference materials and tools for each step.

There are two points of difficulty. The first is step 2's critique of current conditions, where we must take care to avoid negating the purpose of the target process. Without seriously evaluating the current way of doing things, we will be less likely to think of improvements.

If for some reason you are unable to come up with an improvement idea, try drawing a diagram showing the flow of goods in the current line. If you are unable to do that, then diagram the path taken by the workers as they operate the line.

The second point of difficulty is at step 4 — determine the starting point for process razing. While it is seldom a problem when the starting point for process razing is established as a problem in a particular process, when the problem is more abstract, then it might be subjectively understood in different ways by different people. For instance, a worker might consider a certain condition to be a defect in the layout while a manager might consider the same condition to be necessary for preserving harmony among the line workers. Needless to say, such issues can become a source of confusion for layout planners.

In general, when determining the starting point for process razing, consider the following:

1. Start with eliminating waste from each process.

Begin with small improvements and wait until small improvement activities have become an integral part of everyday work activities. Because few small and mid-sized companies have established such daily small improvement activities, starting at this level is especially important.

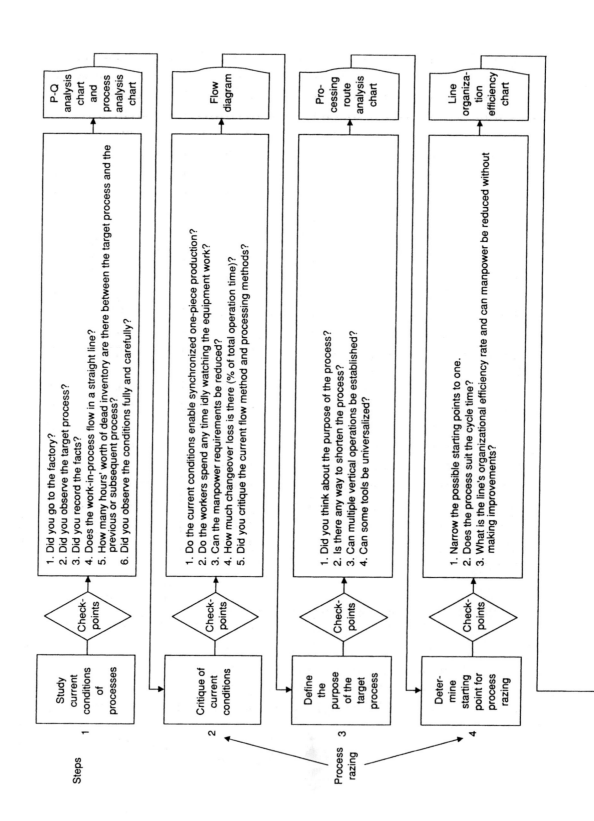

Steps

Process razing

1. Study current conditions of processes

Checkpoints
1. Did you go to the factory?
2. Did you observe the target process?
3. Did you record the facts?
4. Does the work-in-process flow in a straight line?
5. How many hours' worth of dead inventory are there between the target process and the previous or subsequent process?
6. Did you observe the conditions fully and carefully?

P-Q analysis chart and process analysis chart

2. Critique of current conditions

Checkpoints
1. Do the current conditions enable synchronized one-piece production?
2. Do the workers spend any time idly watching the equipment work?
3. Can the manpower requirements be reduced?
4. How much changeover loss is there (% of total operation time)?
5. Did you critique the current flow method and processing methods?

Flow diagram

3. Define the purpose of the target process

Checkpoints
1. Did you think about the purpose of the process?
2. Is there any way to shorten the process?
3. Can multiple vertical operations be established?
4. Can some tools be universalized?

Processing route analysis chart

4. Determine starting point for process razing

Checkpoints
1. Narrow the possible starting points to one.
2. Does the process suit the cycle time?
3. What is the line's organizational efficiency rate and can manpower be reduced without making improvements?

Line organization efficiency chart

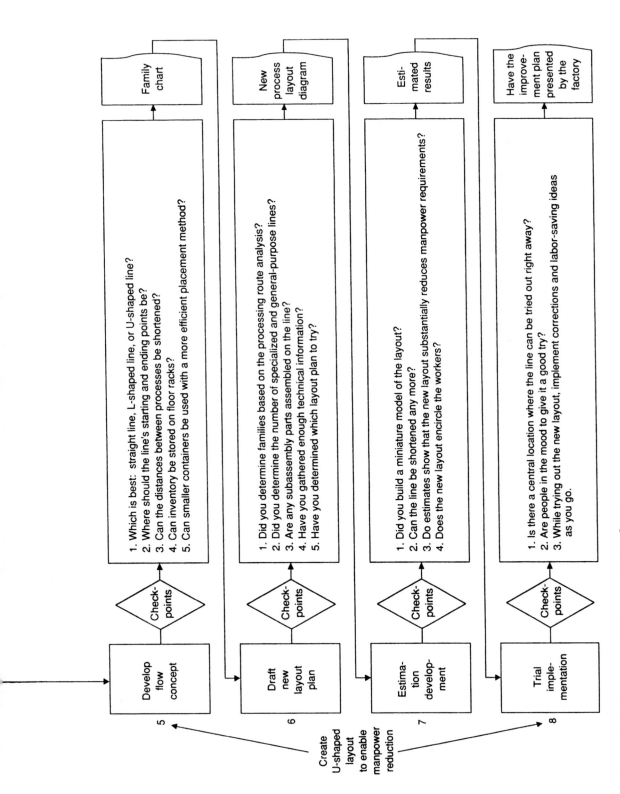

Figure 6-11. Summary of Process-razing Steps

2. Start with reducing standby waste.

One way to approach this is by calculating the line organization efficiency ratio. However, since that requires a certain amount of time and skill, it may be easier to simply observe the workers' motions and watch out for standby instances. Such instances include times when a worker (1) is idly watching the equipment work, (2) has nothing to do because of line imbalances, or (3) is waiting for workpieces that have been delayed due to reworking at upstream processes. The first objective is to eliminate causes of such standby waste.

3. Start with reducing warehouse inventory and in-process inventory waste.

The simplest way to eliminate warehouse inventory and in-process inventory waste is to implement small-lot production. If we attempt to start process razing, however, we are likely to run into a lot of resistance from the factory floor. At this point, small-lot production would have little effect on changeover loss and would make it difficult to meet the daily output requirements.

4. Start with manpower reduction.

Let us suppose, for example, that we decide at this point to create U-shaped cells operated by two workers. We order the entire factory to implement this new layout concept and then evaluate each workshop's improvement implementation effectiveness by the degree to which it has established two-person U-shaped cells. This approach starts from the target concept and pushes the factory toward achieving it.

It has a good chance of success only if the entire company has already become familiar with U-shaped cells and if the workshops have had direct experience in smaller scale U-shaped cell improvements.

5. Start with changeover improvement.

Although most people think that switching to wide-variety small-lot production increases the changeover loss time, this is not the case when we use zero changeover techniques. This approach, while popular among factory workers, is rather timid from the perspective of process razing.

6. Start with eliminating defects and customer complaints.

This is tantamount to starting with a zero-defects campaign. First, we organize the line into U-shaped cells. Then we wait until defect problems occur and take corrective action (such as looking for defect causes via the "5 Whys" approach or by devising mistake-proofing mechanisms for various processes).

7. Start with prevention of missing items.

Missing items are a big problem for assembly processes and, thus, preventing them is a top priority. The two most practical approaches to missing item prevention are: (1) making items continuous (by using the kanban system) and (2) using a tickler system to remind workers when they are running low on an item.

8. Start with preventing intermittent line stops.

Factories that use mechanized or automated devices should keep intermittent line stops within one minute each. Defective items are almost always mixed into the flow of goods immediately before or after such intermittent line stops and will only result in customer complaints if they are shipped.

Ways to prevent intermittent line stops include:

- removing dirt from equipment and preventing its accumulation
- implementing prompt maintenance (for example, by replacing a defective part within three minutes)
- implementing preventive maintenance on a regular basis

9. Start with one-piece production.

We can begin by introducing one-piece production under current conditions at all processes, even those with equipment designed to handle two or more workpieces at once. Certain pieces of equipment, such as large driers designed for large batches of workpieces, will produce energy waste if used for one-piece production. In such cases, we should take the time and trouble to remodel the machine and make it suitable for both one-piece production and zero-defect production.

10. Start with shorter delivery periods.

Process razing is perhaps the most effective way to achieve shorter delivery periods. For example, if we implement process razing for the sake of its advantages for factory management, our process-razing work will necessarily include shortening the distances between processes, often by linking them directly. The more directly linked processes we have, the shorter our delivery period becomes. In fact, the shrinkage in the delivery period is inversely proportional to the number of linked processes; by linking five processes, in effect, we are shortening the delivery period to one-fifth its previous length.

The choice of which of these ten starting points to use for process razing depends on the different needs of the specific processes and industries.

The other process-razing steps will help increase the value-adding performance of a factory and are not difficult. After trying them out a few times, everyone becomes familiar with these process-razing techniques and the steps for their implementation.

7

U-shaped Cells for Assembly Lines

Implementing process razing requires the destruction of the outmoded lot production system and its replacement with U-shaped cells that promote a one-piece flow production and one-piece inspection system. The development of this new system is called "process flow building." If mistakes are made in the way this new system is built, while it may have the form of U-shaped cells, it will not fulfill the function of keeping goods flowing in pace with the cycle time. That is why this chapter first will carefully present the basic principles of process flow building.

WHAT GOES FOR A GARMENT FACTORY GOES FOR A MOTOR ASSEMBLY FACTORY

Building U-shaped cells in processing lines is relatively easy, except in lines that require micro-level parts processing. There are also ways to build joint assembly/processing lines, but we will leave that discussion to later chapters.

In this chapter, we will study U-shaped cell development, allocation of work, and parts feed sequences in sewing assembly lines, a type of assembly line with particularly demanding product changeover requirements. A U-shaped cell built incorrectly will impede the flow of goods, giving rise to standby waste and making it impossible to achieve the estimated production output.

In sewing lines, the most difficult part of changeover is not the switch between product models. Rather, it is the initial production of new or improved products. This makes process razing a daily requirement. If we can successfully build U-shaped cells in a garment factory, we should be able to build them in almost any kind of factory. To illustrate, we shall compare the building of U-shaped cells in a garment factory with that in a motor assembly factory.

A Comparison of Two Factories

First, we shall examine an assembly procedure from each factory: (1) in the motor assembly line, the screw and bolt tightening equipment in the bolt assembly process, and (2) in the sewing line, the assembly of cloth pieces using sewing machines. These assembly operations are similar in principle, differing mainly in the kinds of tools and goods employed. In the former, workpieces are hard pieces of metal; in the latter, they are soft pieces of fabric.

In assembly standards, the first principle is center assembly and the second principle is edge assembly. Some parts can protrude from the edges in motor assembly, but not in sewing.

When it comes to preparing assembly parts, we can compare the main unit of the motor to the front side of the piece of clothing being sewn. We can also compare the motor case to the back side of the clothing, the rotor to the sleeves, the starter to the lining, the coil scopes to the pockets, and so on. In making this comparison, I want to emphasize that, while they differ in the parts and tools used, assembly lines for clothing and motors are basically the same.

One difference worth mentioning is that in motor assembly, once the sequence of assembly operations has been worked out, standardization is relatively easy. In sewing factories that turn out high-fashion apparel for women, for example, the assembly varies according to the operator, making procedures difficult to standardize. In addition, production changes daily. In the case of mass-produced clothing, however, operations are more standardized and similar to motor assembly.

FIXED IDEAS IN SEWING FACTORIES

Figure 7-1 shows a nearly blank assembly process chart. The only things entered on it are the part names (A, B, C, and D), which can symbolize parts for either clothing or motors, or even for wood products or gauges.

After thinking about how his or her own factory's processes might be described by this assembly process chart, I would like the reader to fill in the blank chart's empty circles with assembly process numbers.

Our objective is to discover the critical path. This is the most important set of processes for feeding materials into the line (process 1). For simplicity's sake, we will assume that the required assembly time is one minute at each process. Number the 30 processes as shown in Figure 7-2.

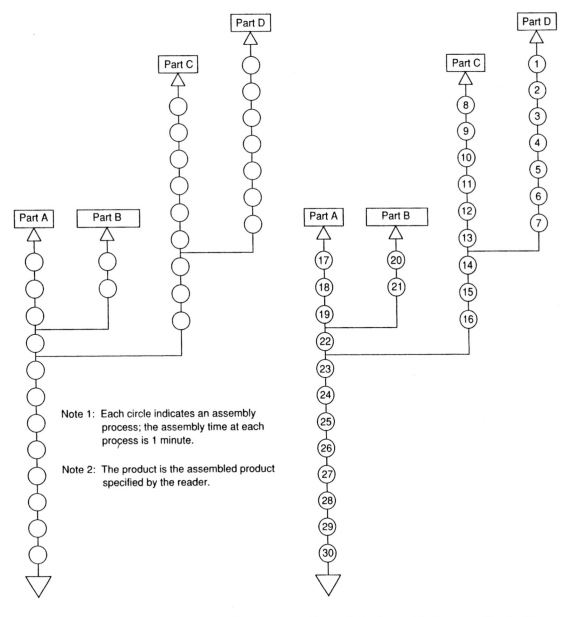

Note 1: Each circle indicates an assembly process; the assembly time at each process is 1 minute.

Note 2: The product is the assembled product specified by the reader.

Figure 7-1. Blank Assembly Process Chart

Figure 7-2. Assembly Process Chart with Process Numbers

I have filled out Figure 7-2 with imaginary processes, which may or may not be completely realistic. In this assembly line, the critical path consists of the processes for part D at the right edge of the chart.

We will now look at an assembly process chart that actually has been used at a garment factory (see Figure 7-3).

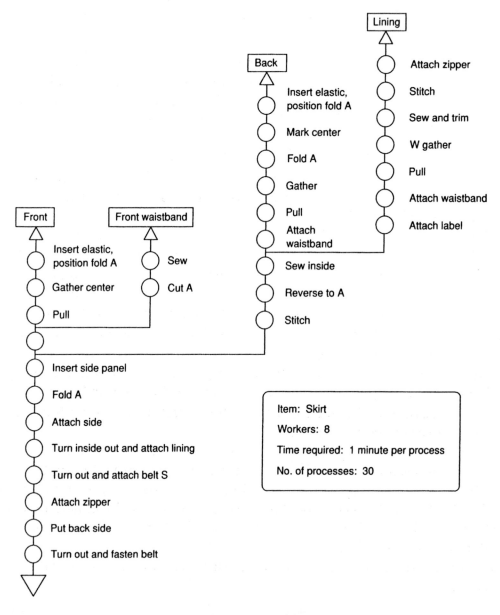

Figure 7-3. Actual Assembly Process Chart (with Process Numbers)

This example, however, presents a problem. As illustrated in Figure 7-3:

- The process numbers have been entered.
- The required time for each process is one minute.
- The line is operated by eight assembly workers, including the leader. The leader is responsible for both the first process (process 1) and the last process (process 30); the other seven operators are each responsible for four processes.

Under these conditions, the 28 processes not handled by the leader have been divided evenly among the seven assembly workers (A, B, C, D, E, and F), making each responsible for four processes. The problem is in deciding which processes should be handled by which workers in order for the line to flow smoothly within the cycle time.

You may wish to think of the solution in terms of the number of minutes per worker (nine minutes, for instance) or in terms of the number of processes handled per hour by each worker. Figure 7-4 presents a solution proposed by a veteran assembly line leader.

The Japanese learn in school that the front of the skirt should always be used as the base, a theory that has become a practice. In her solution, the veteran garment factory leader has forgotten about the importance of finding the critical path, and has instead held onto the fixed idea of the front of the skirt being used as the base. In other words, as soon as the veteran leader saw the "front of skirt" process, she assumed that it should be process 1, as surely as the sun rises in the east. A practice has become dogma.

We must repeatedly ask what is the purpose of each process. In my proposed solution, I assigned processes 2 through 29 in more or less sequential order to the seven workers, according to the direction in which the process numbers were assigned in Figure 7-2.

Figure 7-5 presents my solution. In this case, the first process is the zipper attachment process for the lining. However, in other cases, the first process might be the elastic insertion and position fold A process (process 8), which would be for the leader to handle. Working toward the establishment of a zero-defect line requires the leader to be responsible for the processes that are most crucial for quality assurance.

In my solution, having the lining zipper attachment process as the first process means that:

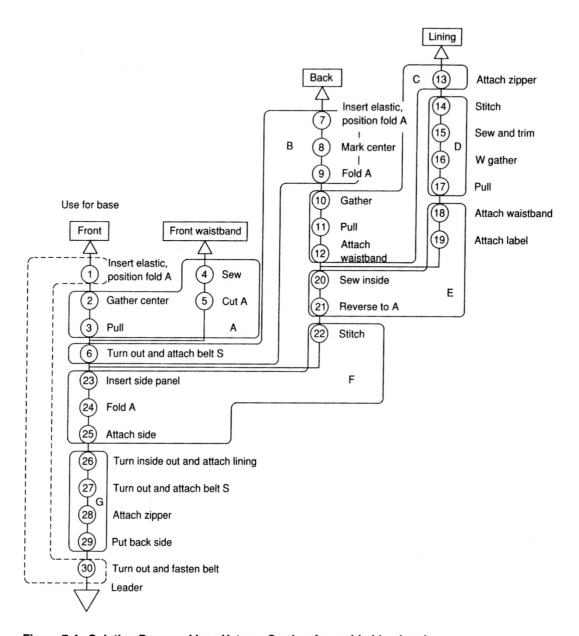

Figure 7-4. Solution Proposed by a Veteran Sewing Assembly Line Leader

1. The first material to be fed to the line is the lining material.
2. The second material to be fed to the line is the back material (for process 8).

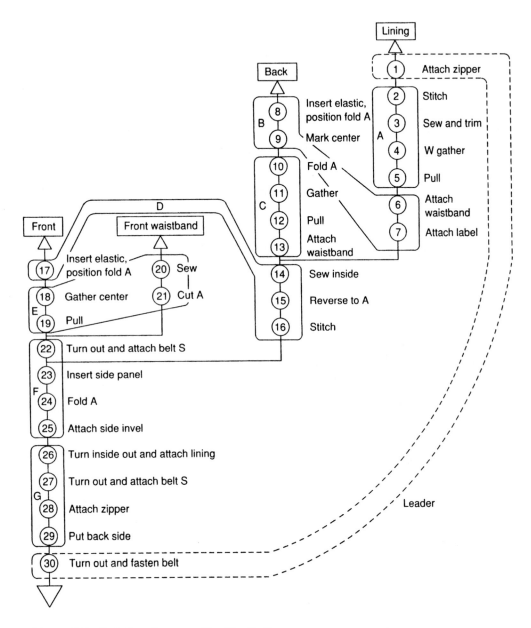

Figure 7-5. Solution Proposed by the Author

3. The third material to be fed to the line is the front material (for process 17).

4. The fourth material to be fed to the line is at the "front waistband" process.

Remember: The purpose of finding the critical path is to prevent standby waste at changeover points in the one-piece flow production system. When we take standby waste as our starting point for process razing, it becomes easier to understand what needs to be done.

It was probably more difficult to discover the critical path in the motor assembly line, since this line did not have branch lines as did the sewing line. Instead, it was a straight line that will be described later in this chapter (see Figure 4-9).

Now consider how to work the time factor into our discovery of the critical path and the order in which parts are fed to the line.

Step 1: Add the total time beginning with the last process (in this case, process 30).

For example:

Process 30 = 240 DM
Process 30 + 29 = (240 + 480 =) 720 DM
Process 30 + 29 + 28 = (240 + 480 + 200 =) 920 DM

To make these sums easier to read, we will refer to the totals in parentheses and to the individual process times without parentheses. Time the processes, preferably with a decimal-minute (DM) stopwatch that divides each minute into 100 decimal seconds.

Step 2: Reassign the process numbers while keeping track of the process time sums.

The difference between Figures 7-5 and 7-6 is the order in which the processes for the front material and the front waistband material are numbered. In Figure 7-5, the process numbers begin with the front material before moving on to the front waistband material processes. When figuring in the time factor, however, we must put the first three front material processes before the front waistband material processes to avoid having standby time.

We must be very careful how we divide up assembly processes. For example, there can be no balance between the process (29) that has the longest process time (480 DM) and the processes (21 and 3) that have the shortest process times (25 DM each). Looking at what these processes involve, we can see that process 29 encompasses a variety of operations while processes 21 and 3 involve relatively simple motions, which means they are easy to divide up as separate processes. This is what prompted me to split up the processes for each operator simply based on a similar number of processes per operator (see Figure 7-5).

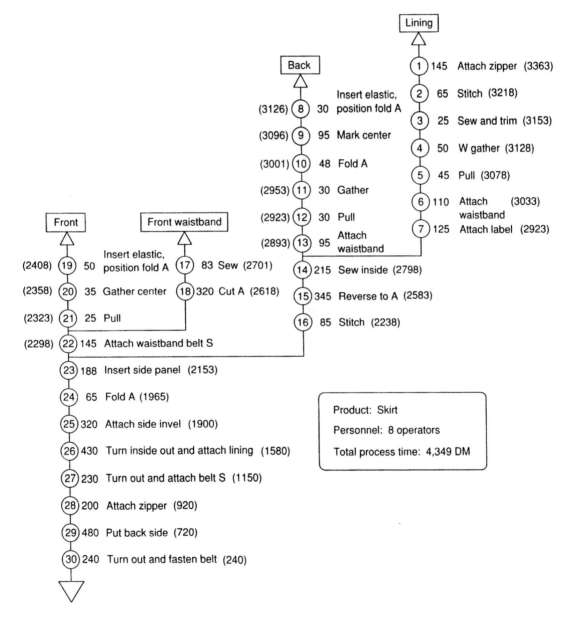

Figure 7-6. Process Times (Accumulated Time)

Step 3: Draw a diagram showing the critical path and material feed sequence, as shown in Figure 7-7.

This kind of diagram only needs to be drawn once, during leader training.

We keep an accumulative record of the process times on the horizontal axis and show the processes on the vertical axis. Mark down the process number, process time, and total time for each part (material). Again, we count the total process time backward — beginning at the last process.

Step 4: Determine the parts feed sequence.

We should begin with the parts feed point having the longest accumulated time and finish with the one having the shortest total time. In the present case, our first feed process, indicated as a pyramid containing the number one, is the lining material feed point. Next is the back material, then the front waistband, and finally the front material.

Actually, the materials in this case are supplied as kits on the supply carts, so we could easily arrange Figure 7-7's process layout according to the parts feed sequence.

Step 5: Assign processes to operators.

As opposed to Figure 7-7, which shows the processes laid out according to the parts feed sequence, the actual layout assigns processes to operators according to the process times.

1. The leader is responsible for the entry and exit processes. The man-hours (process time) of these two processes (240 + 145) equals 385 DM.
2. The remaining 28 processes are divided among the other seven workers. The total time for these 28 processes (4,349 − 385) is 3,964 DM. This is divided into seven equal time segments of 566 DM. The 28 processes should be divided into seven segments that come as close as possible to the 566 DM mark without being impractical. Precision is not important; there can be slight variation in their lengths.
3. After determining the segments, assign the slightly longest segments to the workers who tend to work the fastest.

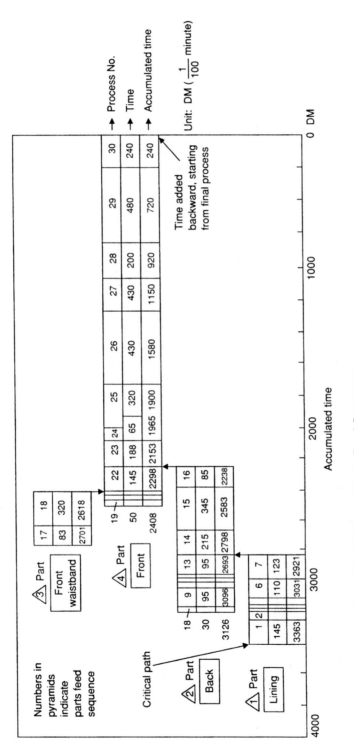

Figure 7-7. Diagram with Critical Path and Parts Feed Sequence

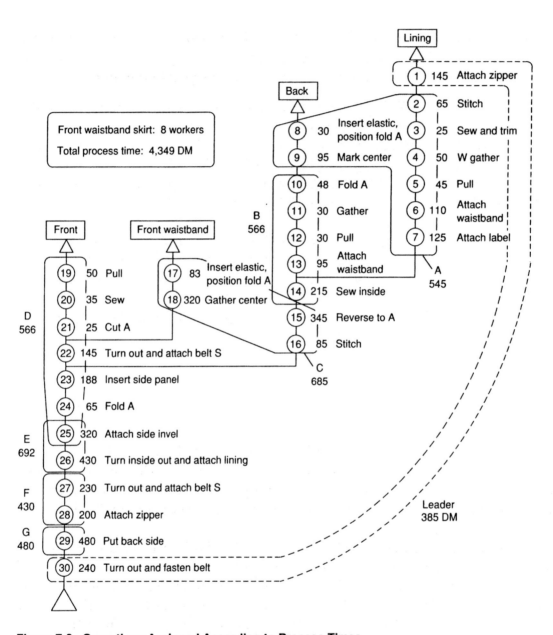

Figure 7-8. Operations Assigned According to Process Times

4. After the workers verbally signal completion of the changeover for a new product, new time measurements should be taken and processes reassigned to prevent certain workers from becoming overtaxed by the different assembly operations for the new product.

5. If imbalances still occur, they also can be remedied by mutual assistance among the line workers. Sometimes, when trying out a new assignment plan, we find that there are still considerable gaps in the time factors.

Compare Figure 7-5 with Figure 7-8. This comparison shows how the assignment of processes to workers changes according to the concept behind the assignment method. Since some processes consist only of simple motions while others involve a variety of operations including changeover, it does not work to simply assign each worker the same number of processes. Troublesome as it can be, we must base process layout and assignment of processes to workers upon the key factor of process times.

Let's move on to Figure 7-9, which shows a motor assembly line process chart. Note that this line contains a relatively large number of linear assembly processes, which makes the line easy to convert into a set of U-shaped cells.

The branching type of assembly line in the garment factory example requires more clever solutions. These will be discussed again in the next chapter.

TEST YOUR SKILLS

Change a five-person line into a four-person line.

Look again at the motor assembly process chart shown in Figure 7-9. You will recall that in Chapter 4 we discussed the important distinction between machine operation time (MT) and human operation time (HT). The more we can substitute MT for HT in an assembly line, the fewer people will be needed to operate the line.

The current layout, shown in Figure 7-10, is a U-shaped cell layout — not a very good one, however, because it includes a lot of standby.

As you can see, currently there are five workers for this line. Our goal is to change this to a U-shaped cell layout that requires only four workers. Give yourself nine minutes to come up with a process-razing solution to this problem. The only restriction in the layout is that the drying oven cannot be moved.

Solution

My solution is shown in Figure 7-11.

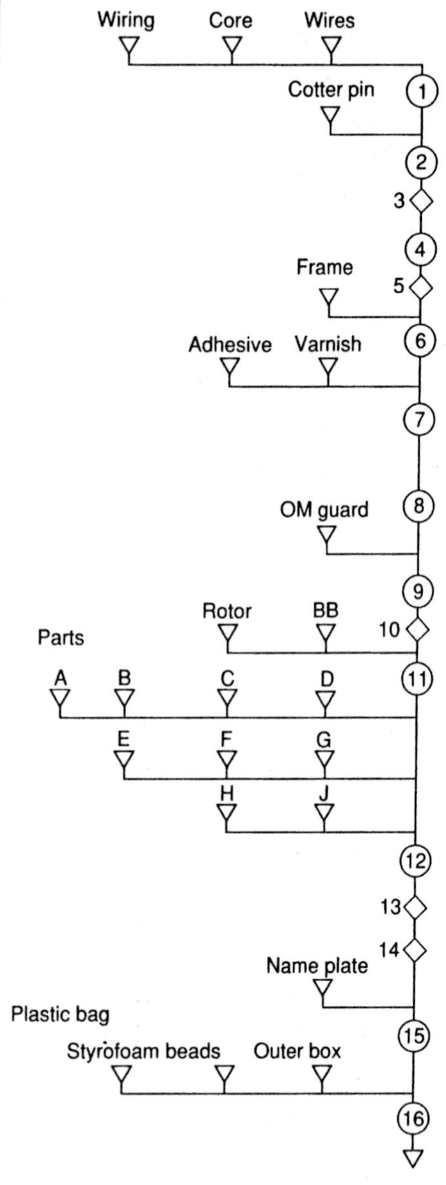

Process Symbol or No.	Process Name	M T	H T
Wiring · Core · Wires			
Cotter pin — ①	Coil	45	57
②	Molding and cotter insertion	13	14
3 ◇			
④	Wire ends		50
Frame — 5 ◇			
⑥	Assembly		19
Adhesive · Varnish	Drip and gluing	25	12
⑦			
	Drying	63	32
OM guard — ⑧			
⑨	Rust-proofing		10
Rotor · BB — 10 ◇	Insert BBs	16	10
Parts — ⑪			
A · B · C · D	Attach rotor		15
E · F · G			
H · J			
⑫	Rotor blades		26
13 ◇	End points		26
14 ◇			
Name plate	Inspection	62	20
Plastic bag · ⑮	Attach name plate	15	6
Styrofoam beads · Outer box			
⑯	Pack into box	10	17
Total		249	314

Figure 7-9. Motor Assembly Process Chart

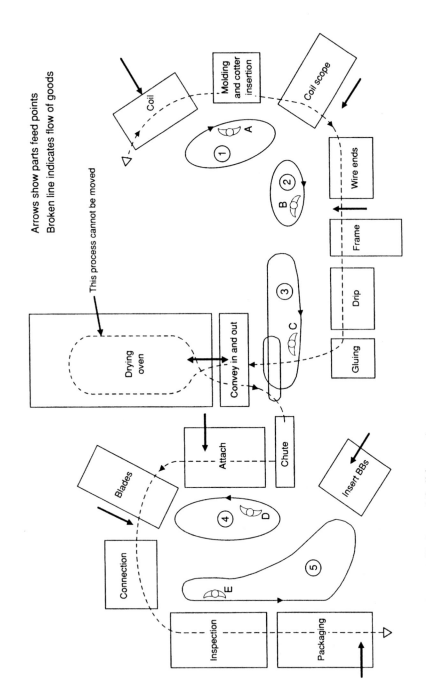

Figure 7-10. Current U-shaped Cell Layout

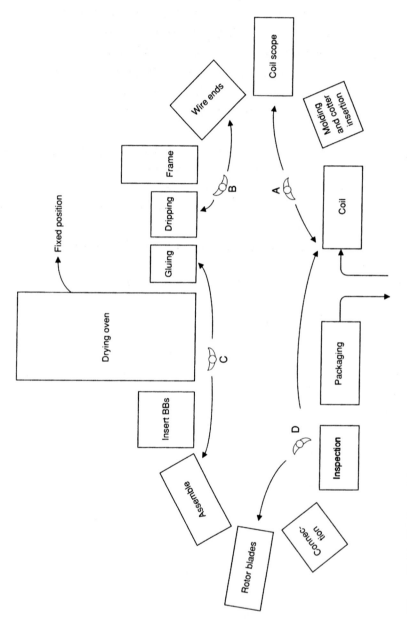

Figure 7-11. U-shaped Cell with Reduced Manpower (from Five to Four Workers)

The following is a step-by-step description of how I developed this solution.

1. I decided to place the immovable drying oven in the center.
2. To build a U pattern, I placed the previous process (coil) on the oven's right and the assembly process on the oven's left.
3. I assigned the leader, veteran worker D, to the entry and exit processes.
4. Since there had been a lot of standby at the assemble process, I took away one worker from this process and tried out the line with only four workers.
5. Using the workers' verbal cues, I measured the process times and divided up the work into equal time segments.
6. I fine-tuned the line balance, checked the standard production per hour (SPH), and worked to make process-razing improvements in processes that were relatively unproductive.

     These improvements were aimed at the following:
   • standby waste
   • waste in picking up and setting down things
   • overspecialization waste
   • workpiece changeover waste

Such process razing was effective in improving the processes. In this case, however, it was best to first approach the problem from the angle of changing the layout to a U-shaped cell layout.

8

Establishing U-shaped Cells
in a Garment Factory

U-SHAPED CELLS FOR ASSEMBLY LINES

Although the title of this chapter concerns garment factory operations, this chapter is essentially a discussion of establishing U-shaped cells for assembly lines. Whether the items being assembled are clothes, motors, or electrical switchboards, the principles are the same. Therefore, the reader is encouraged to see how these principles apply to assembly operations in his or her own company.

We will use the steps for building U-shaped cells that were discussed in Chapter 7 (see Figure 7-5), focusing on the following three steps:

Step 1: Attempt linear layout based on assembly process charts.

We have already seen an example of assembly process charts in Figure 7-5. Figure 8-1 shows another example that is suited to continuous mass production. Consequently, it includes a roller conveyor.

The first process is the entry point for part D. For one-piece flow, however, we need to consider docking for flow mixing points. When part D is being fed to the first process, a signal should be given to the processes where parts A, B, and C are supplied. Although Figure 8-1 does not show the personnel assignments on the line, it does show a variable linear layout that faithfully reflects the assembly process chart. Of course, this is just a theoretical plan, based on what looks good on paper rather than what works best on the factory floor.

One practical problem with the layout in Figure 8-1 is that, in the event of line imbalances, the various line branches are too far apart from each other to

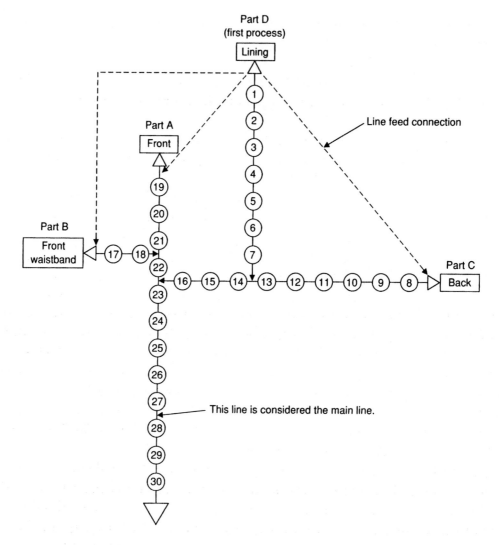

Figure 8-1. Linear Layout

enable mutual assistance among the line workers. Another problem is that using workers in certain processes only makes defect detection and prevention more difficult, and producing defects is an even bigger problem for large-lot production lines such as this one. The biggest drawback of all, however, is that the layout makes it impossible for the same worker to handle the line's entry and exit points. This is a major hindrance to achieving zero defects.

Step 2: Next, redesign the layout so that all processes are on the same conveyor.

To do this, we need to part with the branched line layout shown in Figures 7-5 and 8-1 and rearrange the processes along just one conveyor in the order of the parts feed sequence (see Figure 8-2).

The layout shown in Figure 8-2 is longer than necessary. For this line, the flow method has the assembled product from the part D section carried to process 13, where it is placed under the part C product that is still being assembled. At process 16, this product (now a kit consisting of parts D and C) is taken to process 23, where it is placed under parts B and A. Thus, the closer the assembled product gets to the final process, the larger becomes the kit. Despite this disadvantage, using kits in this way helps to prevent assembly errors.

The greatest risk lies in the "large-lot defects" that tend to occur most easily when conveyors are used. The most likely cause of such defects is excessive division of labor. The second most likely cause is having separate workers handle the line's entry and exit points. This prevents information concerning defective materials or defects inherent in processes from flowing through the line.

Another cause is the speed of the conveyor. For practical reasons, the conveyor must be kept at the pace of the slowest line worker, which means the faster line workers face a lot of standby time. It takes sharp "waste-removal vision" to spot where such standby occurs so that the waste can be reduced. Usually, much standby waste is left unnoticed.

Even though such drawbacks exist, conveyors are still well suited for mass-production lines. They force everyone to maintain a certain pace and production yield tends to reach the estimated levels. Conveyors are not well suited for wide-variety small-lot production lines, however, because they require simultaneous changeover for the whole line — and this creates changeover waste.

Step 3: Create U-shaped cells for the assembly line.

Figure 8-3 shows how the linear layout from Figure 8-2 can be turned into a U-shaped cell to enable the same worker (the line leader) to handle the line's entry and exit points.

The flow method in this U-shaped cell is the same as that in the layout shown in Figure 8-2. The only major difference is that this line uses manual

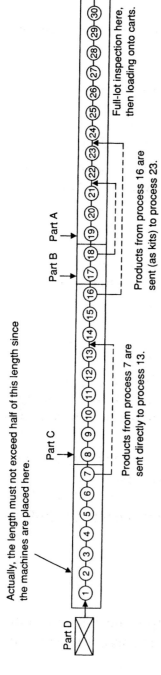

Figure 8-2. Layout Using a Single Conveyor

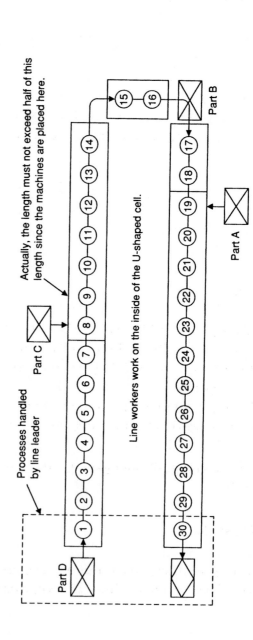

Figure 8-3. U-shaped Cell for a Garment Factory Line

conveyance conducive to one-piece flow, one-piece production, and one-piece inspection. In addition, working on the inside of the U-shaped cell, the line workers are able to give mutual assistance when necessary. Parts are supplied from the outer edge of the U-shaped cell.

This example illustrates us the basic approach and steps for building assembly-line U-shaped cells.

HOW TO IMPROVE THE OPERATION OF ASSEMBLY-LINE U-SHAPED CELLS

After building our U-shaped cell, we need to check the cell's conditions to make sure that it can always operate at the standard production per hour (SPH). In some cases, improvements are needed to ensure SPH-level performance.

Measures Dealing with Missing Items

In assembly processes, missing items are a sure cause of problems. The need to prevent missing items is an important issue.

Kanban

Kanban should be used to keep track of items that are turned out in continuous production lines. For example: the types of items listed in groups A and B in P-Q analysis, even if they are lot-production items produced only five or six times per year.

When management policy dictates a rapid-delivery system, we should begin with kanban for products and later develop kanban for parts.

In wide-variety small-lot production, because the number of parts kanban tends to grow in unmanageable proportions, it is more convenient to use in-factory kanban.

Tickler system

If the product falls into the P-Q category of group C (produced in intermitted lots three or fewer times per year or produced to order only), it is better to use special-order slips. These slips can be issued by computer and thus help prevent errors in parts development when estimating material requirements.

Instead of kanban-based automatic ordering and automated production, we can establish a tickler system that uses order slips to keep track of the daily scheduled provision of materials and parts. Having such a tickler system is important for ensuring the correct timing and quantities of supplied parts and materials, especially when the supplier is an outside company that is not always reliably prompt in making deliveries.

Preventing Rework, Defects, and Operation Errors

The occurrence of defects causes the same kinds of problems as missing parts, which makes preventing defects an equally important principle for assembly-line management activities.

Activity 1: Implement full-lot inspections not only in your own factory's lines but also in lines at supplier factories.

The era of sampling inspections has past. Today we enter the era of zero defects. Zero-defect production downstream cannot exist without zero-defect production upstream. While building zero-defect lines on our own factories, we also must send quality control managers to supplier factories to help them do the same. Simply evaluating suppliers' shipments and checking data from within the confines of one's own factory will not lead to the kind of action needed to establish zero-defect production at supplier factories. The key is for everyone to learn and repeatedly practice the process-razing techniques discussed in Chapter 5.

Activity 2: Play the "5 Why" game.

In order to find the causes of defects, ask "why?" five times. Then, based on your answers, find ways to prevent their recurrence. We will look at some examples of this later.

Activity 3: Establish mistake-proofing.

I cannot overemphasize the importance of mistake-proofing. Because much has already been written about mistake-proofing, I will not discuss it here. Suffice it to say that sensors help greatly to catch human errors.

Horizontal Development of Zero Changeover

The simplest way to reduce product warehouse inventory is by reducing assembly lot sizes. For example, to cut the inventory level by half, we need only reduce the assembly lot by half. In other words, every percentage of reduction in assembly lot size will bring approximately the same percentage of shrinkage in product warehouse inventory. On the other hand, when we increase the changeover time by a factor of N, a conspicuous increase in idle time will result, making it difficult or impossible to maintain the standard daily production (SDP).

Therefore, the precondition for success in reducing assembly lot sizes is to establish and horizontally develop techniques for keeping changeover in machining lines and other assembly parts processing lines to within three minutes (that is, zero changeover).

On the assembly line itself, changeover must be completely successive. To do this, we also must have successful zero changeover. We will take a closer look at zero changeover in forthcoming chapters.

Measures Against Intermittent Line Stops

Intermittent line stops are problems that cause a machine or device on the line to stop briefly (for a minute or less). Such intermittent line stops tend to occur unpredictably for mysterious reasons and they usually coincide roughly with the production of defective goods. This makes intermittent line stops an important problem for quality control managers.

In process industry or automation device factories, the common quality control axiom that "quality is built into the product at each process" has been extended to "quality is built into the product at each device in each process." Therefore, their QC activities generally include:

- establishing a calendar of preventive maintenance activities
- practicing in quick response maintenance (such as replacing parts within three minutes of a breakdown)
- using line-specific and machine-specific data surveys on intermittent stops to aid in eliminating causes and implementing the "5 Why" approach

In addition, there is the building of U-shaped cells, which we discussed earlier on. We should note, however, that these QC activities are basic preconditions for establishing successful U-shaped cells.

ESTABLISHING AN OVERALL PRODUCTION FLOW IN A GARMENT FACTORY

The Toyota Production System (TPS) is, among other things, a way to establish an overall production flow. In fact, no factory's production system is based on the Toyota Production System until it integrates the production flow throughout the factory — not just for certain lines within the factory. This means that even the U-shaped cell shown in the garment factory example in Figure 8-3 cannot be called a TPS application, even though it uses standing-while-working machines and includes vertical multi-process handling.

To become a Toyota Production System example, the three lines must be integrated as one U-shaped cell. First, we must draw up plans for U-shaped cell designs. This should include making paper patterns that meet the production standards and drafting new production standards as required for the U-shaped cell design.

Next, we must figure out how to integrate setup processes in the U-shaped cell. In garment factories, such setup processes can include cutting fabric and manufacturing small parts to be assembled onto the clothing in the main assembly line. We also need to plan for kit carts that can travel along the U-shaped cell.

Finally, we are ready to begin designing the main assembly U-shaped cell. This U-shaped cell will include more than the garment assembly processes shown in Figure 8-3. In fact, in this second process-razing effort, we will need to integrate the finishing machines and other finishing processes (such as thread-tying and button-sewing) as well as pressing, inspection, and packaging. Thus, the entire garment factory becomes one overall U-shaped cell layout.

And don't forget that the same person should handle the cell's entry and exit points. As a rule of thumb, to meet a 20-day delivery deadline, we should plan on one day for making the paper patterns, one day for the setup processes, and three days for the assembly and packaging processes. This means a total of five days for each small-lot production run.

In Chapter 13, we will examine a case study of an apparel manufacturer called MYNAC, which achieved a single-delivery period of nine days and went on to aim for a further reduction to just five days by linking processes and making other improvements to the overall production flow.

The challenge for all garment factories is to create a new garment production system that features an uninterrupted flow from the reception of customer orders to parts processing, parts subassembly, assembly, inspection, packaging, and shipment, all moving at an even speed and a steady cycle time, based on one-piece flow, one-piece production, and one-piece inspection. For MYNAC, the proof of success in taking on this challenge will be the establishment of five-day delivery periods and zero customer complaints.

TEST YOUR SKILLS

What Is Wrong withThis U-shaped Cell Design?

Figure 8-4 shows an assembly process chart for a garment factory. The products are skirts, the line is staffed by eight workers, and, for simplicity's sake, the operation time has been set at two minutes per process. Since there are 31 processes, the total operation time is 62 minutes. We will omit discussion of the cycle time.

This chart has the following characteristics:

1. Going along with the conventional wisdom that the front is the basic piece of fabric, we call the line to which the front piece is supplied the main assembly line. The lines supplying the other three main parts are set apart as branch lines.
2. The layout has machine-specific processes (all process numbers are machine numbers), which means it is a machine-oriented layout. In this layout, operations are grouped around machines, such as ironing operations at the ironing table.

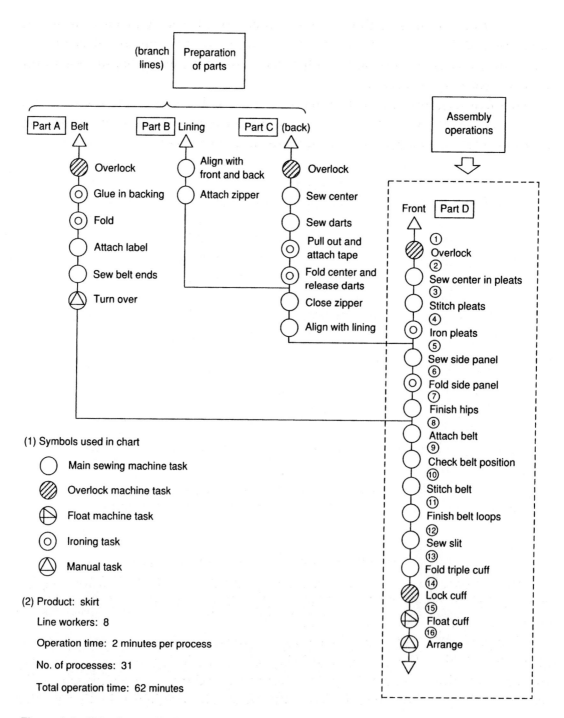

(1) Symbols used in chart

○   Main sewing machine task

◯ (hatched)   Overlock machine task

◉ (float)   Float machine task

⊙   Ironing task

△   Manual task

(2) Product: skirt

Line workers: 8

Operation time: 2 minutes per process

No. of processes: 31

Total operation time: 62 minutes

Figure 8-4. Skirt Assembly Process Chart

Readers unfamiliar with garment factory operations are advised to ignore the various part and process names and to simply think of the parts as parts A, B, C, and D. This should help such readers imagine how this layout might apply to their own factories.

This is a large-lot layout in which the flow is based on the "bundle" system. (Parts are conveyed in lots or "bundles" of ten units each for lot production.) This layout is also shown in Photo 8-1 and Figure 8-5.

Photo 8-1. Classroom-style Layout

As shown in the left side of Photo 8-1, stacks of in-process inventory piled up between each process in the line. This prevented the factory from keeping up with its estimated SPH and resulted in large lots of products needing rework or having irreparable defects.

One garment factory employee noticed these problems and prompted the factory to establish the U-shaped cell layout shown in Figure 8-6 and to carry out process razing. The eight workers were assigned two processes each to distribute the 16 processes evenly. The employee who originally instigated this improvement had a professional understanding of garment factory operations and the new plan suffered few problems. Nevertheless, he sensed that something was wrong with the layout.

I now ask the reader to think of a way to carry out process razing and transform the layout shown in Figure 8-4 into a U-shaped cell. If necessary, refer back to the explanation of process-razing techniques — and use your imagination. There is no need to explain the steps in reaching your conclusions, just jot down the conclusions themselves.

I will give you a few hints:

- Discard the conventional wisdom that the front line (part D) should be the main line and the other parts' lines should be the branch lines.
- Using the assembly process chart, enter process numbers, find the critical path, and mark the start of that path as the first process.
- First draw up an assembly process chart that follows a single straight line, then bend it into a U-shaped cell design.
- Assign the lead worker to the line's entry and exit processes.

Solution

My objective is to create a U-shaped cell for wide-variety small-lot production. While there are several good ways to solve this problem, I propose a solution shown in Figure 8-7 that follows seven steps.

Step 1. I began with the assignment of tasks. Since there are 31 processes altogether, I assigned three processes to the leader and calculated the rest as shown:

31 processes − 3 processes (for leader) = 28 processes
28 processes ÷ 7 other workers = 4 processes per worker

Step 2. I proposed a two-piece production system in which workers handle one set of materials at a time and one set exists as in-process inventory. This is a small-lot production system rather than a one-piece flow system. The one-piece "cushion" of in-process inventory means it is not imperative to have rigidly precise operation times for each process.

Step 3. Once I had drawn up a straight-line layout linking the lines for parts A, B, C, and D, I rearranged them into the U-shaped cell shown in Figure 8-7.

What Is Wrong with These U-shaped Cells?

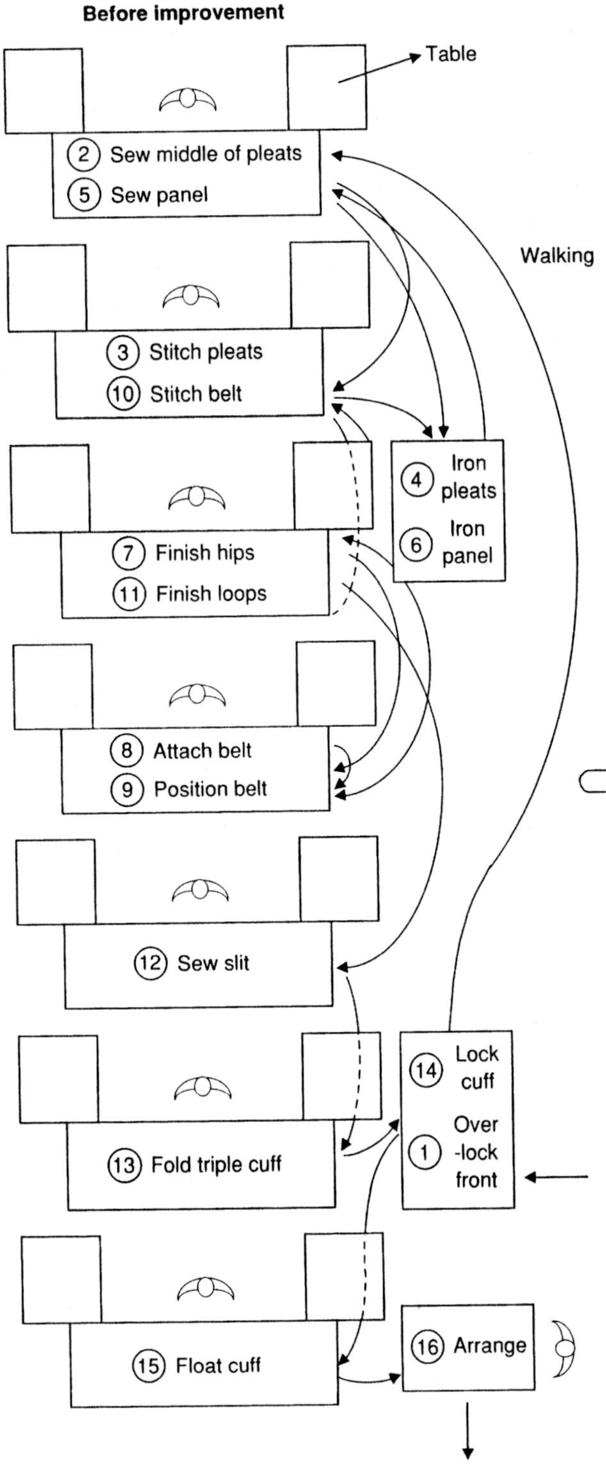

Before improvement

Table

② Sew middle of pleats
⑤ Sew panel

Walking

③ Stitch pleats
⑩ Stitch belt

④ Iron pleats
⑥ Iron panel

⑦ Finish hips
⑪ Finish loops

⑧ Attach belt
⑨ Position belt

⑫ Sew slit

⑭ Lock cuff
① Over-lock front

⑬ Fold triple cuff

⑮ Float cuff

⑯ Arrange

Figure 8-5. Current Classroom-style Layout

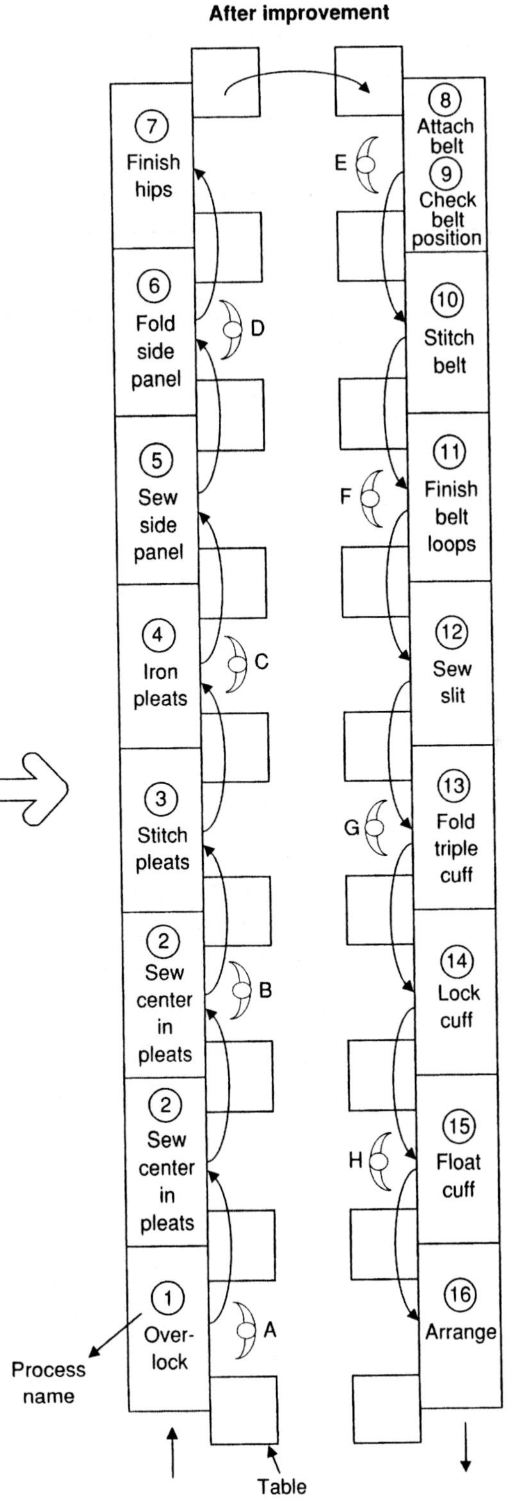

After improvement

⑦ Finish hips

⑧ Attach belt
⑨ Check belt position

E

⑥ Fold side panel

D

⑩ Stitch belt

⑤ Sew side panel

F

⑪ Finish belt loops

④ Iron pleats

C

⑫ Sew slit

③ Stitch pleats

G

⑬ Fold triple cuff

② Sew center in pleats

B

⑭ Lock cuff

② Sew center in pleats

⑮ Float cuff

H

① Over-lock

A

⑯ Arrange

Process name

Table

Figure 8-6. U-shaped Cell for Main Line Only (Eight Workers)

Step 4. I recognized that, as it stands, this layout permits mutual assistance only between adjacent processes.

Step 5. As is also shown in Figure 8-7, I tried to group together similar types of machinery and ironing tables within the U-shaped cell.

Step 6. I made plans to remodel the straight-line and basin sewing machines to include auto-feed (MT) devices.

Step 7. I also planned for partial (10 percent) automation of the presses through the installation of auto-feed (MT) devices.

I must emphasize that one precondition for these improvements is the building of a "quick-response center."

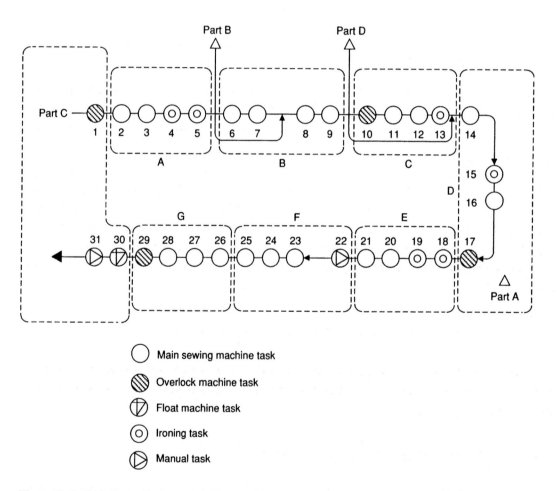

Figure 8-7. Solution: U-shaped Cell for a Garment Factory

9

U-shaped Cells for Electronic Component Assembly

MAMMOTH ASSEMBLY LINES FOR ELECTRONIC COMPONENTS

In just about any electronic component assembly plant that you visit, you will find the kind of mammoth assembly lines shown in Figure 9-1. You will also find an abundance of assembly workers seated alongside the conveyors as they work.

Although such assembly lines have a nice, well-ordered appearance, they are actually full of waste, especially standby waste, wasteful division of work, waste in disorganized positioning of workers, and the like. It is fair to say that the typical electronic component assembly line has about four times more waste than the typical automotive parts assembly line, three times more than the typical motor assembly line, and at least twice more than the typical garment factory.

Process Razing for Electronic Component Assembly Lines

The basic steps in process razing were described in Chapter 6. For review, we will look at them briefly again, this time in the context of an electronic component assembly line.

Step 1: Study current conditions of processes.

Four types of reference materials are needed for this step: (1) a P-Q analysis chart, (2) a flow diagram, (3) an assembly process analysis chart, and (4) a

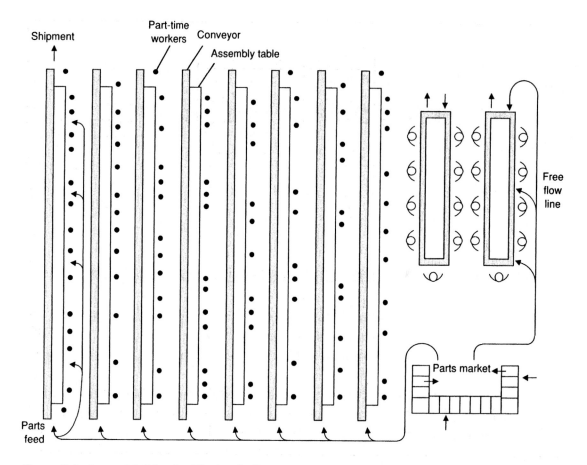

Figure 9-1. Assembly Line for Electronic Components or Electrical Products

line-specific processing route analysis chart. We should begin with a P-Q analysis (or ABC) chart, as illustrated in Figure 9-2, to get a general idea of how to build the line. Electronic component assembly is a highly competitive field where the trend toward wide-variety small-lot production took hold very early on. Consequently, electronic component assembly plants can no longer afford to resist this competitiveness-boosting trend.

In this chart, Group A is the free flow line. By this, however, I do not mean the conventional sort of free flow line that is now obsolete. Instead, I refer to a line where the workers work on the inside and the parts are supplied from the outside. The objective is to reduce manpower needs while establishing a free flow line. Since specialized lines are not good for this purpose, we must use general-purpose lines. We must also establish zero changeover in

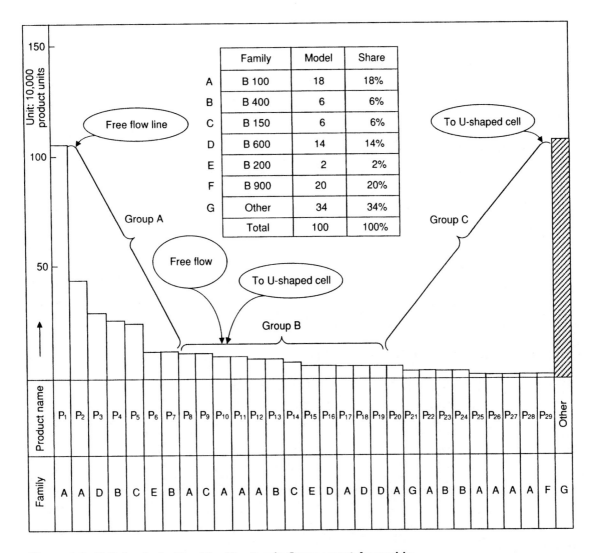

Family	Model	Share
A	B 100	18	18%
B	B 400	6	6%
C	B 150	6	6%
D	B 600	14	14%
E	B 200	2	2%
F	B 900	20	20%
G	Other	34	34%
	Total	100	100%

Figure 9-2. P-Q Analysis Chart for Electronic Component Assembly

which product model changes must be done within three minutes. To do this, we must make sure that zero changeover is incorporated into the order reception and design specification processes.

Group B should be transformed into a U-shaped cell for wide-variety small-lot production. In the beginning, this U-shaped cell should have four workers, then two, and finally just one. Later in this chapter we will see how to accomplish such manpower reduction.

Step 2: Critique current conditions.

Because we are trying to establish wide-variety small-lot production, we first should try to operate the assembly line without the conveyor. The advantages of using conveyors for assembly lines were described in Chapter 3. Here we will look at some disadvantages of using such conveyors:

- the line gets longer (length creates waste)
- more waste in picking things up and putting them down
- sitting-while-working waste (workers cannot help each other)
- defect production waste (goods produced in larger lots contain more defective products when defects occur)
- standby waste (due to line imbalances arising from over-specialized job assignments)
- overstaffing waste (the greatest waste of all)
- waste caused by full-line stops during equipment breakdowns
- waste from lengthy changeover times

These various kinds of waste then can be divided into two types:

1. waste due to large-lot production of defects
2. waste due to employing workers on a conveyor line

Step 3: Define the purpose of the target process.

Since the purpose of the assembly line processes is to assemble parts, all other operations on the line should be regarded as waste. For example, a separate inspection process should be considered as waste, and should be "razed" into a linked process.

Step 4: Determine the starting point for process razing.

Step 4 involves an important process-razing technique. While nothing is wrong with basing our determination of the starting point for making improvements on the problems defined so far, the definition of these problems can differ according to (1) the perspective and approach of the people defining them and (2) their understanding of the relative advantages and disadvantages of the proposed starting points. The process-razing technique, on the other hand, reveals certain patterns that help determine the starting point, identify the improvement points, and check the results of process razing. We only need to choose the pattern that best suits our own factory situation. Some examples are:

- eliminate waste from each process → change human operation time (HT) to machine operation time (MT) → establish U-shaped cell with reduced manpower
- eliminate standby waste → establish U-shaped cell with reduced manpower
- link processes → establish U-shaped cell with reduced manpower
- eliminate in-process inventory waste → establish one-piece production → establish U-shaped cell with reduced manpower
- eliminate warehouse inventory waste → establish smaller lots → establish zero changeover → establish U-shaped cell with reduced manpower
- eliminate defect production waste → establish one-piece production → establish U-shaped cell with reduced manpower
- eliminate late delivery waste → link processes → establish U-shaped cell with reduced manpower

Step 5: Develop a flow concept.

After designing a single straight-line layout based on the assembly process analysis chart, change the layout into a U-shaped cell design. Refer back to Chapter 8's discussion of establishing U-shaped cells at a garment factory.

Step 6: Draft a new layout plan.

It is important to remember that we are not striving for perfection. We simply are trying to come up with a plan for a new layout — a four-worker U-shaped cell, for example — in under ten minutes. It is seldom worth thinking about it longer than this. If we cannot think of a process-razing idea within this time frame, an extra hour is unlikely to make much difference.

Step 7: Estimation development.

Estimation development combines result predictions with detailed planning for process razing. These estimates and plans should be clearly designed to achieve our particular objective.

Step 8: Trial implementation.

If we have not already done it, we should establish a "rapid action" center to carry out trial implementation promptly. The point is to be quick about it and not to worry if the trial fails. It is often only when we see a plan fail that we realize what improvements are needed and can go on to succeed the second time.

FIXED IDEAS AT ELECTRONIC COMPONENT ASSEMBLY LINES

This example is from a case study of Factory B, a subcontractor factory in Osaka. The electronic components being assembled are power supply switches. Their current assembly line layout is a "mammoth line" similar to that shown in Figure 9-1. Figure 9-3 shows an enlarged view of one branch line within that assembly line.

Although it does not include an assembly process chart, we can see that the line section shown in Figure 9-3 includes 13 processes and is operated by 16 workers. We will naturally need to analyze the operation time and categorize it into human operation time (HT) and machine operation time (MT), but we require more information for that. For argument's sake, we will assume that the operation time is 30 seconds per process.

There are several reasons why this factory still retains a conventional "mammoth line." One is that it continues to use conveyors designed for large-lot production even though the times warrant wide-variety small-lot production. Their failure to update their production system may be due to complacency or simply laziness. Perhaps, however, it is because the idea of conveyor-driven assembly is still strongly held within the electrical equipment industry.

A second reason for hanging onto this obsolete type of production system is that conveyors appear to enable greater security and flexibility in response to demand fluctuation. It is felt that sudden surges in demand can be met simply by adding more workers and speed to the conveyor-driven assembly line. For example, although common among automobile assembly plants, apparently electronic component assembly factories have not yet adopted the more cost-efficient management methods that emphasize productivity-boosting improvements to meet demand surges without increasing manpower.

A third reason is that the conveyor encourages manual handling of assembly tasks (HT) rather than machine handling (MT).

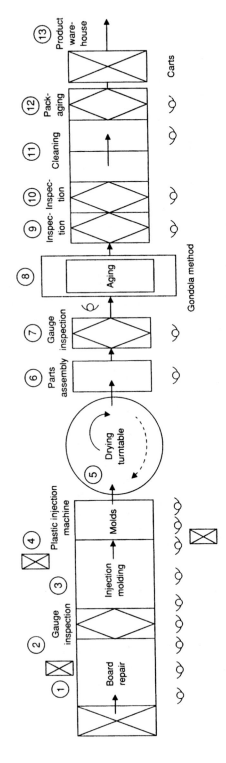

Figure 9-3. Flow Diagram of Section of Mammoth Line at Factory B

A fourth is the fact that while many factory managers give lip service to such modern concepts as flexible and fully automated manufacturing systems, they do not know how to successfully transform their conventional factories into one.

To begin our study of process razing as applied to electronic component and electrical product assembly lines, let us refer to the partial list of improvements to remove waste from specific processes shown in Table 9-1.

Table 9-1. Process-specific Waste Elimination Table

Process no.	Process name	Type of waste	Priority no.	Causes	Waste elimination plan (or hint)
1	Board repairs	Picking up and setting down soldering tools	1	Defect production waste	① Create soldering stand ② Solder at previous process ③ Establish 5-piece flow ④ Eliminate cause for having to pick up and set down soldering tools
2	Gauge inspection	Waste in inserting gauges vertically		Shape of jig's insert slot	① Insert at a sloping angle instead of vertically ② Use a corrective jig
13	Cleaning	Cleaning waste	7	Manual cleaning	① Use brush-cleaning machine (MT) ② Let leader handle entry and exit points

These waste-eliminating measures for specific processes are taken in the following order:

1. Go to the factory and observe the operations first-hand.
2. Consider the purpose of each process. Then consider all operations that do not serve that purpose as wasteful. Now you know from where to begin removing waste. Give yourself no more than nine minutes to think of a way to eliminate waste at each process.
3. The starting point for removing waste is usually the same as the starting point for process razing. The only time they differ is when the waste is related to picking up and setting down things.

4. The objective is to eliminate HT — or at least reduce it — whenever possible.

5. Replace HT with MT; principally, auto-feed devices. For example, install automated screw fastening machines and automatic continuous measuring devices.

6. Divide the new total HT time by the cycle time (CT) to calculate the minimum number of required workers (n).

7. Fill in the waste elimination table as follows:

   (1) Write down the name of the processes ("process name" column). Although in-process inventory should be strictly considered part of the process, we should still omit it from this column.

   (2) Enter the type of waste found in the process ("type of waste" column).

   (3) Enter nothing in the "priority number" column until you complete the rest of the table. This is because the priority numbers are based on a judgment of waste-elimination priority for the entire set of processes.

   (4) Estimate the causes behind the waste ("causes" column).

   (5) Make a note of any plan or idea for eliminating the waste at that process ("waste-elimination plan" column).

The types of waste-removing ideas and plans entered in the "waste-elimination plan" (or "hint") column should be estimated based on experience, sensitivity, and courage. We tend to rely on our intuitive left brain for this kind of thinking. After some practice at this sort of problem-solving, most people find it easier to come up with process-razing plans within the nine-minute deadline.

Now, I ask the reader to take no more than nine minutes to come up with a manpower reduction plan for the line shown in Figure 9-3. Please refer back to the figure, but do not look ahead to the proposed solutions.

Figure 9-4 shows the results of three days of process-razing practice at Company B, as reported by employees at Company C. They also reported their teacher's improvement plan, which is shown in Figure 9-5. The students compared their plan with that of the teacher to help broaden their understanding.

Comparing the two plans, we find very little difference. Company C's employees may be above average, but it is possible to teach almost anyone this pattern-oriented way of thinking. Furthermore, with a positive attitude, a person can become a process-razing improvement expert in a short time.

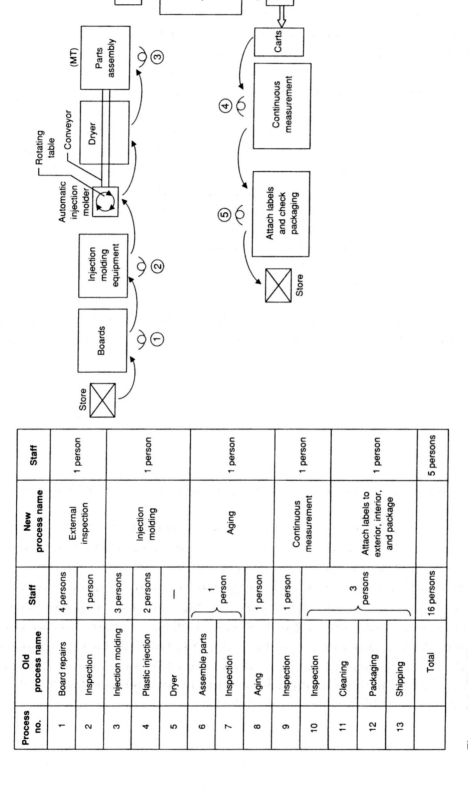

Figure 9-4. The Students' Plan

Process no.	Old process name	Staff	New process name	Staff
1	Board repairs	4 persons	External inspection	1 person
2	Inspection	1 person		
3	Injection molding	3 persons	Injection molding	1 person
4	Plastic injection	2 persons		
5	Dryer	—		
6	Assemble parts	} 1 person	Aging	1 person
7	Inspection			
8	Aging	1 person		
9	Inspection	1 person	Continuous measurement	1 person
10	Inspection	} 3 persons	Attach labels to exterior, interior, and package	1 person
11	Cleaning			
12	Packaging			
13	Shipping			
	Total	16 persons		5 persons

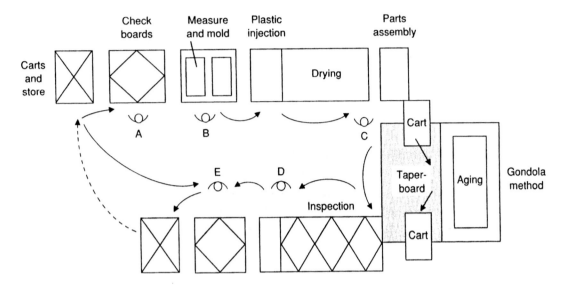

Figure 9-5. The Teacher's Plan

Once they had learned this method, employees at Oriental Motors and members of the Nagano Diversification Council were able to think of ways to reduce manpower requirements by 30 percent and at little or no expense — all within nine minutes. This puts them on the road to becoming process-razing professionals.

TEST YOUR SKILLS

What type of process-razing plan can eliminate these kinds of waste?

Using an example from a different field, it is time for you, the reader, to test what you have learned. Company U has a round conveyor line at which workers sit and insert components into circuit boards (see Figure 9-6).

Following a P-Q analysis like the one shown in Figure 9- 2, this round conveyor initially was deemed suitable for the Group A workpieces, which could be automatically inserted as they were carried one at a time on the conveyor. Group C workpieces, however, came in 50-unit lots with 100 parts per unit and required 20 changeovers per day. This made the five-worker round conveyor line unsuitable for small-lot production. Looking for types of waste to eliminate, the improvement team listed the following:

1. changeover waste due to simultaneous changeover throughout the line
2. standby waste (line imbalances due to different degrees of difficulty in inserting components)
3. Waste in incorrect positioning of parts due to a poor work angle (sitting while working)
4. careless errors (such as defects caused by inserting the wrong component)
5. waste in finding and selecting positions for components
6. waste due to a lack of organization in parts insertion sequence planning (due to failure to use assembly process analysis charts)
7. waste due to a failure to make kits of common parts
8. waste due to a lack of mutual assistance among workers (due to sitting while working)

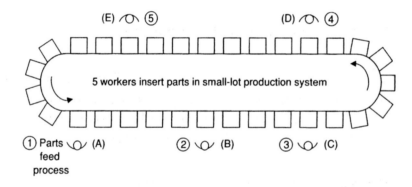

Figure 9-6. Small-lot Parts Assembly Using a Round Conveyor

Solution

In this case of a factory where electronic components are inserted into circuit boards, I again recommend the use of P-Q analysis. It is the best tool for aiding our understanding of wide-variety small-lot conditions and for estimating the kind of equipment investment necessary for the future.

Step 1. I proposed installing an automatic insertion machine for the Group A products and a U-shaped cell in which the processes are linked, as shown in Figure 9-7.

We should always let machines do the kind of work they do better. For example, the positioning work described in Table 9-2 is simple, repetitive, and

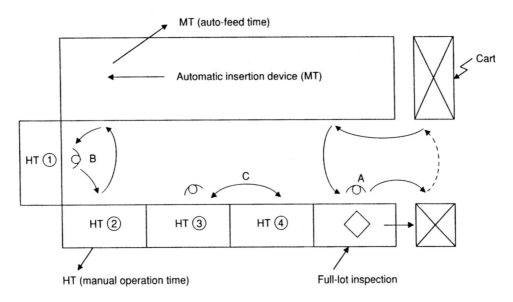

Figure 9-7. U-shaped Cell with Automatic Insertion Device

involves many parts, which makes it a prime candidate for mechanization. Conversely, some tasks are better left to human workers. For instance, humans generally do a better job of difficult positioning tasks that involve only a few parts, such as in the 470-ohm 10K part listed in Table 9-2.

Table 9-2. Parts to Be Inserted in Circuit Boards

Part name	Positioning	Quantity	Handled by
220 ohms	Easy	16	Machine
Ceramic 10K	"	13	"
1K	"	10	"
470 ohms	Difficult	2	Human
10K	"	1	"
and so on . . .			

Step 2. For Group B, I proposed a free flow line, as shown in Figure 9-8.

In this layout, the workers stand while working and are on the inside of the U-shaped cell. The production system is a one-piece flow, one-piece insertion, and one-piece in-process inventory system that keeps pace with the cycle time. All conveyance can be done manually.

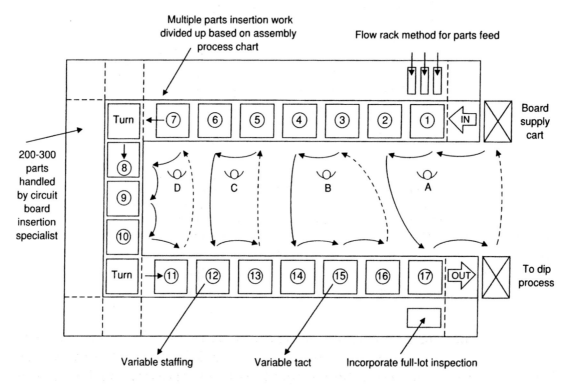

Figure 9-8. Wide-variety Small-lot Free Flow Line Using Manual Insertion

Parts are fed to the cell from the outside via a flow rack, and can be fed in kits for small-lot production. The processes are laid out to enable fluctuation in both manpower and pitch. Once zero-defect conditions have been established, this cell can be linked to the dip process.

Step 3. Since group C is also a small-lot production group, I proposed a manual-feed one-piece flow U-shaped cell with three- to five-piece insertion (see Figure 9-9).

Parts insertion lines, ordinary assembly lines, and garment factory lines are basically all the same. Their work tables are jigs with fixed bases, and any box

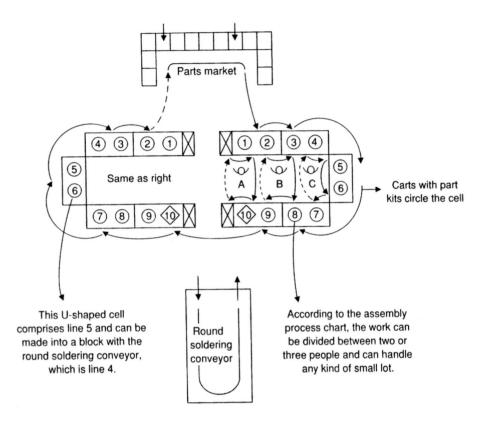

Figure 9-9. Three- to Five-Piece Insertion U-shaped Cell Using Manual Feed

full of parts moving downstream can be considered a kit. The mammoth lines can be broken down into three, four, or five small lines operated by two or three workers each and consisting of about ten processes each. The lines all use prefabricated patterns or molds to aid in the positioning of parts. Their block organization consists of up to five U-shaped cells and, in some cases, one dip conveyor cell for the soldering process.

Step 4. No matter what proposal is made, it should include the elimination of waste caused by having the round conveyor. Table 9-3 shows a process-specific waste elimination table for the electronic component insertion line. Armed with this table, we do not need to be trained in industrial engineering or quality control methods to see where waste should be removed. As long as we are willing to make the effort, we can certainly discover where the waste is.

In order of priority, the following summarizes the waste discovered in the component insertion line that used a round conveyor.

Table 9-3. Waste Elimination Table for Wide-variety Small-lot Component Insertion Line

Process no.	Type of waste	Priority no.	Causes	Waste removal plan
1	Waste due to incorrect insertion angle	3	Sitting while working	① Switch to standing while working ② First parts to be inserted should be the ones with the longest legs ③ Review size of holes
2	Standby waste	2	Poor work allocation	① Switch to one-piece flow, with 3-5 workers and takt-based flow ② Create an assembly process chart ③ Use verbal cues
3	Changeover waste	6	Round conveyor is designed for large-lot production	① Unified changeover in Plan A, successive changeover in Plan B, and 5-line/4-line operation in Plan C ② Prepare for zero changeover
4	Waste due to creation of defect causes	1	1. Careless mistakes 2. Loose parts, incorrect insertion angle	① Organization of insertion sequence ② Work allocation based on assembly process chart ③ Create parts list based on specific processes and insertion sequences ④ Install mistake-proofing devices for parts handling
5	Waste due to lack of mutual assistance	4	Sitting while working	Create a line designed for wide-variety small-lot parts insertion (e.g., Plan C)
6	Positioning waste	5	Long wires	① Adjust wire length to suit holes ② Use paper pattern to guide insertion ③ Practice using left hand
7	Waste due to missing items	7	Inadequate changeover	① Establish tickler-style production setup board ② Prepare item kits ③ Create a parts market

- Priority 1: Waste due to the creation of defect causes.

     The remote cause for this is sitting while working, which is the natural working position when using a round conveyor. The responses to this are listed in the waste elimination table shown in Table 9-3.

- Priority 2: Standby waste.

     The cause for this is allocating work without having first drawn up an assembly process chart for the parts insertion processes.

- Priority 3: Waste due to an incorrect insertion angle.

     The cause for this is the round conveyor, since its forward motion makes it difficult to insert parts correctly.

- Priority 4: Waste due to a lack of mutual assistance.

     Again, underscores the disadvantages of using a round conveyor that obliges workers to sit separately while working instead of having the mobility to help each other.

- Priority 5: Positioning waste.

     This is generally due to an imbalance between the size of the insert hole and the width and/or length of the "leg" section of the part to be inserted. Waste is also caused by having to look around for parts when there is no jig for organizing them. Insertion work is also made more difficult when the insertion sequence is not well organized and standardized.

- Priority 6: Changeover waste.

     See Table 9-3.

- Priority 7: Missing item waste.

     See Table 9-3.

After examining all of these disadvantages of using round conveyors for inserting components into circuit boards, one might wonder why they were ever developed in the first place. The unfortunate fact is that this round conveyor system was developed in the United States as an expedient solution to the problem of using immigrant line workers who had little or no training and who often did not speak the same language. As we have just seen, this type of system is not very well suited for the generally well-trained and interactive workers of Japan. Therefore, Japanese companies would probably choose Plan A for the situation shown in Figure 9-7, Plan B for that shown in Figure 9-8, and Plan C for that shown in Figure 9-9.

10

Techniques for Removing
Waste from Factories

This chapter presents an overall discussion of removing waste from factories, which is, after all, the basic activity underlying process razing.

For present purposes, waste refers to behavior, methods, and motions that do not serve the specified objective. For example, in assembly operations the specified objective is to assemble products. All motions within those assembly operations that add value to the product being assembled are called V motions. Strictly speaking, all other motions are waste.

A more lenient definition of waste recognizes certain motions related to the assembly work as "semi-waste" instead of full-fledged waste. Such motions include positioning, picking up, and setting down parts or workpieces.

This leaves various other non-V motions as pure and simple waste: searching for tools, finding them, selecting them, standby, reading charts, and thinking. This is the three-part definition of V (or non-waste) motions, semi-waste, and waste that we will use in this book.

REMOVING WASTE FROM BRICKLAYING OPERATIONS

The pioneer in removing waste from work motions was a man named Frank Gilbreth. In 1885, Gilbreth, then only 17 years old, joined a construction company as an apprentice bricklayer.

In those days, companies all over the world believed that training in manual labor consisted merely of showing the apprentice how things were done. Gilbreth's boss no doubt said something like, "Look, just watch how I do it and then you do it the same way." His boss worked so quickly, however, that

Gilbreth missed much of the technique he was supposed to be observing. Wanting to keep his job, Gilbreth later drew a diagram of the bricklaying process to help himself understand it better. He tried to note every motion involved in the process.

In those days, they did not have video cameras to record the process frame-by-frame. Nonetheless, let us suppose that they did and that Gilbreth made a videotape of the bricklaying process (see Figure 10-1).

When we look at the 18 frames illustrated in Figure 10-1, the entire process seems complicated. It becomes easier to understand if we summarize it in an assembly process chart, such as shown in Figure 10-2.

Let us follow Gilbreth's approach as we ask ourselves what kind of waste exists at each assembly process, what the causes are, and how we should remove the waste.

The Process of Picking Up a Brick

The first thing we might notice is the worker's poor posture; bending at the hip is a wasteful way of working. The cause of this wasteful motion is that the scaffold platform is too low; it should be at a height where the worker does not have bend down or stretch up to work comfortably. Figure 10-3 shows a platform with a height adjustment device to remove this cause of waste.

"Walking waste" is another form of waste in this bricklaying process. The causes of this waste are (1) that the task of spreading mortar onto the brick wall has been separated from the task of scooping up mortar with the trowel and (2) that both tasks are being done using only one hand. Figure 10-3 shows how this can be improved by using two hands to simultaneously scoop up some mortar and pick up a brick.

Assembly Process

Although it appears to be a value-adding motion, the step at which the bricklayer inspects the brick he has picked up can be called "inspection waste." It appears to add value because it ensures that the brick's best-looking side will be the one showing on the brick wall. However, we can remove the waste from this process by combining the inspecting and positioning of the bricks with unloading them from the supply truck to the platform. This way, the bricklayer does not have to check for the "good" side when laying the bricks.

Figure 10-1. Imaginary Videotape Recording of Gilbreth's Bricklaying Work

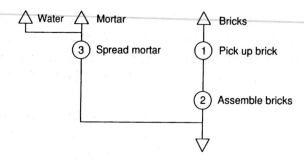

Figure 10-2. Assembly Process Chart for Bricklaying

① Pick up brick in left hand and scoop mortar with trowel in right hand

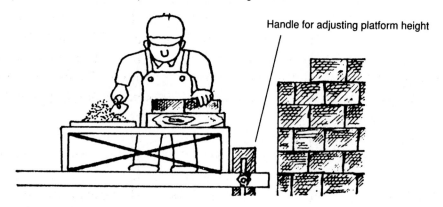

Handle for adjusting platform height

Figure 10-3. Platform with Height Adjustment Device

Mortar Spreading Process

A fourth type of waste in the bricklaying process is the repetitious checking and adjustment of the mortar mix. As you probably know, like cement, mortar is mixed with water to make it spreadable. Daily temperature and humidity variations affect the consistency of the mortar mix, making it difficult to maintain a good mix without frequent checking. One way to reduce this kind of waste is to find out which bricklayer in the company is most efficient at maintaining a good mortar mix and having all other bricklayers learn his or her method.

These are the four major types of waste for this bricklaying process. We might consider a fifth type of waste: changeover waste. In this case, the changeover waste occurs because of the difficulties posed by the steadily increasing height of the brick wall being laid, the need to replenish stacks of bricks, and the preparation of fresh mortar, all of which are left up to the brick-layers to handle. We could reduce some of this waste by assigning a changeover specialist to handle these tasks for all the bricklayers so that they can work without such interruptions.

A sixth minor type of waste is conveyance waste. Currently, the bricks are simply unloaded from the truck into large stacks. We could improve the process by making special containers that line bricks up in neat ten-brick stacks (i.e., small lots) and by having the person unloading the bricks make sure that their "good" sides are all facing the same way.

A seventh form of waste concerns the practice of checking the evenness of the brick wall being laid. After laying each layer of bricks, the bricklayer stands back a few yards and visually checks how level the top of the wall is, making adjustments if necessary. We could eliminate some of this waste by driving posts in at the right and left sides of the wall, with height scales marked on each post. The bricklayer can then accurately judge the wall's levelness without having to step back. The bricklayer could even stretch a string between the two posts to make even more precise measurements.

There are other types of waste in this process and ways to remove them, but we will stop here. Let us note that by making improvements such as those just described, Gilbreth was able to raise his bricklayers' standard output per hour (SPH) from 120 bricks to 350 bricks. Table 10-1 shows a process-specific waste elimination table for this case. The reader should be familiar with this table and the meaning of its column headings from our discussion of such tables in Chapter 9.

MOTION STUDY FOR ASSEMBLY LINES

Following his success in removing waste from bricklaying operations, Gilbreth went on to develop a group of symbols to indicate specific types of motion. He used the following symbols, for example, to describe bricklaying:

1. Search for brick → look around → ◌
2. Find brick → look straight ahead → ◌
3. Extend arm (reach) → arm → ◡
4. Grasp → fingers grasping → ∩
5. Carry → palm of hand → ◡

Table 10-1. Waste Elimination Table for Bricklaying Process

Process no.	Process name	Type of waste	Priority no.	Causes	Waste removal plan
1	Picking up and setting down bricks	① Waste in bending over ② Walking waste ⑤ Changeover waste ⑥ Waste in conveying bricks	3 4 5 7	Difficulty in adjusting height of scaffold platform, division of labor, one-handed operations, leaving too much for the bricklayer to do, unloading bricks in a disorganized manner	Install a height adjustment device on scaffold and establish symmetrical two-handed operations (see Figure 10-3) Assign specialized workers to unload and arrange bricks
2	Assembly	③ Inspection waste ⑦ Waste in adjusting wall height after laying each layer of bricks	6 2	Must check during bricklaying, must visually check height from a distance	Use specialized worker to arrange bricks, use scaled poles and stretched strings to simplify height checking
3	Mortar spreading	④ Must constantly check and adjust mortar mix	1	Variation in mix conditions and methods	Learn best method from most efficient mortar mixer

6. Adjust position ⟶ moving ⟶ ♪
7. Set brick down ⟶ assemble ⟶ #

Actually, the above series of seven distinct motions describes only part of the bricklaying process, namely picking up a brick and setting it down, all of which takes no more than two seconds. If we divide two seconds by seven, we can see that each motion happens very quickly, taking an average of about 0.3 seconds each.

We can simplify this set of motions by summarizing them as follows.

1. Grasp brick (reach and grasp brick)
2. Carry brick
3. Set brick down (includes positioning the brick)

Even when simplified into three motions, we should recognize that each motion averages only about 0.6 seconds.

These motion symbols do not describe the entire array of "motion elements." Gilbreth eventually developed a list of 17 such symbols, and called them "therblig" symbols (an approximate reverse spelling of his own name).

Figure 10-4 lists the modern arrangement of therbligs as used by today's motion study researchers when studying assembly lines. The reader may wish to become familiar with their symbols as we continue our discussion of work motions. I have selected a few of them for further description.

---

2. Finding (discovering an object)

4. Walking (walking waste is to be expected in all assembly lines as they switch to standing-while-working)

13. Adjusting (basically, this means rework, which is almost always a part of assembly line work)

14. Talking (talking is necessary for certain complicated assembly operations)

18. Waiting off the job (an external factor, such as a missing part or line-stop breakdown, has caused the operator to wait)

19. Waiting on the job (an internal factor, such as waiting for the machine to finish its work, has caused the operator to wait)

The following is a breakdown of the 21 assembly motions described in Figure 10-4 in terms of their categorization as V (value-adding) motions, semi-waste motions, and waste motions.

Operation No.	Symbol	Description of Symbol	Example	Category
1. Searching		Eye looking around	Looking for a misplaced screw	Waste
2. Finding		Eye looking at object	Eye has found what it was searching for	Waste
3. Choosing		Arrow indicates direction of attention toward objects	Operator chooses whichever suitable object is easiest to pick up	Waste
4. Walking		Symbol is like the "W" in "Walk"	Operator walks to next process	Waste
5. Reaching		Symbol looks like an empty hand	Operator reaches to grasp a screw	Semi-waste
6. Grasping		Symbol looks like extended thumb and index finger	Operator grasps object between the fingers	Semi-waste
7. Carrying (transporting)		Symbol looks like an object being carried in the palm	Operator carries an object	Semi-waste
8. Positioning		Motion of changing the position of the object being held	Operator changes the position of an object before inserting it into a hole	Waste
9. Assemble		Symbol looks like one object connected with another	Operator inserts a screw into a screw hole	Value
10. Using		Symbol looks like the "U" in "Use"	Operator uses a screwdriver to turn the screw into the screw hole	Value
11. Disassemble		Symbol looks like "assemble" symbol with one part removed	Operator peels off adhesive tape from object	Waste
12. Checking		Symbol is standard flow-chart symbol for inspection processes	Operator measures, externally inspects, or otherwise checks an object	Waste
13. Adjusting		Symbol implies repetitive adjustments	Operator performs adjustments, reworks, or starts over again	Waste
14. Talking		Symbol looks like lips	Operator chats with another operator	Waste
15. Holding		Symbol looks like fingers holding an object	Operator holds onto a tool or part while doing work	Semi-waste
16. Releasing		Symbol looks like upside-down palm dropping object	Operator lets go of a screwdriver	Semi-waste
17. Pre-positioning		Symbol looks like two parts lined up together	Operator sets up objects for next process	Semi-waste
18. Waiting off the job		Symbol looks like person giving up in despair due to problem outside of normal line operations	Operator stops working due to missing parts or an intermittent line stop (breakdown)	Waste
19. Waiting on the job		Symbol looks like person standing idle	Operator stops working and watches machine (auto-feed mechanism, etc.) work	Waste
20. Thinking		Symbol looks like hand raised to forehead in thought	Operator studies diagrams and thinks	Waste
21. Resting		Symbol shows person lying down	Operator decides to take a rest even though it is not break time	Waste

Figure 10-4. Motion Study Chart for Assembly Line

- V motions: 2   (9.5 percent)
- Semi-waste motions: 6   (28.6 percent)
- Waste motions: 13   (61.9 percent)
   Total   21 (100.0 percent)

As you can see, the majority of the motions described are wasteful motions, which clearly suggests that there is a lot of waste that can be removed from assembly line operations. In relation to the wasteful motions in an assembly line, the value-adding motions are more analogous to the edible part of a pomegranate than to the edible part of an orange or banana. Virtually every manufacturing company has the following things in common when it comes to wasteful motions in assembly line operations.

1. Wasteful motions such as searching for parts in parts bins, finding them, carrying them, and removing them.
2. Positioning motions when assembling parts.
3. Operations such as removing or peeling off adhesive tape are easily overlooked.
4. The most waste is in rework, repairs, and adjustments, which can create the causes of further defects.
5. Standby waste is the second most common type of waste, since it includes both waiting off the job (for missing items or line stops) and waiting on the job (for machine work or delays caused by line imbalances). This distinction between off-job and on-job waiting is important for analyzing and eliminating waste.

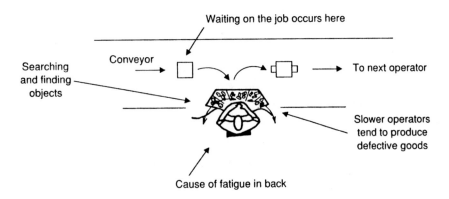

Figure 10-5. The Conveyor Line as a Source of Waste on the Assembly Line

6. Talking waste is another major form of waste on assembly lines, and especially on those lines where workers sit in a circle and are able to talk as if seated around a banquet table.
7. The root source of much assembly line waste is the arrangement of workers seated along a conveyor line. The disadvantages of this layout were described in Chapters 6 and 9.

The techniques used for making improvements based on motion study are not easy for amateurs to master. Such improvements involve painstaking studies of right-hand and left-hand motions and the time required for each motion, using the symbols shown in Figure 10-4. Subsequently, the improvements are made by eliminating unnecessary and wasteful motions.

For example, looking at the conveyor-driven assembly operations shown in Figure 10-5, let us assume a 20-second pitch time and a total of 33 motions. On the average, it would take about one hour to do the motion study analysis of these 33 motions and another three hours to organize the data and propose an improvement plan. (The rule of thumb is that this phase takes three times as long as the motion study analysis phase.) That makes a total of four hours for a motion study of one worker's assembly process. If there are ten workers on the line, we will need 40 hours just for the motion study. Not too many managers can spare this amount of time either from their own schedules or from those of their line workers.

WASTE ELIMINATION VERSUS MOTION STUDY

For practical purposes, I recommend removing waste over motion study. When we get involved in motion study, the motion study process becomes our objective and we tend to lose sight of the real objective, which is to comprehensively remove waste from the assembly line.

In 1960, I made serious efforts to use motion study as a means of removing waste from assembly operations. Soon, however, I found myself wasting a lot of time on technical subtleties and other extraneous details. The motion study method itself became the main challenge and I lost sight of the real challenge of eliminating waste from the assembly processes. In the meantime, I caused a lot of unneeded trouble for the assembly workers and others involved in the motion study.

Having learned a valuable lesson the hard way, I will mention two points in hopes that others will not have to repeat that unfortunate experience:

1. The assembly line motion study symbols and methods described in Figure 10-4 do not teach us anything that is not already obvious. Neither does the motion study method teach us how to improve our visual perception so that we can easily identify motions lasting an average of 0.6 seconds.
2. Generally, 90 percent of all motions in assembly line work are at least partially wasteful motions. Therefore, as an investigative method, motion study is not very illuminating. We can work more efficiently simply by devising ways to eliminate waste.

I began by eliminating waste from specific processes in the assembly line. Table 10-1 lists the format for this waste-removing method. Japanese improvement teams have the benefit of a long-established cultural tradition that places a high value on efficient work and that scorns waste of any kind. I always encourage these improvement teams to put those cultural values to work when removing waste from assembly processes — an activity that anyone can be successful at, regardless of technical training.

Working with various types of companies and industries throughout Japan, I have seen many workers who knew very little about industrial engineering yet who quickly picked up the knack of removing waste from processes. This amazing phenomenon remains a source of joy for me.

Figure 10-6 shows a checklist for removing waste from the factory. This checklist is being used in courses at Company K's training center.

When starting waste-removing efforts, we should use a table such as that shown in Table 10-1 and gradually get the hang of it by practicing it again and again in our own factories. The key to becoming an old hand at eliminating waste is to learn the principles of removing waste so well that they become second nature.

TEST YOUR SKILLS

Our hypothetical improvement group has just used a checklist similar to the one shown in Figure 10-6 to find out what kind of waste exists in one of their assembly processes. The results show that the most prevalent kind of waste is walking waste, followed, in order of decreasing prevalence, by waste in operations, conveyance waste, defect production waste, idle observation waste, changeover waste, and waste in stopping work to make arrangements.

Factory name:			Date:

◎ can make immediate improvement   ○ needs improvement   △ needs further study | Improvement group |

Category	Type of waste	Evaluation	Example
Waste in operations	1. Waste in picking up and setting down items		
	2. Waste in motions		
	3. Walking waste		
	4. Standby waste		
	5. Waste in stopping work to make arrangements		
	6. Waste in rework, defects, and operation errors		
	7. Waste in idle observation		
	8. Changeover waste		
	9. Waste in one-hand operations		
	10. Waste in sitting while working		
Waste in layout	1. Waste in over-division of work		
	2. Waste in two-person tasks		
	3. Waste in in-process inventory and warehouse inventory		
	4. Waste in conveyance distances		
	5. Waste in trans-shipment		
	6. Waste in redundant transport		
Waste in the flow of goods	1. Overproduction waste		
	2. Waste in missing items		
	3. Waste in invisible abnormalities		
	4. Searching waste		
	5. Waste in failure to meet standard output per hour (SPH)		
Waste in equipment and other types of waste	1. Waste in disposal of unused equipment		
	2. Waste in idle equipment		
	3. Waste in broken-down equipment		
	4. Waste in line stops		
	5. Waste in the use of materials and by-products		
	6. Waste in production yield		
	7. Waste in the use of water, oil, electricity, and gas		
	8. Waste in lack of proper arrangement (*seiri*) and orderliness (*seiton*)		
	9. Waste in unnecessary meetings		
	10. Waste in unnecessary questions (including telephone consultation)		
Total	◎ - 3 points ○ - 2 points △ - 1 point		

Figure 10-6. Checklist for Removing Waste from the Factory

Figure 10-7 shows the general layout of the target process, including a sketch of the walking route. As you can see, the layout looks like a nest centered on the assembly work. In all, there are 27 parts whose retrieval requires a worker to walk five or more steps. Now, please take a few minutes to think of a process-razing idea to eliminate waste — particularly walking waste — from this process.

Hints:

- Ask whether it is people or things that need to be moving.
- The overall layout should be U-shaped.
- It is best to use kit carts.

Solution

In the case of trying to eliminate walking waste, we should start by thinking in terms of moving things instead of people. The cause of walking waste is that objects are in fixed positions and require that people walk to retrieve them. This point applies not only to walking waste, but also, on a more subtle level, to other kinds of waste, such as searching, finding, choosing, and carrying waste.

My specific steps for eliminating waste are:

1. Carefully create an assembly process chart.
2. Determine the flow unit (one-piece flow, two-piece flow, etc.) and the flow sequence.
3. Create a U-shaped cell layout plan.
4. Attach smaller U-shaped cells to the outside of the main cell as subassembly processes arranged according to the processing sequence.
5. Have objects moved around the U-shaped cells on a roller conveyor whose frame is built at floor level (see Figure 10-8).

If certain objects cannot be moved because of their weight, shape, or location, we have no choice but to have the people move. Figure 10-9 shows such a layout, in which the main assembly table is in the center and the subassembly processes encircle it.

In both plans, the policy toward missing items is to use different withdrawal kanban for each product model number and to have a keeper use the instructions on these kanban as he or she takes the required parts from the parts market to the subassembly processes by making rounds with a kit cart.

Supplier kanban should be used at the parts market to keep the supplier factories informed of parts requirements.

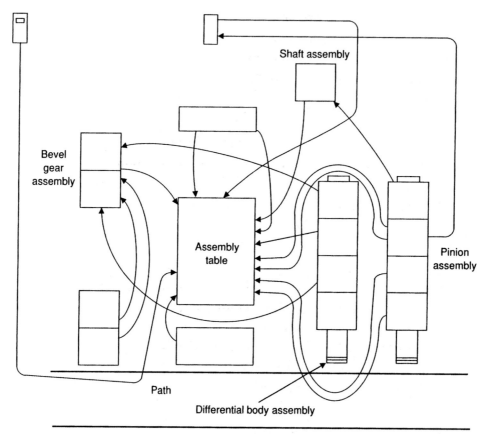

Parts that require 5 or more steps to retrieve

	Differential body assembly	Bevel gear assembly	Pinion assembly	Shaft assembly
1	Shaft assembly	Cage	Pinion gear	Shaft
2	Cover	Sun gear	Bearing	Case
3	M10 bolt	Spider	Coupling	Bearing
4	M12 bolt	Pinion gear	Bolt	Retainer
5	Oil (330)	Bearing A	Washer	
6	Crane hook	Bearing B	Cage	
7	Impact		Spacer	
8	Washer		Yoke	
9	Checksheet			

Figure 10-7. Process Razing to Eliminate Walking Waste

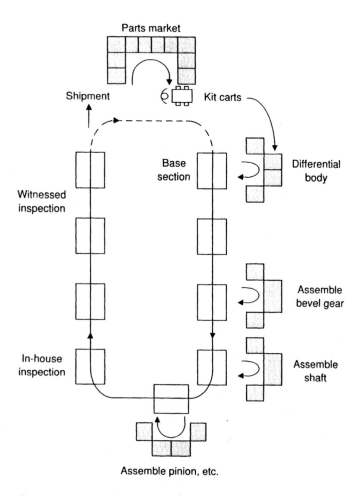

Figure 10-8. Conveyance Layout

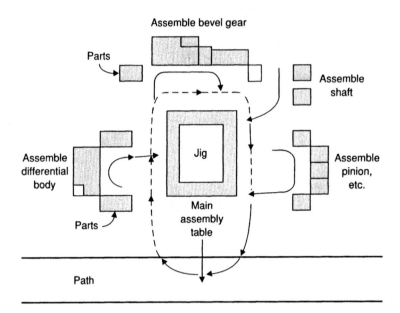

Figure 10-9. Layout with Some Worker Movement

Part II
Application

11

Color Changeover Improvement at Japan's Oldest Plastics Company: The Case of Starlight Industries

In this chapter, we will change the subject and study changeover improvements at a plastic molding factory. We will examine the challenge of color changeover improvement and present a case study of a successful improvement in this area.

Changeover improvements can be broken down into five categories:

1. improving metal die changeover (such as press dies)
2. improving processing standards and related changeover of general-purpose and automated machinery
3. improving parts replacement and product model changeover in assembly processes
4. improving changeover of materials and raw materials used in cleaning process industry factories
5. improving preparatory work (such as trial operation, production start-up, and demonstrations at exhibits)

The fourth category is the most difficult because it is mainly done as part of cleaning activities. Two other types of changeover improvement are single changeover (changeover within nine minutes) and zero changeover (within three minutes). These both are goals of improvement groups who have mastered the rules and principles of making improvements.

STARLIGHT INDUSTRIES

Starlight Industries, or Company S, has been a pioneer in Japan's plastic molding industry. Founded in 1936, it is Japan's oldest plastics company.

161

Company S is currently capitalized at $3.5 million, employs 650 people, and has recorded $107 million in total annual sales. Besides the head office in Osaka, Company S has three production facilities: the Ritto plant in Shiga Prefecture, Tokuan plant in Higashi Osaka, and the Hiroshima plant. Photo 11-1 shows the Ritto plant, where improvement teams took on the challenge of establishing zero changeover.

Photo 11-1. Starlight Industries' Ritto plant, where improvement teams took on the challenge of establishing zero changeover.

Photo 11-2 shows some of Company S's products, which include interior automotive parts, office equipment housing, spindle bearings, friction liners, brake linings, bins for kitchen food storage wells, safety helmets, and plastic toilets for public facilities.

Company S is best known for its skills in manufacturing large molded plastic products as well as difficult-to-make plastic items. It is also known for its assembly and silk printing technologies that enable the company to supply various molded items as subassembly products. A third source of fame for the company is its wide-variety small-lot assembly line system that uses kanban for prompt delivery of products to clients in the automotive and office equipment industries.

Photos 11-3 and 11-4 show parts of the assembly line. Figure 11-1 describes the layout of a process on the line. The line's welding press includes silk printing. All line workers, most of them part-time employees, stand while working. The line has from six to ten assembly processes, uses from five to 30 assembly parts, and has many U-shaped cells each handled by one to three workers.

Photo 11-2. Products of Company S

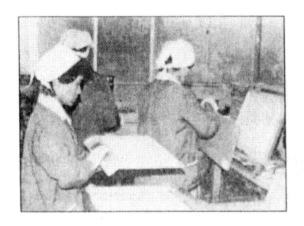

Photo 11-3. A U-shaped Cell in an Assembly Line

Photo 11-4. Auto-feed Welding Press in a U-shaped Cell

LINKING THE ASSEMBLY LINE WITH THE PLASTIC MOLDING EQUIPMENT

In plastic molding factories, a successful transition to a wide-variety small-lot assembly line consisting mainly of U-shaped cells requires that upstream processes supply only what is needed for assembly when it is needed, and only in the amount needed. This just-in-time supply method, however, increases the number of changeover operations.

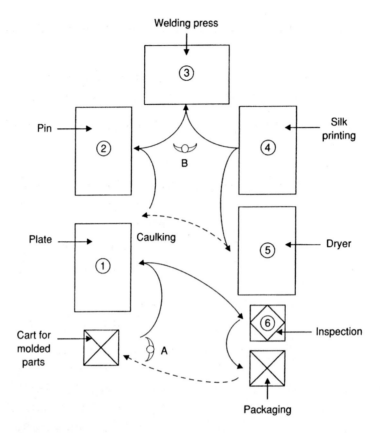

Figure 11-1. U-shaped Cell Process Diagram

The cause-and-effect relationship is really quite simple: more frequent changeover means more time lost to changeover, and this leads to a drop in daily output. Eventually, it leads to a drop in overall sales and lower profits. Although to say this is working backward from the conclusion, the basic response to this situation is to reduce the number of changeovers by linking the assembly line with the molding process.

The following steps describe how we can do this:

Step 1. On the second floor of the factory, build a wide-variety small-lot assembly line consisting of U-shaped cells grouped into families. (While family groupings are usually client-specific, they can also be grouped according to the assembly line's processing path.)

Step 2. On the factory's first floor, set up molding equipment to form a block with a specific family of assembly line cells. For example, we might link U-shaped cell 6 on the assembly line with a molding machine to form a block. We call this kind of line organization "block organization."

This type of layout enables the second-floor assembly lines to receive workpieces from first-floor molding equipment on a just-in-time basis. As a result:

- In-process inventory (dead inventory) is reduced to zero and there is no longer any need to retain parts for assembly, although a product storage area is still needed.
- The elimination of in-process inventory and dead inventory (especially inventory that has been processed by subcontractors) reduces defects and eliminates downstream quality complaints.
- The simplest way to reduce inventory is to shrink assembly lot sizes. For example, if we want to cut inventory in half, we need only cut our current assembly lot size in half.
- Ways can often be found to enable the assembly line workers to monitor the molding equipment as they work on the assembly line.

The more we are able to combine tasks (i.e., monitoring molding equipment while working on the assembly line), the more we can operate the molding equipment with little or no manpower. Accordingly, it is better to work out a block organization plan to link the molding equipment with the assembly processes it supplies and to avoid having separate factories for the two stages. The following are two methods for establishing such block organization:

1. *Block organization based on similar materials.*

    This method involves setting up molding machines that supply similar materials to specific assembly line families (U-shaped cells). Although this method requires frequent mold changeover, it completely avoids changeover of materials and thus can be established rather easily.
2. *Block organization based on different materials.*

    This method sets up molding machines not only to supply similar materials to specific families but also to supply different types of materials to other families.

While it reduces mold changeover and enables more freedom in color changes, this second method does not enable zero changeover, and ends up requiring the sharing of molding equipment among various families. Company S formed a changeover improvement study group to look for ways to overcome the two hurdles just described.

LARGE MOLD CHANGEOVER: SINGLE CHANGEOVER
WITHIN SIX MONTHS

This mold changeover was made more visible and easier to understand by the operation analysis shown in Table 11-1, which was created with the help of a video camera. Normally, this kind of operation analysis requires some knowledge of time-based analysis, but not if we use a video camera. People can easily learn how to operate a video camera and a VCR, which allow them to view each step in the changeover over and over. The following are some basic steps for using video cameras and a VCR to discover waste in changeover operations.

Step 1: Use the video camera to gather data on current conditions.

Ask the changeover workers to work at a slow pace. Since the goal is to discover waste in the changeover procedures, time is not a factor here. The changeover workers should be told this and should just work slowly and carefully. The other members of the changeover group should be watching the changeover operations as they are recorded.

Step 2: After recording the changeover, start the process of finding and eliminating waste.

The video recording should be shown not only to the changeover group members but also to the changeover workers. At this point, the goal is to get people to observe how the work is done and to consider possible better alternatives. Ideas should be recorded on a waste elimination checklist (see Table 11-2).

Step 3: Devise waste elimination plans.

As shown in Table 11-2, we have divided waste into four categories: setup waste, changeover waste (waste in attaching and removing items), cleaning waste, and adjustment waste. The next step is to look at the examples of waste in the table and devise small, medium, or large improvement plans to eliminate the waste. If you watch the video recording while devising these waste elimination plans, there will be little argument about the facts of the matter. They will

Table 11-1. Changeover Operation Analysis Chart

Factory: Injection Mold Factory 2   **Date: July 18, 1983**

Process:	Color change from PP (black) to ABS (white)	Person responsible:		Umekage	Item:		Housing
Machine name:	Mitsubishi Natoko	No. of operators:		1	Changeover time:		96 minutes, 50 seconds
Machine no.	$800	Changeovers/ month:			Measured by:		Watari

No.	Changeover steps	Time		Changeover			Improvement points
		Total	Step	Internal	External	Waste	
	Startup of color changeover	0.00					
1	Get up on platform and clean hopper with air blower.	32'00"	32'00"		✓		Can something smaller than the 150 kg hopper be used? Plastic granules get spread all around.
2	Step down from platform to get cleanser to put into hopper.	34'00"	2'00"		✓		Find a place to keep cleanser that does not require operator to step down from platform.
3	Keep cleaning injector and gauge until cleaning machine stops.	52'00"	18'00"	✓			The screw stop position has not been standardized. Need to find a way to avoid having to walk to switch.
4	Feed ABS pigment to hopper, operate injector, and gauge repeatedly until pigment runs out.	60'00"	8'00"			✓	This step (always just a formality) is probably unnecessary.
5	Use air blower to clean out hopper, then use loader to load specified dry materials into hopper.	67'00"	7'00"		✓		Try using cassette-type mini hoppers.
6	Do a free shot, injecting plastic into the mold during the color change and note the change in colors.	96'50"	29'50"			✓	Injections into metal molds do not reduce the change-over time. Molds with 25-kg capacity are still too large. This step is unnecessary.

Table 11-2. Waste Elimination Checklist for Large Plastic Molding Machine

Category	Time	Types of Waste	a (small improvements)	b (medium improvements)	c (large improvements)
Setup waste	20 minutes	① Missing materials ② Tools ③ Anti-rust painting ④ Use pipe wrench ⑤ Layout (walking waste)	① Use kanban for changeover ② Set up 7 tool plates ③ Unify bolt sizes ④ Install ladders on the main unit and extractor unit	① Assign 1 person the job of inspecting mold repairs ② Use hoist or 2 cranes for changeover	① Double hopper ② Mold position ③ Temporary storage site for materials
Waste in removing and attaching items	25 minutes	⑥ Waste in removing and attaching hardware, bolts, nuts, and washers ⑦ Attach eject rod ⑧ Removing and inserting items from top of machine ⑨ Connecting and disconnecting hoses ⑩ Positioning hoses	⑤ Build and install spring-loaded mapper ⑥ Hang next to air hose hopper ⑦ Remove dirt (prevent foreign matter from accumulating)	③ Unify mold attachment thickness (on sides) ④ Centralize coolant hoses ⑤ Use right-angle design at exit ports for scraps	④ Use side-load, side-removal roller conveyor so that eject rods do not have to be removed ⑤ Perform changeover on front cap section only
Cleaning (color change) from black to white	90 minutes	⑪ Waste in excess screw turning ⑫ Cleaning sequence ⑬ Cleaning method ⑭ Method for using cleaning fluid ⑮ Scraps thrown on floor ⑯ Removal of grouped items	⑧ Prepare filter for external changeover ⑨ Cut off excess screw threads ⑩ Use labels to indicate proper cleaning sequence ⑪ Use 3 types of cleaning fluid (and get them ready beforehand) ⑫ Install scrap bins	⑥ Establish optimal conditions for cleaning method (a) Amounts of cleaning fluid (b) Types of cleaning fluid (c) Amount of materials (d) Types of materials (e) Insertion pressure (f) Extraction speed (g) Temperature of plastic resin	① Cleaning fluid A for white to white changeover ② Cleaning fluid C for white to black changeover ③ Cleaning fluid B for white to gray changeover ⑥ Introduce a right-angle design that does not stop at the front cap section ⑦ Use double device for material hopper to enable cassette method ⑧ Establish periodic changeover program for screw section
Adjustment waste (waste in adjustment for standards)	25 minutes	⑰ Adjustment in mold clamping ⑱ Adjustment in protrusion amount ⑲ Standard instructions are difficult to see ⑳ Limited-run samples are not checked	⑬ Use gauge to measure mold clamping (opening and closing) ⑭ Devise block gauges for protrusion amount and mold opening amount ⑮ Use cards to display mold standards	⑦ Inspect first of limited-run lot and stamp for approval	⑨ Use conveyor instead of group item removal
Total	160 minutes	㉑ Cleaning of filter ㉒ Straddling or climbing on the machine		⑧ Study feasibility of 2 lines (one black and one white with hopper and dryer)	

be plain to see. This should make for a productive and harmonious improvement planning session.

Step 4: Once the waste elimination planning is over, apply flag development to Table 11-2.

Here, we begin to put together the improvement implementation schedule. The "flags" used in flag development are notices that specific improvements have been planned. For instance, it has been decided who is to carry out the improvement, what items are involved, and when the improvement is due to be finished. Small improvements can be handled by the factory floor staff as part of its daily duties. Medium improvements should be referred to the rapid action center and large improvements to the production engineers. The result should be an improvement assignment list, such as the one shown in Table 11-3, where improvements are listed along with the persons responsible and the deadlines, organized from a companywide perspective.

At this step, concrete planning is very important. Improvement efforts that are not backed by solid planning are likely to end in confusion. Even with the risk of increased careless mistakes, it is still better to leave the concrete planning to the people responsible for making the improvement.

Using the four steps just described, the changeover group managed within six months to establish single changeover for the mold changeover, which had previously required 70 minutes. Table 11-3 lists only the supply line that feeds black and white materials to the materials tank, jet loader, and hopper-dryer. Figure 11-2 shows how the cleaning process was changed to an external changeover process.

SINGLE CHANGEOVER FOR COLOR CHANGES ACHIEVED IN SIX MONTHS

Having found that videotaping could not help them with parts of the equipment that were hidden from view, the changeover group studied the structural diagrams of those parts and implemented an operation analysis, as was shown in Table 11-1. Figure 11-3 shows external views of the plastic molding equipment and the injection molding machine. The plastic molding equipment model is a Mitsubishi Natoko 800-ton unit. The injection molding machine

Table 11-3. Improvement Assignment List

	Item	Period and Person Responsible
①	Right-angle design for bottom drip cap section	June 20, Shimabayashi and Watari
②	Mini hopper sliding platform	June 18-19, Watari
③	Remodel mini hoppers	June 20, Shimabayashi
④	Nozzle taper design, test nozzle	June 23, Tozaka
5	Centralize coolant hoses on molding machine	June 20, Shimabayashi
⑥	Scrap bin	June 20, Shimabayashi
⑦	Clean and organize area around molding machine, test color changing method	June 24 by Umekage and test on June 4 by Anda
⑧	Materials tank (150 kg)	
⑨	Attach casters	
⑩	Jet roller (3 units)	Filter size = φ0.8 to φ1.0
⑪	Hopper-dryer (100 kg)	
12	Cylinder head and spare parts	Changeover during day 8 of periodic molding machine overalls
13	Chamfer cylinder seat	
⑭	Introduce labels for cleaning inspection, establish standard sequence	June 20, Umekage
15	Review and improve air hoses	June 20, Shimabayashi and Watari

includes a hopper that sits atop the machine's heated cylinder and feeds materials to the cylinder. Inside the cylinder, a screw turns and presses the heat-softened plastic material toward the nozzle. The screw stops when it reaches its forward limit, after which a piston is used to expel the plastic through the injection nozzle. At this point, a small amount of oxidized gas remains stuck in the front of the cylinder, which makes it difficult to change colors.

As was shown in the operation analysis in Table 11-1, when changing from the black material (polypropylene resin) to the white material (ABS resin), it takes almost 100 minutes to get a completely white plastic from the molding machine. The more frequent the changeovers (N), the greater this correspond-

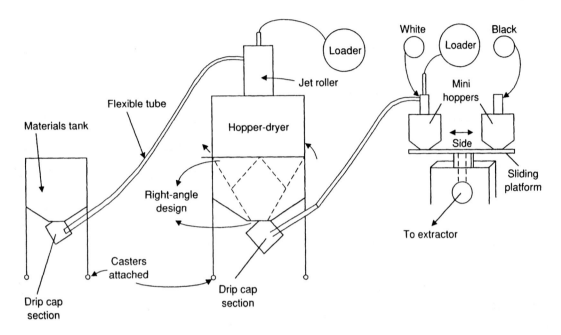

Figure 11-2. Supply Line for Black and White Materials

ing time loss becomes. This situation clearly points to a need for changeover improvement. Let us consider the following improvement steps:

Step 1: Study current conditions.

At this step, we study the current situation and draw up an operation analysis table, such as shown in Table 11-1.

Step 2: Critique the current methods.

Ask what the purpose of each operation is and ask if the operation is really necessary and if there is some way to do without it.

Step 3: Try out ideas on the factory floor.

To find out which changeover conditions get the job done in the shortest time, we should combine our ideas concerning improved changeover methods and procedures and test them in the factory.

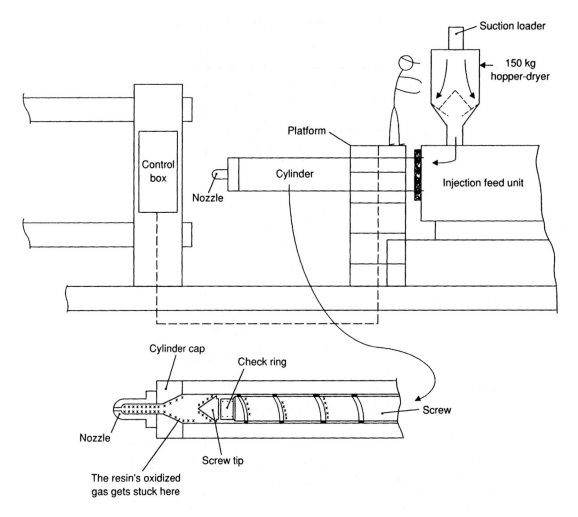

Figure 11-3. Why Color Changes Take So Long

The changeover group's ideas concerned the use of a cleanser and changes in the way the molding equipment was operated. They drew up a testing schedule to try out these ideas and track their causes and effects. Then they started testing the ideas. The testing schedule is shown in Table 11-4. They measured the success of these tests in terms of how many injection shots it took to change completely from black to white material, the corresponding time period, general impressions, ranking of tests, and so on. They also noted the processing conditions. Two people carried out these tests together, one working as the molding machine operator and the other as the cleaner.

Table 11-4. Combined Tests to Determine the Shortest Changeover Time

Test No.	A Scrub Cleanser Brand	C Quantity	B Cylinder Temperature °C	Finish Cleanser Brand	D No. of Screw Rotations rpm	E Gauge Stroke mm	Data — No. of shots: Free shots	Total shots	Data — Time: Free shots	Total shots	General Impression	Ranking
1	S	S 400g	220	ABS	50	25	21	40	5'30"	22'55"	Not clean enough	8
2		ABS 2kg	220	"	72	50	13	42	5'00"	27'40"	"	7
3		S 400g	210	"	72	50	23	38	13'00"	20'40"	"	5
4		ABS 2kg	210	"	50	25	41	65	10'00"	30'30"	"	6
5	H	H 500g	220	"	50	50	22	42	4'05"	21'05"	OK	2
6		H 1kg	220	"	72	25	14	40	4'00"	25'50"	OK	4
7		H 500g	210	"	72	25	8	27	2'15"	18'00"	OK	1
8		H 1kg	210	"	50	50	16	43	3'40"	25'20"	Not quite enough	3

Notes (and other conditions)

Injection pressure: Primary = 100 kg/cm^2, secondary = 80 kg/cm^2, tertiary = 5 kg/cm^2

Cycle time: injection = 10 seconds, loading = 5 seconds, curing = 30 seconds

Injection speed: Medium speed

ABS must go from black to clear

Note: A small molding machine was used for these tests.

Step 4: Determine the shortest changeover time based on the test result data.

We can use the following formulas to calculate the total changeover times in minutes (') and seconds ("). Caution is needed to avoid making careless errors in arithmetic.

(Formula A) Results of coarse cleanser brand tests

$$\{(1) + (2) + (3) + (4) - (5) + (6) + (7) + (8)\}$$

$$= \frac{6105''}{4} - \frac{5415''}{4} = 1526'' - 1354'' = 172'' \text{ (H is best)}$$

(Formula B) Results of cylinder temperature tests

$$\{(1) + (2) + (5) + (6) - (3) + (4) + (7) + (8)\}$$

$$= \frac{5850''}{4} - \frac{5670''}{4} = 1462.5'' - 1417.5'' = 44'' \text{ (higher temperature may be better)}$$

(Formula C) Results of finish cleaner quantity tests

$$\{(1) + (3) + (5) + (7) - (2) + (4) + (6) + (8)\}$$

$$= \frac{4960''}{4} - \frac{6560''}{4} = 1240'' - 1640'' = 400'' \text{ (smallest quantity is best)}$$

(Formula D) Results of screw rotation tests

$$\{(1) + (4) + (5) + (8) - (2) + (3) + (6) + (7)\}$$

$$= \frac{5990''}{4} - \frac{5530''}{4} = 1498'' - 1383'' = 115'' \text{ (higher rotation number may be better)}$$

(Formula E) Results of gauge stroke (internal cleanliness check) tests

$$\{(1) + (4) + (6) + (7) - (2) + (3) + (5) + (8)\}$$

$$= \frac{5835''}{4} - \frac{5685''}{4} = 1459'' - 1421'' = 38'' \text{ (better if the inside is completely clean)}$$

The results of these calculations are shown in graph form in Figure 11-4. The encircled dots indicate preferable levels for each factor. As shown in the figure, these are A2, B2, C1, D2, and E2.

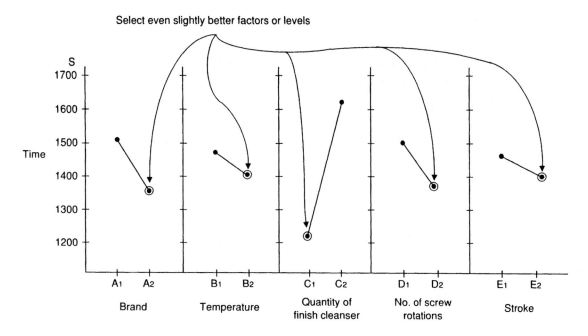

Figure 11-4. Selection of Optimal Changeover Conditions

Specifically:

- Coarse cleanser brand H is preferable.
- It is better to have a somewhat low cylinder temperature.
- It is better to use only a little finish cleanser.
- It is better to have more screw rotations.
- It is better to have a shorter stroke (internal wash).

We can now determine the shortest changeover time (T) as follows:

$$T = 1354" + 1417" + 1240" + 1383" + 1421" - \frac{11{,}520}{8} \times 4$$

$$= 6815' - 5760'$$

$$= 1055"$$

$$= 17' \text{ (minutes) } 35" \text{ (seconds)}$$

We can see that test 7 resulted in a changeover time of 18 minutes, achieving almost as short a time as determined by the previous calculations. It is important to remember that in carrying out these tests, our objective is to select rather than to verify. Our concern should be to choose the best method — not to verify the statistical significance of our calculations.

Back in 1955, I participated in some factory floor testing where we did distribution analyses using square sum calculations. To make sure we had not made any errors in our calculations, we checked the statistical significance of all of the factors. Giving ourselves a 5 percent margin for error, we accepted all factors that could be shown to be statistically significant and rejected all those that were not statistically significant. I advocated this approach to everyone at the time.

Later, after I had thought about it some more, I realized that since the purpose of factory floor testing was to find out which of the tested methods worked best, we could simply choose and combine the better factors on an empirical basis and not worry about their statistical significance. We may not come up with the best possible combination of factors the first time, but subsequent improvements can always be made until we reach our target.

In order not to repeat past mistakes, I instructed the changeover group for the changeover improvement just described to focus solely on picking all of the better methods. If we were to check for statistical significance, we might well find that the only significant improvement was to reduce the amount of finishing cleanser, or that even that might not qualify as statistically significant.

It is essential that we take a practical approach by recognizing these factory floor tests as a positive step toward optimizing changeover conditions and other factory conditions. Success depends not so much on the speed of the progress as it does on the enthusiasm of the improvement group.

Step 5: Determine the next step for further improvements.

So far, the changeover group's efforts have established a minimum changeover time of 18 minutes, which is still double the target value of nine minutes (the "single changeover" period). Therefore, further improvements were needed.

The group focused on two factors as steps toward further improvements: (1) the sequence and (2) the pace of changeover operations. They had already established the changeover operation standards through their factory floor tests.

Because the factory workers wanted input from each section of the factory, they formed a new changeover group that included one person from each line in the factory. This nine-member group is shown in Photo 11-5.

Photo 11-5. Members of the Changeover Group

Step 6: Determine the changeover sequence.

Following the changeover improvement principle that "moving the hands is OK, but moving the feet is not," group members drew up a walking route diagram and analyzed it in search of walking waste. They found they could reduce walking waste by moving all of the switches to a single control box.

The broken line in Figure 11-5 shows the path walked during changeover operations. Next, they listed the changeover procedure as shown in Figure 11-6. (Although this chart contains some in-house terminology, we show it in its original form.)

Step 7: Self-directed practice prior to changeover demonstration.

Using the procedure described in the chart, the changeover group's leader had group members practice the procedure several times until they were proficient enough at it to get close to their target time of ten minutes. Once they had reached that point, they demonstrated their new changeover procedure to other workers.

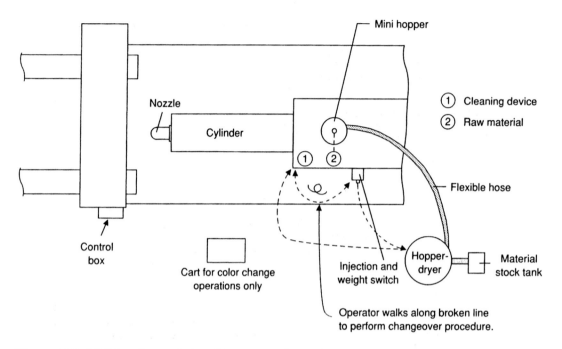

Figure 11-5. Walking Route during Changeover Operations

Step 8: Horizontal development via changeover demonstration.

The goal of the changeover demonstration is to help operators learn new skills by watching an example of the new changeover procedure. It is counterproductive to create a standard operations chart for the new changeover procedure and to order the operators to perform the changeover within a certain period of time. This is particularly true at factories that employ a lot of operators.

At Company S, they distributed the changeover procedure list to all factory floor employees, following which the rapid action center's leader held a changeover demonstration (see Figure 11-6). Photos 11-6 and 11-7 were taken at the demonstration. The demonstration changeover was completed in eight minutes and 25 seconds, which led one observer to remark, "Why haven't we ever learned this way before? It's so fast and looks so easy!"

This demonstration fostered rapid horizontal development of the new changeover procedures (see Figure 11-7). The workers began vying with each other to devise further small improvements in machinery and skills. Eventually the fastest changeover time was reduced to just five minutes and 40 seconds —

(1) Setup for resin change
 (a) HP 2.5 to 3.0 kg, 500 to 850 tons
     2.0 to 2.5 kg, 100 to 400 tons
 (b) Amount of material used next: 2.5 to 3.0 kg
 (c) Two 3-kg containers (for loading mini hopper)

(2) Steps in changing resins and colors
 (a) Perform setup for resin and color changes
 (b) Change molds
 (c) Set molding conditions
 (d) Change resin and colors

(3) Resin-changing method
 (a) Perform free shot to discharge all remaining resin from cylinder
 (b) Load specified amount of HP into mini hopper
 (c) Turn screw back 3 or 4 rotations, turn screw forward to about 1 centimeter short of the full
   forward position, then repeat reverse rotations.
 (d) When part of the screw is visible from above the mini hopper, immediately refill the mini hopper
   with the specified amount of the next material (to enable continuous operation of the screw).
   Repeat steps (c) and (d) until all of the HP has been used.
 (e) Clean out the mini hopper

(4) Caution points
 (a) Never stop the forward or reverse screw rotation when there is still HP in the mini hopper.
 (b) Do not advance the screw to the full forward position — stop about 1 centimeter before
   that point.
 (c) If the nozzle becomes clogged, do not use a burner to heat the nozzle.
 (d) Make sure the supply containers are kept full of HP and whatever material is being used next.
 (e) Always have an experienced worker check the setup before the resin and color change
   operation is performed.

Figure 11-6. Resin Changeover and Color Changeover Standards

Photo 11-6. Demonstration of New Changeover Procedure at Company S

Photo 11-7. Demonstration Was Followed by Hands-on Practice Session

well within the single changeover time of nine minutes, but not yet down to the zero-changeover level of three minutes.

Without listing the full benefits of the changeover time reduction, suffice it to mention that since this changeover is performed about 270 times per month, the work-hour savings per month comes to 24,300 minutes (90 minutes × 270) or 405 hours (about 50 worker days). The amount of material used per changeover was reduced from 25 kilograms to just 5 kilograms, producing a net material savings of 5,400 kilograms (20 kg × 270) per month.

The biggest benefit of all, however, is that this changeover improvement enables the assembly line to be linked with the molding process. As a further improvement, the rapid action center's leader later proposed that the cylinder cap changeover procedure could be improved by using the method shown in Figure 11-8, in which a bayonet device similar to screw-on camera lenses would speed up the cylinder cap changeover. This method was still being tested at the time of this writing but, if successful, it promises to reduce the color changeover time to within the zero-changeover limit of three minutes.

So ends the tale of Company S's changeover improvement efforts. In this chapter, I have tried to convey four key points concerning color changeovers — the most difficult kind of changeover for plastic processing factories:

1. Find which cleanser works best for cleaning out cylinders.
2. Find out what the optimum conditions are for color changeover.

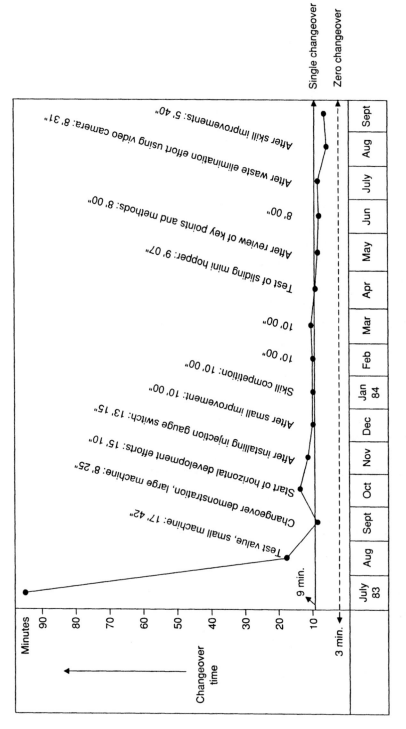

Figure 11-7. Reduction of Changeover Time for Color Change in Large Molding Machine

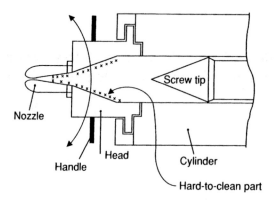

Figure 11-8. Proposed Bayonet Method

3. Once an improvement has worked, try to reproduce it right away.
4. Use changeover demonstrations to launch lateral development of improvements.

If we put these points into practice, we can eventually reduce color changeover time to under three minutes (zero changeover) for virtually any color changeover operation. I hope that this chapter will prove instructive not only for people who work in plastic processing factories but also for people in various types of device-industry factories.

TEST YOUR SKILLS

Determine the optimal free shot conditions and the minimum number of shots.

Using the data in Table 11-4, here are some hints:

- Find the free shot totals for each changeover factor and level.
- Make graphs to better understand the data (such as the graph shown in Figure 11-4).
- For each level, find out what the shortest free shot level is, then calculate the minimum number of free shots as the optimal conditions.

Solution

Omitting the calculations and graphs used to work out this solution, I suggest the minimum number of shots is five, defined as A2 + B1 + C1 + D2 + E2 − 4 × overall average.

12

Establishing One-Piece Flow at a Factory that Produces Small Lots on a Customer-order Basis: The Case of Oriental Motor

Many case studies show how successful the Toyota Production System (TPS) has been when used for mass-production purposes. Very few case studies, however, show similar successes at factories that produce small lots on a customer-order basis. This chapter describes one of these few small-lot successes: Oriental Motor's establishment of one-piece production for its immense array of 60,000 product models.

REDUCING INVENTORY TO ONE-SIXTH THE PREVIOUS LEVEL

Several years ago, an adviser at Oriental Motor's bank reviewed the company's management statistics and commented, "I wonder why your inventory levels are so high in comparison to your sales levels." He then suggested the company might find better use for the money that was tied up in inventory.

Today, the bankers ask Oriental Motor executives why their inventory levels are so low relative to their sales levels. This time around, the bankers want in on the company's secret for boosting profitability by suppressing inventory.

Figure 12-1 shows a "management yardstick" that I proposed for midsized companies wanting to introduce the Toyota Production System. The key consideration when studying the introduction of TPS is where to begin. To answer that question, we must first consider the kinds of tools we need.

Let us take a look at some management figures from Oriental Motor's T production operations division. Before introducing TPS (i.e., before improvement), the division had an inventory level of $2 million and its total sales averaged $1 million a month. This meant that the division's inventory was

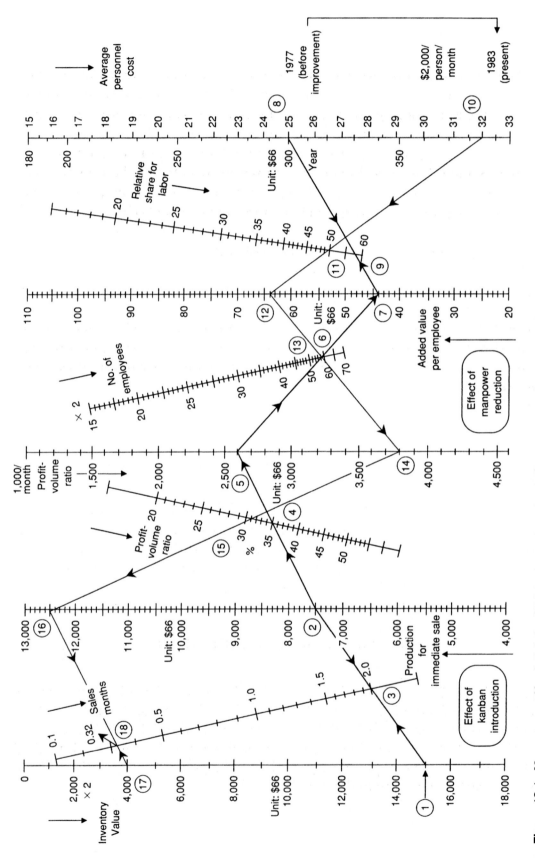

Figure 12-1. Management Yardstick for TPS Introduction (Figures from T Production Operations Division)

equivalent to two months' sales — and we can understand the banker's concern. One reason for the division's large inventory level was a management policy that stressed keeping an ample inventory to avoid loading-related losses that occur when orders for small motors cannot be filled quickly enough.

At the time, Toyota was able to handle many thousands of parts at its factories while maintaining only three days' supply of inventory. When he became aware of this fact, Oriental Motor's President Kuraishi became convinced that "warehouse inventory and in-process inventory were the root of all evil" and he got the ball rolling to introduce TPS at his company. The lines in Figure 12-1's graph show just how well this new strategy paid off.

Photo 12-1 shows some of Oriental Motor's products, which include various high-precision compact motors. Oriental Motor produces about 3,000 basic models of motors; factoring in the variables (such as reduction gears), the total product variety comes to about 60,000 types. These motors find uses in products ranging from computers, photocopiers, and other business machines to farm equipment, amusement rides, as well as various instrumentation and drive systems.

Photo 12-1. Motors Produced by Oriental Motor

Founded in 1885, Oriental Motor has long been a specialist in motor manufacturing. One of the most important chapters in its history came in 1951, when Oriental Motor began standardizing its parts and organizing product series using the greatest common denominators whenever possible. A second turning point came when the company integrated all of its production operations, from forging to parts processing and assembly.

In recent years, user needs for manpower reduction, more compact size, and higher performance have spurred the development of new products at Oriental Motor. At the time of this writing, the company was turning out over 3,000 types of standard products, including power motors with output ranging from 0.5W to 150W, stepping motors for control devices, DC flangeless motors, and reduction gear mechanisms. These motors were finding their way into display devices, computers, and various other products. Oriental Motor had already built up a solid reputation in the industry as a stable supplier of highly reliable products.

In 1982, Oriental Motor was capitalized at $2.4 million, posted total annual sales of $10 million, and employed 850 persons, whose average age was 30. For the 1983 business year, the company aimed to achieve $12 million in total sales, on the way toward its longer-term goal of reaching the $13.3 million sales mark by 1985. The production operations division includes five factories; one each in Toyoshiki (Chiba Prefecture), Tsuchiura (Ibaraki Prefecture), Tsuruoka (Yamagata Prefecture), Takamatsu (Kaga Prefecture), and Kofu (Yamanashi Prefecture). The sales and service network is composed of 20 domestic offices and six overseas offices, which together serve over 5,000 client companies in Japan and abroad (see Photo 12-2).

Photo 12-2. Oriental Motor's Factory in Tsuchiura, Japan

Referring back to the graph shown in Figure 12-1, we can sum up the advantages and disadvantages in overall productivity for Oriental Motor's production division by noting that rises in productivity correspond to rises in added value per employee. This in turn relates to the processing costs per employee. The high added value per employee shown in the figure therefore indicates high productivity. In 1977, the output value was $3,000 per month per person and the relative share for labor was a high 58 percent (see number 8 in Figure 12-1). In 1983, these figures changed to the levels shown by numbers 10 through 18 in Figure 12-1. The difference between the levels shown by numbers 8 and 10 in the figure reflects the increase in personnel costs between 1977 and 1983. The difference between numbers 9 and 11 is the relative share of labor, which shows how well these higher personnel costs were absorbed. The difference between numbers 7 and 12 shows the increase in value-adding productivity for the division as a whole. The difference between numbers 6 and 13 shows the change in the number of personnel, which in this case is zero. (Actually, part-time hiring during this period can be interpreted as an increase of 0.6 workers.)

We can draw our conclusions concerning the changes made in Oriental Motor's production operations division by making the following comparisons. The most impressive change shown by Figure 12-1 is the difference between the levels numbered as 3 and 18. It was this change that amazed the company's banker. By 1983, Oriental Motor had reduced its inventory to one-sixth its 1977 level; from the equivalent of two months' output to just 0.32 months.

For simplicity's sake, if we assume that a month consists of 22 working days and that inventory can be divided into equal thirds (as product inventory, in-process inventory, and materials inventory), the amount of in-process inventory would stand at two days' worth, which is still not very close to Toyota's level of 0.7 days. The production lead time comes to 16 hours, which is fairly close to Toyota's 10 hours. Oriental Motor did not fully meet the challenge of duplicating Toyota's success, but the improvements still made a considerable impact on the division's management statistics.

THE CHALLENGE OF ESTABLISHING ONE-PIECE PRODUCTION

Oriental Motor's President Kuraishi made a distinction between one-piece production and the one-piece flow production method. His idea of one-piece production was based on the realization that it is better for the sake of long-term management efficiency to fill 100 orders for 100 customers one at a time than it is to fill an order for 100 products from just one customer. Naturally, the ideal is to have a one-piece flow production system that includes various automation devices or that is a complete flexible manufacturing system (FMS) to handle similar types of products. In the Toyota Production System, mass-produced products are divided up into small lots to establish one-piece flow through mixed production, which makes for the greatest efficiency.

Incidentally, Oriental Motor's small-motor customers prefer (1) to order their motors one at a time and (2) to receive prompt delivery in order to keep their own warehouse inventory levels down. To meet these customer demands, Oriental Motor needed to adopt a "product-out, customer-in" approach that gives customer convenience first priority over production convenience. This led to the idea of establishing one-piece everything: from receiving orders to production and inspection. Therefore, one-piece production is a custom-made orientation that stresses individual care for products as they are manufactured and inspected, in pursuit of the goal of a zero-defect production system.

The reason why President Kuraishi recognized one-piece production as preferable over the long term is simple. Even though one-piece production (ideally, one order each for 100 companies) will lower production efficiency during the short term, the timely provision of 100 percent defect-free products to 100 companies will bring a large base of satisfied customers. This will eventually reap the reward of expanded orders.

In 1977, few managers were keen on abandoning the mass-production approach. After all, keeping a large inventory enabled companies to avoid the heavy changeover cost burden, complexities, and additional labor costs of small-lot production systems. As a result, most managers still firmly believed that mass-production with ample inventories was the best possible system.

This helps explain why, as shown in Figure 12-1, Oriental Motor maintained inventory equal to two months' output in 1977. Thus, in adopting the one-piece production policy, Oriental Motor's president knew he was asking a lot of his managers and factory workers. They accepted the challenge of introducing the Toyota Production System by pooling together everyone's experience-based know-how to build a stronger workplace and a stronger management.

Another of President Kuraishi's goals was to completely eliminate warehouse inventory. The two simplest methods for doing this are: Materials Requirement Planning (MRP) and Operations Planning (OP) methods. Kuraishi recognized, however, that a small-lot method, such as the "ten-unit lot production" method, might work even better for building up the factory flow. Accordingly, he decided to modify his approach to one-piece production by making it a ten-unit U-shaped cell production system in which each cell followed the one-piece production method. He made this decision out of consideration for the fact that failure to establish very quick changeover operations in the production cells would lead to very heavy labor costs.

For example, if it takes nine minutes (single changeover) for the changeover of a small press and takes 30 seconds to process ten workpieces in the press, the loss due to changeover for 100 products would be 1,800 percent (540 seconds ÷ 30 seconds × 100), an 18-fold increase in loss. Therefore, the one-piece production system requires zero changeover in order to remain profitable.

Table 12-1 describes the process by which Oriental Motor established zero changeover.

As can be seen in the table, Oriental Motor began studying jobsite industrial engineering (IE) and new product systems in 1977.

In 1978, the company adopted a stock market system (in which all parts are supplied in kits) to prevent missing parts, and also introduced the use of kanban for assembly and processing processes.

In 1979, it stopped using belt conveyors for its motor assembly line and switched to one-piece production on a line where all workpieces were sent downstream manually. The layout of the test line at this time was similar to an "S" shape, and became known as the "S line." (This type of layout will be described later.)

In 1980, 30 managers were selected to attend hands-on practice sessions at other companies to help build stronger factories and factory management at Oriental Motor. This training helped the managers gain the skills necessary to lead improvement projects.

In 1981, after the S-shaped line that had been set up as a test line began outperforming the conveyor-belt lines, the company decided to switch over to S-shaped lines throughout each factory.

In 1982, the whole company switched over to one-piece production based on ten-unit lots. This brought inventory down to one-sixth its 1977 level. At the same time, they discovered how switching from S-shaped lines to U-shaped cells can help achieve zero defects and manpower reduction. They therefore introduced waste elimination techniques and process razing throughout each factory as part of the switchover to U-shaped cells.

In 1983, they found that establishing one-piece production based on ten-unit lots went a long way toward achieving zero warehouse inventory. At the same time, it raised the problem of increased loss due to changeover. To reduce this type of loss, the company formed a U-shaped cell promotion study group

Table 12-1. Progress in Establishing a One-Piece Production System

1977	1978	1979	1980	1981	1982	1983
① Formed group to study new production systems	① Abolished the inspection department and built a process-integrated quality assurance organization	① Employed female part-time workers in all factory workshops	① Separated production planning from head office operations	① Separated purchasing division from head office operations	① Conducted waste elimination analysis	① Established zero changeover (3 minutes or less)
② Developed spare workers	② Adopted cock market system	② Abolished belt conveyor assembly system	② Quality circle activities	② Established test line for wide-variety small-lot production	② Studied process razing	② Established U-shaped cell promotion group (for entire factory)
③ Established andon system	③ Studied kanban systems	③ Studied one-piece production on specialized lines (A, B, C, D)	③ Thoroughly implemented pull production	③ Shortened lead time for parts	③ Introduced waste elimination techniques	③ Adopted 2-person assembly method
④ Trained single-skill workers to become multi-skill workers	④ Switched from monthly to weekly production schedules	④ Introduced NC lathe and adopted Maru analysis	④ Established joint lines	④ Prepared for one-piece production in machining lines	④ Switched to 10-unit lots	④ Introduced zero-defect production system
⑤ Developed female inspection workers	⑤ Abolished product code-specific shipping charts and switches to production vouchers	⑤ Introduced kanban for product warehousing	⑤ Introduced standard lot sizes in product warehouse	⑤ Employed S-shaped layout throughout factory	⑤ Established U-shaped cells	⑤ Thoroughly implemented SPH
⑥ Formed group to study jobsite IE	⑥ Introduced kanban for parts management	⑥ Established cock parts	⑥ Held hands-on training sessions in-house and at outside sources		⑥ Adopted back number system for products and parts	

to help introduce zero-changeover techniques (for making improvements to enable changeover within three minutes) and two-person assembly techniques throughout the company.

Figure 12-2 shows a flow chart description of Oriental Motor's introduction of kanban for its U-shaped cells. To adopt a new production system in a factory that makes products to order, the new system must focus on the flow of goods in the factory.

ORGANIZATION AND OPERATION OF U-SHAPED CELL PRODUCTION STUDY GROUP

The first and most important consideration when introducing a new production system and implementing substantial improvements is to establish a solid consensus among the relevant managers. This consensus does not mean merely going along with what top management has ordered, it means reaching understanding and agreement among everyone concerned prior to taking action. Unless this preliminary step of consensus-building is taken, there is little chance that top management's orders will be fully understood or well implemented.

For example, let us suppose that the president of a certain company has just announced a "mass production/mini sales" policy. What this means is that the production system is geared toward the efficiency lent by mass production but that it can still be used for small-lot sales based on one-piece order reception, production, and sales. The company's middle managers interpret this concept to mean that they should recognize the need for small-lot services to customers but should still basically reject small-lot production as less efficient than mass production. Oriental Motor suffered a similar misunderstanding among its managers, which underscores the importance of consensus building.

The second most important consideration is to build a promotional organization to help improvement groups reach their goals. At Oriental Motor, a company-wide U-shaped cell production study group (or "U Study Group") was formed to help people study and practice one-piece production activities. The organization and operation of the U Study Group developed along the following lines:

1. The U Study Group's purpose is to help the company establish a companywide one-piece production system based on U-shaped cells. The ultimate goal is to establish zero-defect lines.

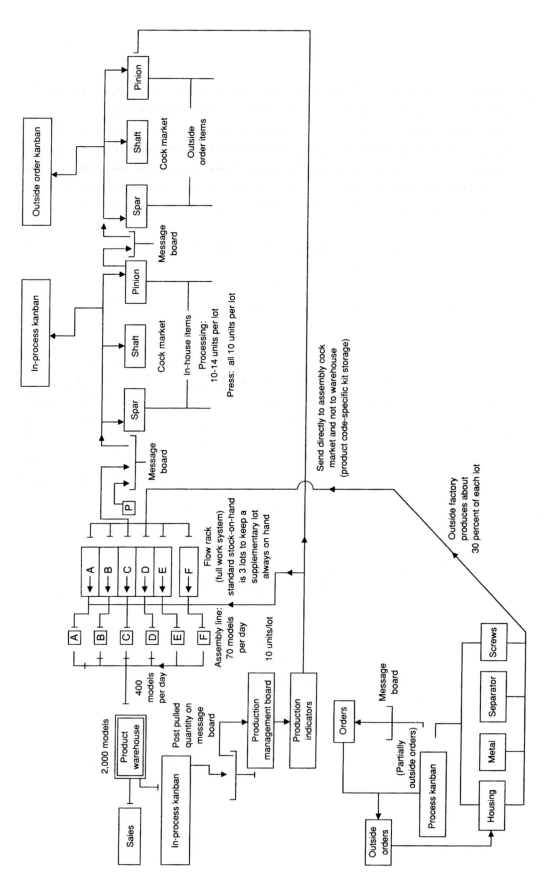

Figure 12-2. Use of Kanban in U-shaped Cells

2. As people work to establish zero-defect lines, they will also be strengthening the company's management and its production lines.

3. The U Study Group's members included at least three people selected from each factory. The U Study Group spent four days of each month touring production facilities. The meeting place was rotated among the factories, and at each factory the superintendent and the person in charge of one-piece production were responsible for reporting to the group.

   The U Study Group membership included full members and partial members. The partial members were appointed by managers at their respective factories. Therefore, in addition to the full members appointed by the company's factory superintendents, the group included other members from each factory, for a total of about 30 members.

4. The U Study Group bases its operations on a theme that is decided upon by the relevant factory superintendent. They hold seminars and lectures related to the theme, make factory visits, propose improvement plans, compare members' improvement plans with those proposed by more experienced lecturers and foremen, and so on. Consequently, certain talented or well-experienced managers or production engineers are sometimes asked to give lectures to the U Study Group. Photo 12-3 shows an improvement plan comparison session.

Photo 12-3. Improvement Plan Comparison Session by U Study Group

5. The improvement plans proposed by the U Study Group members are sent to the relevant factories for further study and possible implementation. No matter how enthusiastic the U Study Group is about any particular improvement plan, it is up to the relevant line's managers to decide whether or not to implement it. This rule makes it all the more important that the U Study Group strive to educate managers about one-piece production based on U- shaped cells.

6. As of this writing, the types of improvement themes proposed and their success rates have varied from factory to factory, but can be summed up as follows:
   • one-piece production based on ten-unit lots (an 80 percent success rate)
   • cultivating an eye for identifying waste and practice in removing waste (90 percent)
   • using process-razing techniques for U-shaped cells (50 percent)
   • achieving zero changeover (three-minute changeover or sequential changeover in assembly) (50 percent)
   • building a zero-defects line (50 percent)

Recently, the company managed to achieve the "zero warehouse" goal. The remaining major themes are achieving zero changeover, zero defects, zero breakdowns, and zero missing parts.

7. The basic training included only the topics needed for understanding one-piece production based on ten-unit lots and dispensed with many of the traditional topics covered by ordinary IE or QC training courses.

The following is a list of the main topics covered by Oriental Motor's basic training program prior to introducing the new production system.

   i. The basic training included an explanation of the P-Q analysis approach. (See Chapter 3 for a detailed description of this approach.)
   ii. It also covered the development of processing families via part-specific processing route analysis. For assembly lines, we use assembly process analysis to discover the critical path in each assembly line.
   iii. They also studied process flow diagrams. Here, the trainees learned how to chart the flow of goods in processes and the paths walked by process operators.

iv. The trainees learned how operation analysis can be used to study current conditions, after which they were able to practice removing waste.

v. They practiced devising process-razing plans and eliminating wasteful manual operations. They also began to propose improvement plans and study automation techniques.

vi. They learned about establishing manpower reduction goals centered on the cycle time and about ways to design for multi-unit handling.

vii. They studied the composition and layout of U-shaped cells designed for manpower reduction.

viii. They learned how to incorporate full-lot inspection into U-shaped cells and how to use past downstream complaints to help determine future inspection points.

ix. They got to practice asking "Why" five times to identify the underlying causes of problems or defects.

x. They learned how to develop and install mistake-proofing devices.

The somewhat different production systems adopted by each factory will be introduced in this chapter according to their themes:

- Takamatsu factory: One-piece motor assembly production using U-shaped cells. (It is centered on building U-shaped cells and devising mistake-proofing improvements.)

- Tsuchiura factory: U-shaped cells for ten-unit lot production. (This is chiefly about establishing zero changeover to enable ten-unit lot production.)

- Toyoshiki factory: Steps in U-shaped cell development for rotor assembly. (This focuses on steps, since the orthodox type of line is acceptable in this case.)

- Tsuruoka factory: Using U-shaped cells for single-operator assembly. (A brave attempt to achieve the goal of single-operator assembly lines.)

ONE-PIECE MOTOR ASSEMBLY PRODUCTION USING U-SHAPED CELLS

At the Takamatsu factory, the aim was to achieve zero defects by perfecting a one-piece production system based on U-shaped cells. This factory features an integrated production line for small precision motors, and they planned to develop one-piece production centered on linked assembly and processing lines. This production system uses one-piece flow, one-piece manufacturing, and one-piece full-lot inspection. Figure 12-3 shows the type of U-shaped cell the factory was already using even before making improvements. This layout used "shish-kabob" lot production, which made it difficult to identify defects when they occurred. The in-process defect rate was as high as 1 percent, and they occasionally received complaints from customers.

Their policy toward improving this type of U-shaped cell layout included these points:

1. Adopt one-piece flow, one-piece manufacturing, and one-piece full-lot inspection.
2. Maintain one-piece in-process inventory centered on the cycle time. Whenever a defect occurs, immediately look for the causes.

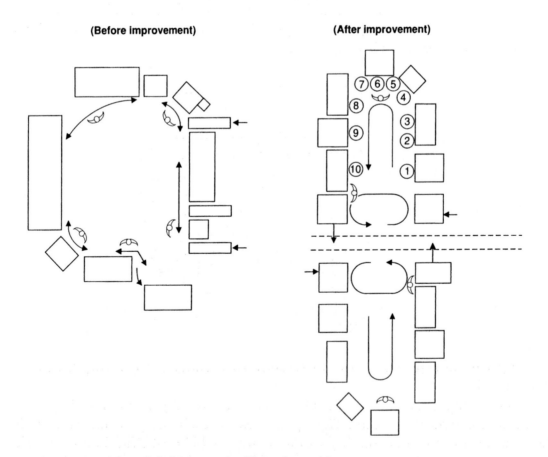

Figure 12-3. U-shaped Cell Layouts for Motor Assembly

3. The standard assembly lot size is ten units, with a maximum of 30 units.

4. The line workers are to be given the right to stop the line whenever they notice anything unusual, and should be encouraged to do so.

5. Jigs should be devised to improve production efficiency and as mistake-proofing devices.

6. Clear standards need to be written concerning the conditions that produce nondefective goods and the conditions that produce defective goods.

7. The same line worker should operate the cell's entry and exit points so that one unit of materials is fed only when one nondefective product is produced.

The factory used this basic approach to redesign its U-shaped cells. Figure 12-3 shows the "before" and "after" improvement cell designs. The assembly line cell is operated by two persons. Figure 12-4 shows the standard operations design for the improved U-shaped cell.

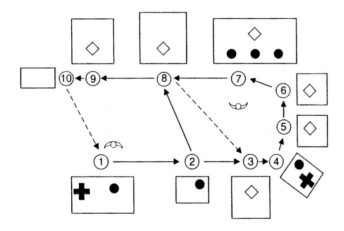

Figure 12-4. Standard Operations Chart for U-shaped Cell

Figure 12-5 shows a line efficiency rate chart for the improved U-shaped cell.

Before improvement, the line efficiency rate was 72 percent; after improvement, it was over 95 percent. Their goal was to reach 100 percent. And while keeping the number of assembly workers low would boost efficiency, the workers were also needed to help ensure zero defects. In the U-shaped cell shown in

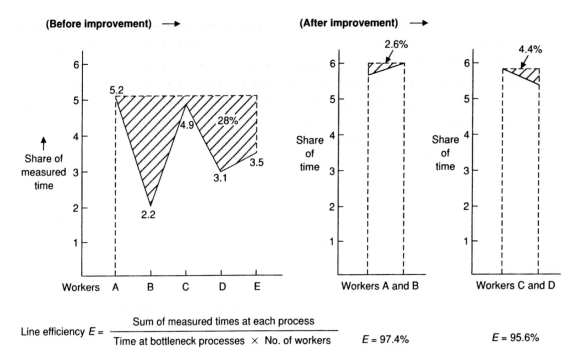

Line efficiency $E = \dfrac{\text{Sum of measured times at each process}}{\text{Time at bottleneck processes} \times \text{No. of workers}}$

Figure 12-5. Line Efficiency Rate Chart for Assembly U-shaped Cell

Figure 12-4, there are two workers on the line and six units of in-process inventory. They made the following suggestions concerning mistake-proofing:

- Make it so that the workpiece cannot fit into the jig when an error occurs.
- Make it so that the start switch does not work when the processing is done out of order.
- Make it so that the machines automatically stop when an error is made, and equip the machines with devices that notify the operators of the error's occurrence.

As mentioned, the Takamatsu factory staff developed devices (or machines) for assembly and inspection or equipment that automatically stop the equipment whenever a defect occurs. They also added mistake-proofing devices to processes that involved manual operations, and implemented full-lot inspections so that any defects that did occur would remain within the factory and would not get shipped to customers.

For example, let us consider two auto-stop devices: the ball-bearing insertion device shown in Photo 12-4 and the bracket/case alignment device shown in Photo 12-5.

These devices include insertion pressure control circuits that enable the machines to stop whenever the alignment is not right. Figure 12-6 shows an auto-stop device that also notifies the operator of the line stop.

Photo 12-6 shows an auto-inspection device that conducts wire connection tests and aging tests on motors to check the motor's characteristics, wiring, and pressure resistance. When any of these automatic tests detect an abnormality, the auto-inspection device notifies an operator.

Photo 12-4.
Ball-bearing
Insertion Device

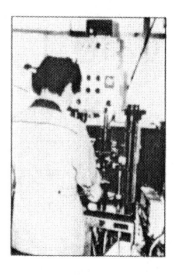

Photo 12-5.
Bracket/Case
Alignment Device

Photo 12-6.
Auto-inspection
Device

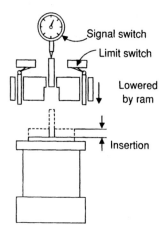

Figure 12-6. Auto-stop Device

Mistake-proofing devices can be thought of as a means to equip processes with jigs that perform "full lot inspections" by using sensors to detect the kind of careless mistakes that used to go unnoticed, such as forgetting to attach labels and nameplates, omitting a capacitor or two, forgetting to install a brake shoe, and so on.

Figures 12-7, 12-8, 12-9, and 12-10 and Photos 12-7, 12-8, 12-9, and 12-10 show various kinds of mistake-proofing devices.

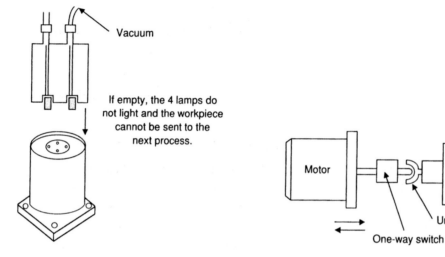

Figure 12-7. **Mistake-proofing Device to Prevent Brake Shoe Omission**

Figure 12-8. **Rotation Direction Sensor**

Photo 12-7. **Mistake-proofing Device to Detect Assembly Omissions**

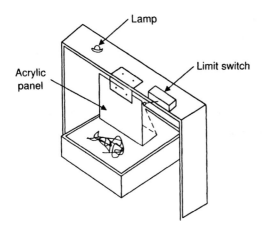

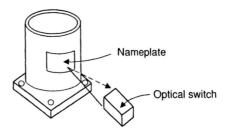

Figure 12-9. Mistake-proofing Device for Parts Assembly Omission

Figure 12-10. Mistake-proofing Device for Nameplate Omission

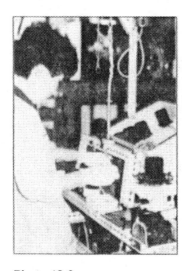

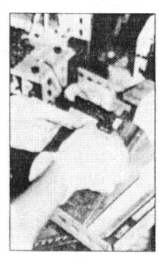

Photo 12-8. Rotation Direction

Photo 12-9. Parts Assembly Omission

Photo 12-10. Nameplate Assembly Omission

The key point is that instead of having to admonish people against making careless mistakes, devices can be developed that enforce the rule against making mistakes by detecting them and preventing defective items from being passed to the next process. In other words, the devices themselves are carrying out a type of full-lot inspection — a worthwhile improvement indeed. Looking, for example, at the mistake-proofing device for detecting brake shoe omissions (see Figure 12-7), we can easily imagine how similar devices can be developed to detect not only missing brake shoes but also other missing parts or even extra parts. Looking at it from another angle, one could even go as far as to say that a factory that fails to make improvements using such mistake-proofing devices is a factory that suffers from careless management mistakes! This chapter should help managers come up with their own ideas for mistake-proofing devices, such as devices that feed brake shoes to the assembly process in batches of four, that handle them one at a time, that move them to another jig, or that automatically insert them. Such an approach is bound to be more successful that merely being critical toward operator errors.

In the final analysis, perhaps the best idea proposed by the Takamatsu factory managers was the vacuum pump-powered auto-insertion device shown in Figure 12-7. The devices in Photos 12-7 through 12-10 are shown as they appear on the production line.

The results of these improvements aimed at achieving zero defects on the motor assembly line are shown in Figure 12-11. Not only was manpower reduced, but productivity per worker was raised and the in-process defect rate was cut 80 percent. They also came to understand how important one-piece flow and one-piece production are for maintaining quality.

This six-month improvement effort got the Takamatsu factory onto the right track for developing U-shaped cells factory-wide and reduced the number of customer complaints to zero. For the future, they planned to combine certain assembly jigs, develop more automation devices, automate the conveyance (connections) among assembly processes, and pursue various other improvement themes.

U-SHAPED CELLS FOR TEN-UNIT LOT PRODUCTION

The Tsuchiura factory can be characterized by the ten-unit lot production system it uses regardless of the lot size of the customer orders.

Why ten-unit lots? First, as shown in Figure 12-12, 82 percent of the factory's orders for a given month are for quantities of ten or fewer units. Second, the factory has a very short delivery period of one or two days that requires a rapid-delivery system.

Figure 12-13 shows how the factory's product warehouse inventory compares to orders (in terms of product shipments). Even with this product warehouse inventory, the factory was troubled by delivery delays and sales overruns due to fluctuation in the amounts and types of products ordered. The

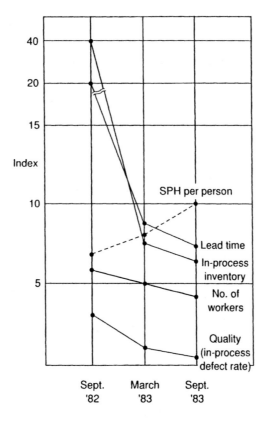

**Figure 12-11. Results of U-shaped
Assembly Cell
Improvement**

factory's managers decided to adopt a new production system in order to solve these chronic problems.

Their starting point was to find a production system that would work within the established framework of ten-unit lot production. To do this, they followed these steps:

1. Remove waste from the existing lines and study new processing methods.
2. Link processes and develop integrated processing and assembly lines.
3. Reduce inventory between processes to just one unit.
4. Shorten changeover times.
5. Improve line layout and establish one-piece production based on U-shaped cells wherever possible.

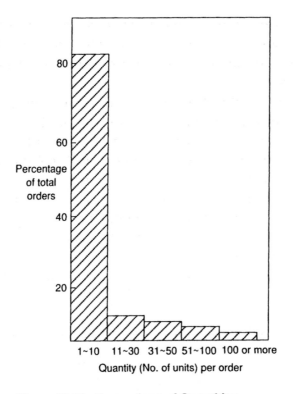

Figure 12-12. Comparison of Quantities
Ordered in One Month

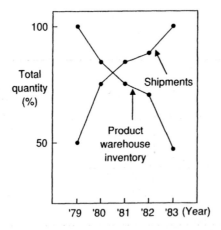

Figure 12-13. Comparison of Product
Warehouse Inventory and
Product Shipments

I would like to describe the Tsuchiura factory's improvement theme, in which they gradually established one-piece production based on ten-unit lots without overlapping too much with our examination of the Takamatsu factory's improvement example.

Since the Tsuchiura factory's improvement turned out to be easy to develop horizontally throughout the factory, the improvement items were all described on improvement sheets. Having these improvement sheets as reference resources sparked people in other workshops in the factory to make similar improvements. This reached the point where workshops on different lines were actually competing to see who could make the improvements first. For brevity's sake, I will include here only some of the descriptions from the improvement sheets and only the "before and after" improvement figures.

Figures 12-14 and 12-15 are from the sheets describing waste-removing improvements. In Figure 12-14, the improvement eliminates walking waste and is based on the rule of thumb that "it is OK to move your hands but not your

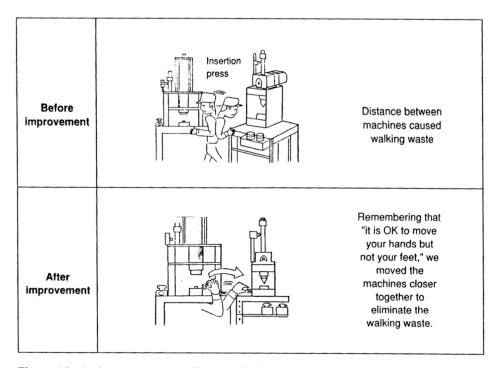

Figure 12-14. Improvement to Remove Walking Waste

feet." In Figure 12-15, the installation of a revolving workpiece storage shelf eliminated waste in picking up, setting down, and piling up objects.

The press in Figure 12-15 had been used for stand-alone operations and was later integrated into the assembly line shown in Figure 12-22. Figure 12-16 shows how changeover loss increased sharply when one-piece production was implemented for the factory's ten-unit lot production system. Although these figures support the view that large lots make more sense economically, we must not give this consideration too much weight. Improvements can negate the economic disadvantages of small lot production. Figure 12-16 also hits the improvement activities that were carried out to reduce the change-over loss by achieving zero changeover. These improvements are not always made, and it is important that workshops that do make them hold report meetings and/or demonstrations to encourage other workshops to make similar improvements. Every improvement effort should make use of an improvement schedule such as that shown in Figure 12-16.

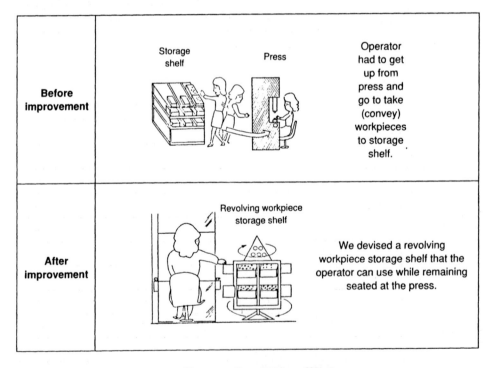

Figure 12-15. Improvement to Remove Conveyance Waste

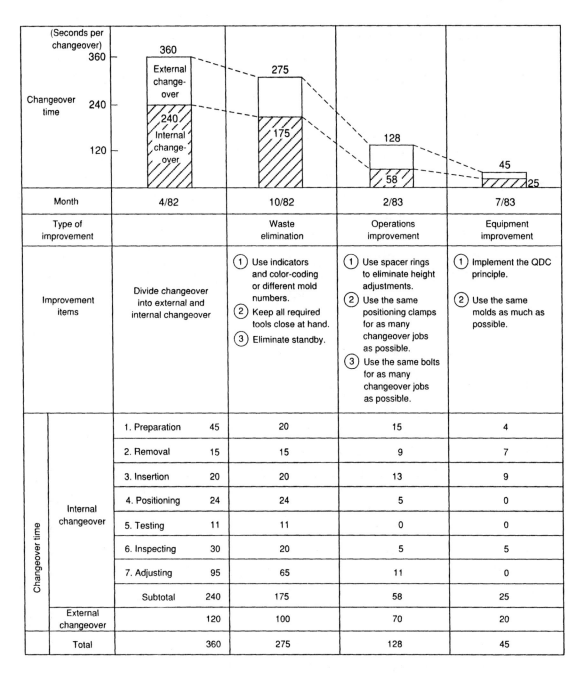

Figure 12-16. Press Changeover Improvement Schedule

Determined to attain the goal of zero changeover (changeover time of three minutes or less) for their one-piece production system using ten-unit lots, they took the following steps in addressing changeover problems:

Step 1. Conduct an operation analysis of the current changeover operations to better understand them.

We have omitted the description of this operation analysis for this chapter.

Step 2. Use the results of the operation analysis to develop a waste elimination chart for the changeover operations.

The important thing is to use the operation analysis results to divide changeover waste into three categories: preparation waste, waste in removing and attaching items, and adjustment waste. After that, the group is ready to carry out waste-removing improvements.

Step 3. The basic concept behind eliminating waste is the idea that "zero changeover can be achieved." Let this idea guide your improvement activities.

We human beings have an apparently unique gift for working toward an ideal, and we should certainly make the most of it.

Step 4. Draft waste-removing plans for the different types of waste. Then draw up an improvement schedule such as shown in Figure 12-16 that reflects the following priorities:
- Start with small improvements that can be carried out immediately.
- Also pursue slightly larger-scale improvements that might incur some expenses, such as installing fastening tools.
- Save the more expensive, large-scale improvements (such as new molds or equipment remodeling) for last.

Figure 12-16's improvement schedule describes the improvements made at the Tsuchiura factory to attain zero changeover. Before these improvements were made, the total changeover time was 360 seconds. After the improvements, it was 70 seconds.

Figure 12-17 shows an example of a changeover process in which "zero changeover" has been achieved. The mold changeover does not require any mold exchanges. Only the light caddy section needs to be changed, and the operators had no trouble doing it. As of this writing, the factory is working on achieving zero changeover for all of its changeover operations, including those involving processing equipment.

Changeover Improvement Sheet

Operation	Zero changeover for press changeover operations (25 seconds)		
Problem	Since this changeover operation is done at the same time as the assembly operation, it must be completed within 30 seconds.		
Description of improvement	Use boltless fasteners and change only the caddy section.		
Before improvement		The entire mold was exchanged, requiring a strong operator to lift the heavy molds.	
After improvement	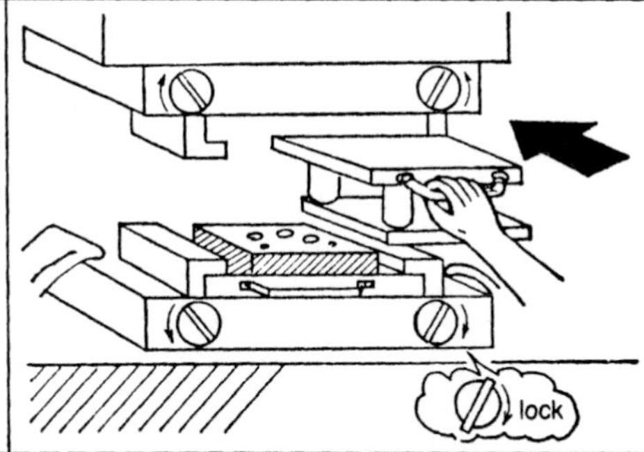	Only the caddy section needs to be changed; the rest of the mold can be left alone. The caddy exchange is done without bolts and uses a lock dial switch instead, enabling an operator to handle the operation.	
Costs and benefits	① The mold changeover time was reduced to 25 seconds. ② The mold changeover was able to be synchronized with assembly, thus eliminating the need for in-process inventory. ③ The new mold was fabricated in-house at a cost of no more than $200.		
Comments	The press could be integrated into the assembly line.		
Company name	Oriental Motor	Factory name	Tsuchiura Factory
Dept.	Dept. No. 1	Month/year	Jan. '83
Sheet by:	Kenji Takaoka	Category	

Figure 12-17. Improvement to Achieve Zero Changeover for Press Changeover Operation

Figure 12-18 illustrates a positioning improvement involving a dog that is used as a position-checking aid on a press.

Figure 12-19 shows an improvement where a boltless fastener was added. In this case, the fastening tool is a ball plunger.

Figure 12-20 shows how using a compound mold enabled four processes to be combined as one process (one machine).

Figure 12-21 shows an example of establishing standing while working and multi-process handling on a shaft and pinion machining line. Before the improvement, four workers were each assigned a different machine, such as a lathe, grinder, or gear cutter. After turning this line into a U-shaped cell, two workers were able to handle all of the processes by standing while working, with fewer workers, more daily output, and reduced changeover times.

Figure 12-22 shows an improvement where an assembly conveyor was eliminated and replaced by an S-shaped layout. This was then changed to a U-shaped cell layout. Since the U-shaped cell that was used as a test line was successful, the factory managers decided that all lines should be redesigned as U-shaped cells.

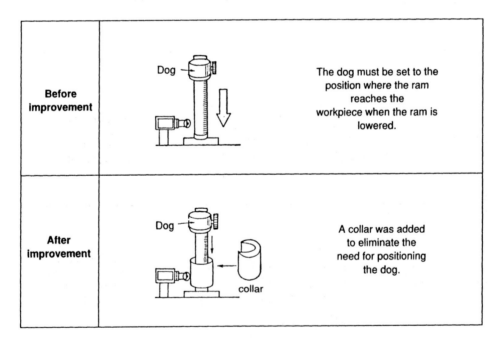

Figure 12-18. Improvement Using Position-checking Dog

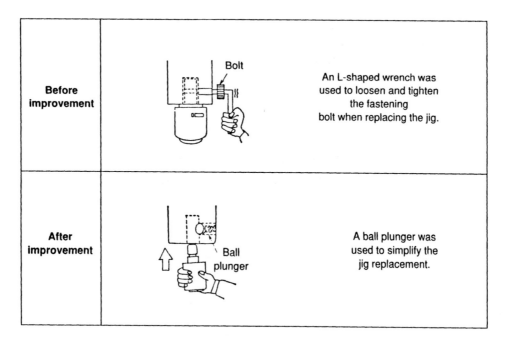

Figure 12-19. Improvement to Simplify Jig Replacement Operation

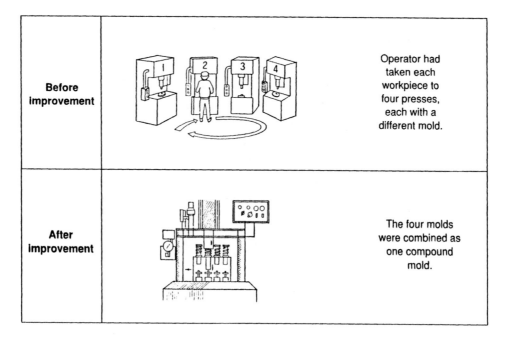

Figure 12-20. Use of Compound Mold for Combining Processes

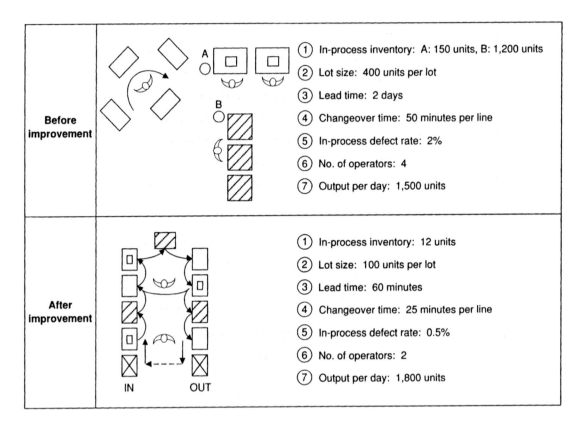

Before improvement		① In-process inventory: A: 150 units, B: 1,200 units

Before improvement
- ① In-process inventory: A: 150 units, B: 1,200 units
- ② Lot size: 400 units per lot
- ③ Lead time: 2 days
- ④ Changeover time: 50 minutes per line
- ⑤ In-process defect rate: 2%
- ⑥ No. of operators: 4
- ⑦ Output per day: 1,500 units

After improvement
- ① In-process inventory: 12 units
- ② Lot size: 100 units per lot
- ③ Lead time: 60 minutes
- ④ Changeover time: 25 minutes per line
- ⑤ In-process defect rate: 0.5%
- ⑥ No. of operators: 2
- ⑦ Output per day: 1,800 units

IN   OUT

Figure 12-21. Layout Improvement in Machining Line

The main purpose of making U-shaped cells is to facilitate the attainment of zero-defect production, but achieving zero defects also requires such measures as full-lot inspections, thorough investigation into defect causes using the "5 Why" approach, mistake-proofing devices, prevention of variation in supplied materials and parts, and improvements in production start-up.

For factory managers, these improvements made the following points:

1. The creation of U-shaped cells for one-piece production using ten-unit lots is an effective means of building zero-defect lines.
2. Manpower reduction can be a big productivity booster. Per-person output figures rose more than 30 percent.
3. It is possible to have zero product warehouse inventory and still maintain a rapid delivery system.

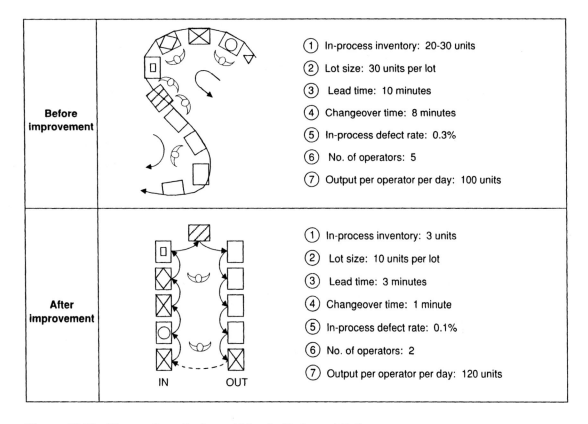

Before improvement		(1) In-process inventory: 20-30 units
		(2) Lot size: 30 units per lot
		(3) Lead time: 10 minutes
		(4) Changeover time: 8 minutes
		(5) In-process defect rate: 0.3%
		(6) No. of operators: 5
		(7) Output per operator per day: 100 units
After improvement		(1) In-process inventory: 3 units
		(2) Lot size: 10 units per lot
		(3) Lead time: 3 minutes
		(4) Changeover time: 1 minute
		(5) In-process defect rate: 0.1%
		(6) No. of operators: 2
	IN OUT	(7) Output per operator per day: 120 units

Figure 12-22. Change from S-shaped Line to U-shaped Cell

4. Small waste-removing improvements in U-shaped cells can produce big ripple effects.
5. The U Study Group's success implanted a "can do" attitude in the minds of the factory managers that promised to spread companywide.

The thoroughness of the U Study Group's waste-removing efforts got people to develop a sharper eye for recognizing waste, and primed their enthusiasm for further improvements.

STEPS IN INTEGRATING A ROTOR ASSEMBLY LINE

We have just seen the process by which the U Study Group got the establishment of one-piece production off to a good start. The following describes the steps they took toward building a U-shaped cell at the Tsuruoka factory.

Their four goals in establishing one-piece production using a U-shaped cell were:

1. to raise the output per day
2. to shorten the production lead time
3. to reduce dead inventory
4. to establish zero-defect production

Step 1: Study the Current Conditions in Wide-variety Small-lot Production

To find out what kind of line they should build, they conducted a P-Q analysis, such as the one we see in Figure 12-23.

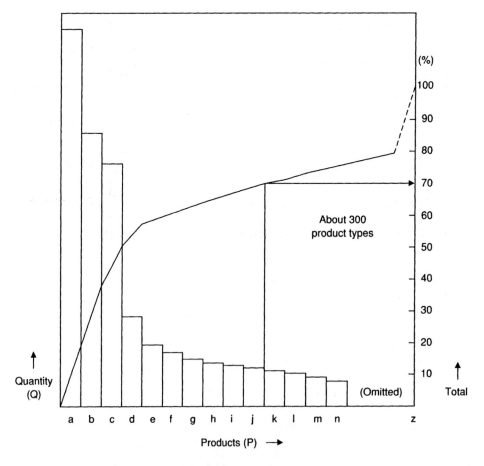

Figure 12-23. P-Q Analysis for Product Groups

Next, they drew up a process analysis chart. For convenience, the assembly process analysis chart shown as Figure 12-24 includes figures for both before and after improvement. Note how much longer the process was prior to improvement. It should be obvious here that joining processes and shortening lines are a key part of making improvements.

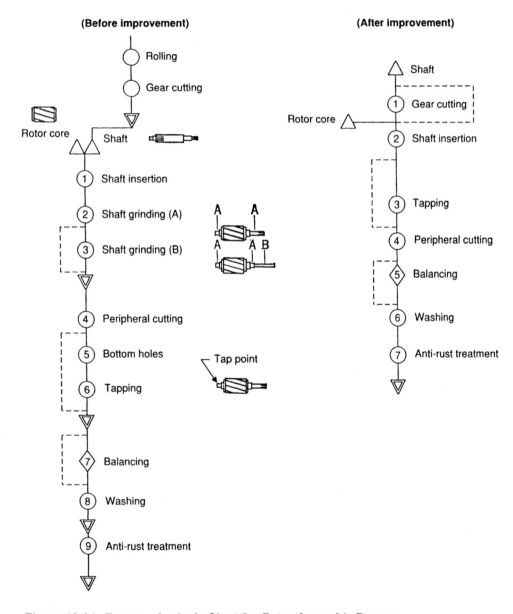

Figure 12-24. Process Analysis Chart for Rotor Assembly Process

The group then drew up a flow diagram. As shown in Figure 12-25, the machines were all laid out in straight lines, but the goods flowed along various curved lines that required a lot of complicated walking patterns.

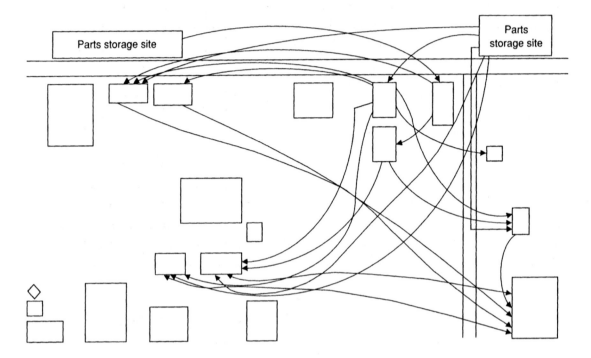

Figure 12-25. Flow Diagram and Walking Routes for Rotor Assembly Line

After the flow diagram, they drew up a processing route analysis chart and began devising ways to shorten and standardize the processing route. Figure 12-26 shows both the "before improvement" and "after improvement" statistics. There is an obvious contrast between the complexity of the former and simplicity of the latter.

Step 2: Study the Line to Discover Waste

The first principle in process razing (removing waste) in production lines to build U-shaped cells is to have a close, firsthand look at the current operations. We need to see exactly how things are being made — how the workpieces are being reshaped during production. This requires close study of the production line operations.

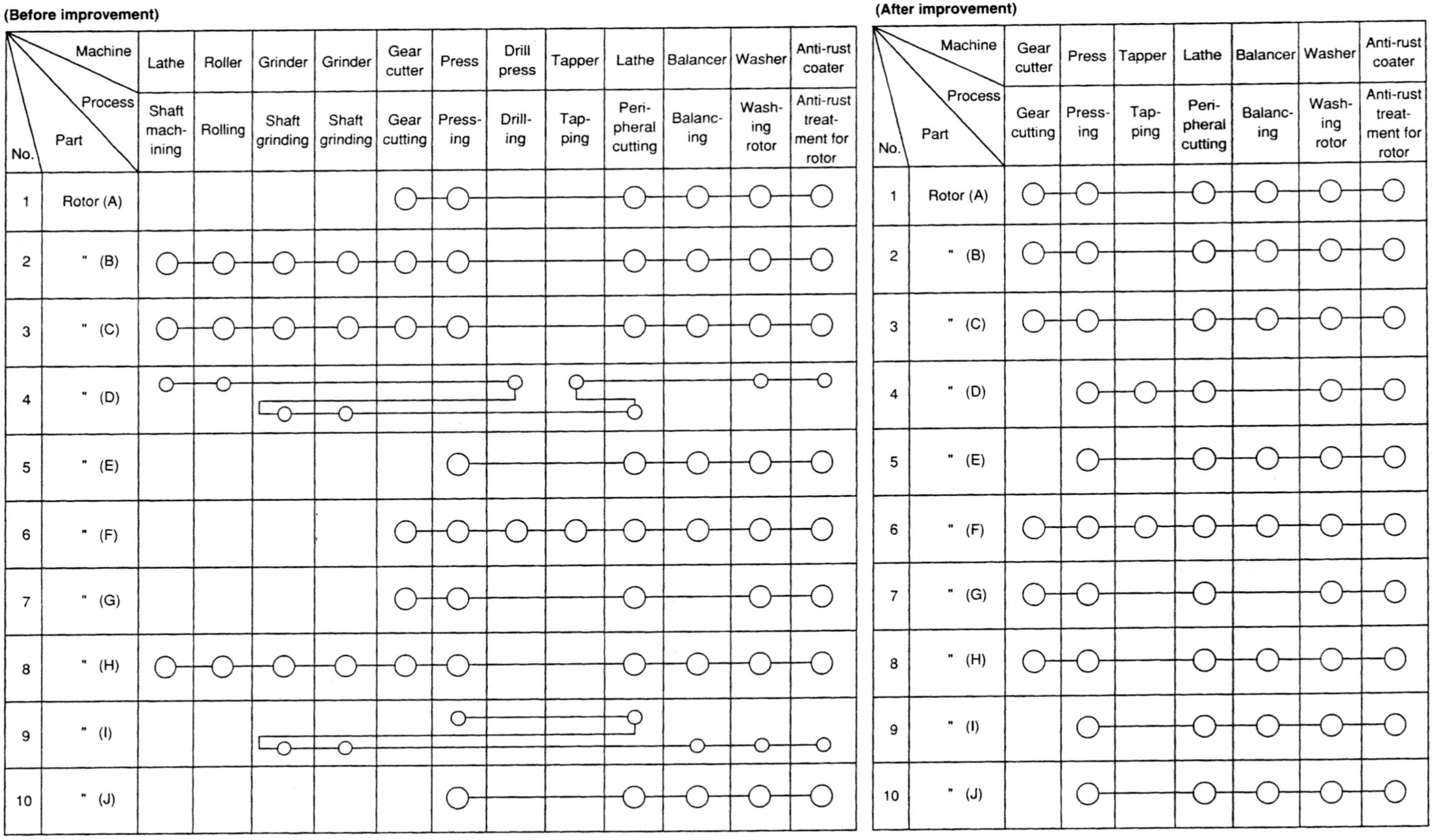

No.	Part	Lathe / Shaft machining	Roller / Rolling	Grinder / Shaft grinding	Grinder / Shaft grinding	Gear cutter / Gear cutting	Press / Pressing	Drill press / Drilling	Tapper / Tapping	Lathe / Peripheral cutting	Balancer / Balancing	Washer / Washing rotor	Anti-rust coater / Anti-rust treatment for rotor
1	Rotor (A)		○			○	○			○	○	○	○
2	" (B)	○	○	○		○	○			○	○	○	○
3	" (C)	○	○	○		○	○			○	○	○	○
4	" (D)	○	○		○			○	○	○	○	○	○
5	" (E)					○	○		○	○	○	○	○
6	" (F)					○	○			○	○	○	○
7	" (G)					○	○			○	○	○	○
8	" (H)	○	○	○		○	○			○	○	○	○
9	" (I)			○	○		○			○	○	○	○
10	" (J)						○			○	○	○	○

(After improvement)

No.	Part	Gear cutter / Gear cutting	Press / Pressing	Tapper / Tapping	Lathe / Peripheral cutting	Balancer / Balancing	Washer / Washing rotor	Anti-rust coater / Anti-rust treatment for rotor
1	Rotor (A)	○	○		○	○	○	○
2	" (B)	○	○		○	○	○	○
3	" (C)	○	○		○	○	○	○
4	" (D)		○	○	○	○	○	○
5	" (E)		○		○	○	○	○
6	" (F)	○	○	○	○	○	○	○
7	" (G)	○	○		○	○	○	○
8	" (H)	○	○		○	○	○	○
9	" (I)				○	○	○	○
10	" (J)		○		○	○	○	○

Figure 12-26. Processing Route Analysis Chart

Prior to improvement, the improvement group noted the following types of waste in the rotor assembly line:

1. Waste due to the accumulation of dead inventory.

   When items get put into piles, those at the bottom become obscured by those on top, making it difficult to keep track of their types and quantities. There is also the risk that the items on the bottom will suffer damage due to the weight of the items on top, especially since the bottom items are generally the last used. This type of dead inventory accumulation tends to occur at large-lot processes, such as washing and drying processes.

2. Waste due to overemphasis on capacity utilization.

   Often, it is not clear whether the primary goal is to meet the SPH target or to raise the equipment's capacity utilization rate. When too much emphasis is given to capacity utilization, the production line begins to accumulate dead inventory due to lack of balance between processes.

3. Waste due to failure to identify causes of defects.

   When a line includes a lot of dead inventory, it is difficult to pinpoint the causes of defects, since defective goods sit unnoticed alongside nondefective products in the dead inventory piles.

4. Conveyance waste.

   As suggested by the flow diagram shown in Figure 12-25, the line included unnecessary conveyance and transfers.

5. Waste due to lack of tool organization.

   Since this line was unable to use a centralized grinding system, the operators had to set up their tools for each changeover. This caused increased changeover loss and more downtime for the equipment.

6. Changeover waste.

   It took 20 minutes to do the grinder changeover operation and 15 minutes to set up the line for a different product model.

Step 3: Implement Waste-removing Improvements

They began the waste-removing improvements that would facilitate the building of a U-shaped cell by removing waste in the form of unnecessary manual operations.

Figure 12-27 shows an improvement the group made on a rotor assembly jig. Before improvement, the upper and lower jigs and the reference guide had to be changed. The improvement simplified this changeover step by using a die-setting type of guide. The improvement group also came up with several mistake-proofing devices for the line, which are not described here.

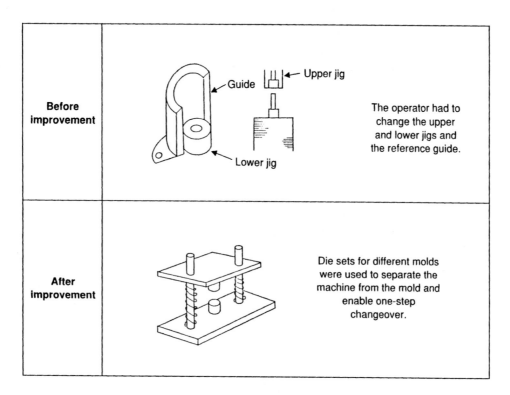

Figure 12-27. Improvement of Rotor Assembly Jig

Step 4: Implement Process Razing

At this step, the improvement group formed a U-shaped cell and tested it. When such tests are successful, the U-shaped cells can be immediately tried out elsewhere in the factory (horizontal development).

Figure 12-28 shows the "before" and "after" improvement layouts for the rotor assembly line. Before improvement, the flow of goods depended upon which product model was being made. After improvement, the line was a U-shaped cell using one-piece flow, one-piece production, and one-piece (full-lot) inspection for zero defects.

- The same operator was in charge of the cell's entry and exit processes.
- The cycle time is a little longer when two operators handle the assembly processes.

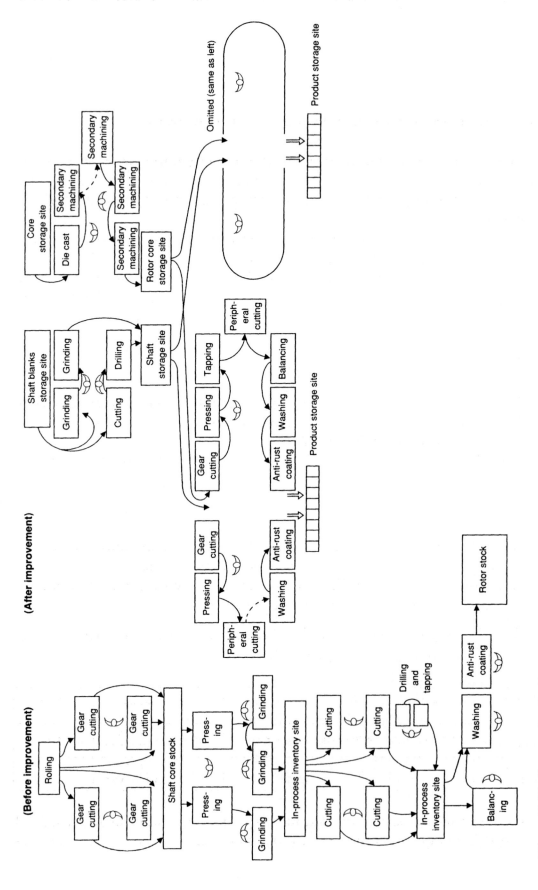

Figure 12-28. Process Razing (U-shaped Cell Development) for Rotor Assembly Line

Step 5: Establish the SPH and Organize the U-shaped Cell

Once the line has been organized, the leader should operate it to see whether or not he or she can keep up with the cycle time. If not, the group must find out why the target values are not being met and look for additional improvements to remove waste.

Some types of improvements that may bear repeating are removal of manual handling waste, walking waste, methods for storing and handling parts, switch positions, measurement methods, and the distances between machines. It may be helpful to record the operations using a video camera so that they can be studied more closely.

Step 6: Develop and Maintain Standard Operation Forms

Figure 12-29 shows a standard operation form for the rotor assembly process. This form was made based on the information in the standard operation combination chart shown in Figure 12-30.

The following lists some key points for maintaining standard operations in U-shaped cells.

- Clarify the target workpieces on each line (family grouping with a focus on changeover operations).
- Display the target values and the target output total (in hourly units).
- Clearly define the scope of the leader's responsibilities.
- Be thorough in responding to defects (find the causes and eliminate them) and develop rules to prevent recurrences.

The following chart compares the "before" and "after" improvement figures for various production line quality statistics.

Compared items	SPH	Dead inventory	Lead time	No. of workers	Output	In-process defects
Before improvement	1,000 units	4,500 units	4 days	14	71 units/ person/day	1.2%
After improvement	2,000 units	1,000 units	0.5 days	16	125 units/ person/day	0.1%

As illustrated, productivity (output per person per day) was increased 1.8 fold. Dead inventory (relative to output) was reduced to one-ninth its before-

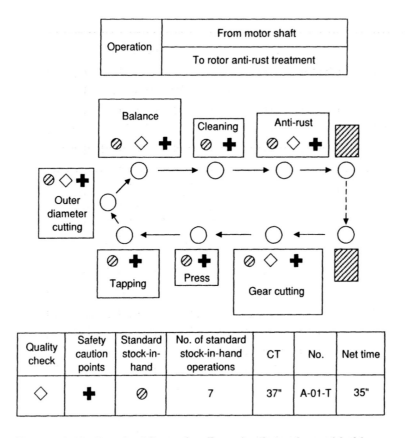

Figure 12-29. Standard Operation Form for Rotor Assembly Line

improvement level; lead time shrank to one-eighth its former level; and the in-process defect rate fell to one-twelfth its former level.

USING U-SHAPED CELLS FOR SINGLE-OPERATOR ASSEMBLY

The ideal assembly line is one that can be operated by one person without producing any defects. This cannot be done unless the line is a one-piece flow line and changeover is successive in order to keep the line working within the cycle time. Today such lines are basic at Oriental Motor's Tsuruoka factory.

From a conveyor line to a U-shaped cell run by several operators.

Before introducing a new production system, the Tsuruoka factory used conveyor lines such as the one shown in the left part of Figure 12-31. The con-

Part or item			Standard Operation Combination Chart			Date of manufacture		Required quantity per day	750			Manual operation Auto-feed Walking

Process						Department		465 Required quantity		37"		

				Time				Operation time				

Operation sequence		Operation name	Manual	Auto								
1		Take materials from pallet	1"									
2		Gear cutting	3"	27"								
3		Press	3"	9"								
4		Tapping	3"	9"								
5		Outer diameter cutting	5"	9"								
6		Balance	3"	18"								
7		Cleaning	2"	26"								
8		Anti-rust	3"	7"								
9		Place finished item on pallet	2"									

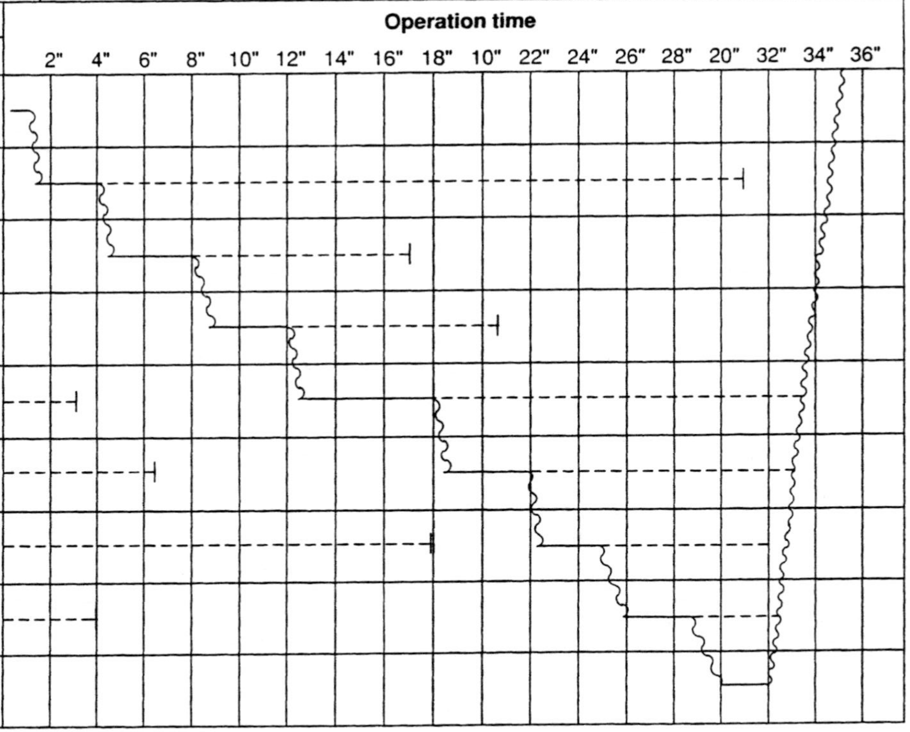

Manual operations:	25 seconds
Auto-feed:	115 seconds
Walking:	10 seconds

Figure 12-30. Standard Operation Combination Chart for Rotor Assembly Line

veyors kept the large lots flowing in an era during which large-lot production was thought to be the most efficient type of production.

After doing a P-Q analysis (similar to the one shown in Figure 12-23) of their conveyor-based small motor assembly line, they found that in the dawning era of wide-variety small-lot production, their pallet and conveyor system was no longer efficient. Their P-Q ratio had increased from 2-to-8 to 4-to-6, resulting in a number of conveyor-induced disadvantages:

1. Warehouse inventory piles up (see Figure 12-1).
2. The lines tend to overproduce.
3. Entire lots of defective goods (discovered at the final process' general inspection) tend to occur and their causes are hard to trace.
4. The line balance must be set according to the slowest operator's speed. The line efficiency rate is usually no higher than 70 percent. The conveyor system also tends to mask standby waste.
5. Changeover loss is high.
6. While it works well for specialized operations, the conveyor line is not very flexible when it comes to changing product models.
7. Conveyor assembly-line workers sit while working. This makes it difficult for them to lend mutual assistance and is also hard on their backs and hip joints.

When viewed from the walkways that factory tour guests use, conveyor operations look well-ordered and efficient. If we look closer, however, we can discover mountains of waste in every conveyor line. This realization led the Tsuruoka factory to try out a five-person U-shaped cell design for its small motor assembly line. As shown in Figure 12-31, this U-shaped cell contained several processes.

Next, they took a critical look at their new U-shaped cell and discovered still more waste:

1. The warehouse inventory had not shrunk, because they were using the same large lot sizes as before.
2. Various problems arose concerning changeover. For instance, defects tended to occur immediately after changeovers. (Since these defects were largely due to overly lenient changeover setting standards, their causes were difficult to pinpoint.) The amount of standby and downtime also rose sharply, lowering the SPH.
3. In-process inventory began to accumulate. The need for manual conveyance was much greater than when the line had a conveyor.

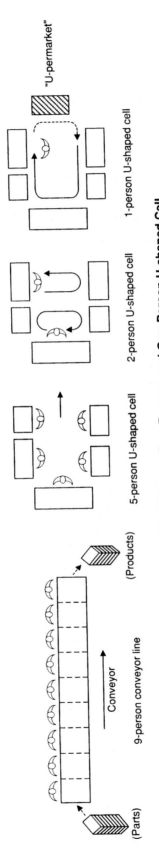

Figure 12-31. Transition from Conveyor Assembly to Five-Person, Two-Person, and One-Person U-shaped Cell

4. Although a clear division of labor had been established, the definitions became fuzzy and operators tended to make careless mistakes (such as incomplete processing or omitting labels) when they got behind schedule.

5. Workers had trouble mastering the skills required for multi-process operations. (It was difficult to train part-time workers in these skills.)

6. It was difficult to keep to the cycle time because no one was accustomed to working with either a cycle time or a one-piece flow system.

7. Different people were in charge of the U-shaped cell's entry and exit points, and supplying the line with workpieces was left up to an operator.

8. Goods spent more time in manual conveyance and retention than in being processed.

This is not to say that the initial U-shaped cell design did not produce any advantages. Productivity was up, for instance, and defects were down.

From a five-person U-shaped cell to a two-person U-shaped cell and, finally, to a one-person U-shaped cell.

Photo 12-11 shows the two-person U-shaped cell that was devised after the improvement group had considered the problems concerning the five-person cell. While reducing the manpower, this new cell design also used a smaller lot size (30 units instead of 60), which cut the warehouse inventory in half. Naturally, this new design meant there had to be more lines and substantial sums invested in additional equipment. These drawbacks, however, were more than compensated for by the advantages gained. The Toyoshiki factory's approach took a middle road between these advantages and disadvantages, differing in that it bravely went a step further by establishing a highly automated one-person line (see Photo 12-12).

The ideas that arose concerning a one-person U-shaped cell were:

• If the U-shaped cell can be operated by just one operator, it must be a one-piece production, one-piece flow line. It must also use one-piece inspection. This means it will have full-lot inspection and will be a zero-defect line.

• The line efficiency rate would be 100 percent. To confirm that, we need only consider that since the line can keep up with the SPH, it does not

Photo 12-11. Two-Person Assembly Line   **Photo 12-12. One-Person Assembly Line**

require outside management. (It would be organized well enough to do without management.)
• It would require fewer changeovers. Ideally, it should be improved to the point of zero changeover, but a simple reduction in changeover is also welcome.
• The scope of job duties would be very clear, and no one could shift his or her own duties onto someone else.

Obviously, a one-person U-shaped cell also has disadvantages, but these will be easily apparent when they arise and can be dealt with then.

Opening a "U-permarket."

The Tsuruoka factory's improvement group leader coined the word "U-permarket." It is a name for the U-shaped cell's directly linked "supermarket," which eliminates the need not only for a parts warehouse but also for a stock market of model-specific production kits. The U-permarket supplies just those parts the U-shaped cell needs, just when it needs them, and in just the right amounts, with no missing items.

Also, the U-permarket keeps the supply of parts under such close control that only three kanban cards are needed. The kanban keep tabs on the flow of goods between the U-shaped cell and its related outside manufacturers and parts suppliers so that there is no need for a parts warehouse and parts are never omitted. Instead, the cell uses a simple flow rack, designed for first in, first out (FIFO) transfer of parts.

Because they are basically similar to the improvements already described in this chapter, I will not go into the other improvements made at these factories (such as other waste-removing improvements, zero missing-parts campaigns, and zero changeover improvements). As of this writing, the factory was looking forward to reporting on its success in building automated assembly lines.

ONE-PIECE PRODUCTION SYSTEMS: FUTURE ISSUES

The main purpose of one-piece production using U-shaped cells is to achieve zero-defect production. Oriental Motor reported that it had not yet fully established its one-piece production system, but felt it had firmly laid its foundation.

As of 1983, Oriental Motor planned to pursue the following steps toward fully establishing a companywide one-piece production system.

Step 1. Incorporate full-lot inspection into every U-shaped cell and fix causes of defects.

Step 2. As part of the above process, select items that have been subject to customer complaints and establish them as intermediate inspection items. Also review the list of inspection items for products made by outside manufacturers.

Step 3. Teach everyone to use the 5-Why approach to find the underlying causes of defects.

Step 4. Establish a mistake-proofing program.

Step 5. Find ways to prevent defects and operation errors related to changeover.

Step 6. Find ways to prevent variation in parts from outside suppliers. (Help supplier companies establish U-shaped cells.)

Step 7. Develop improved methods for starting up new equipment models.

The company listed six more relatively minor items that are omitted here. If Oriental Motor effectively implements these seven steps, it will indeed have a very strong companywide one-piece production system.

13

"Single" Delivery at MYNAC: From Order to Delivery in Nine Days

MYNAC is located in the Japanese town of Iida, Nagano Prefecture, in a rural mountainous area famous for its apple orchards. MYNAC's products include a wide variety of ready-to-wear women's apparel. These include skirts, coats, one-piece dresses, suits, blouses, and pants. Known as a jack-of-all-trades in the sewing business, the company enjoys a reputation for its skill in handling custom orders for just about anything that requires sewing. Their materials run the gamut from cotton to knits, leather, wool, and synthetics.

It employs 22 men, of whom five are college graduates, and 100 women, of whom 12 are either two- or four-year college graduates and 12 are part-time workers, for a total of 134 employees. The staff is young, with an average age of only 27.5 years.

The company name MYNAC is an abbreviation of:

- MY
- N (Nippon or Nagano)
- A (Apparel)
- C (Company)

The company name thus carries the meaning "my company" which is largely true, in that most of the company's shareholders are its employees. MYNAC's president works mainly as a salesman for the company, and vertical relations among the upper and lower echelons of staff are so close that the company hardly needs small-group activities.

WHAT IS "SINGLE DELIVERY"?

Before improving its production system, MYNAC had a delivery lead time of 15 to 30 days after receiving the rolls of cloth. This range reflects differences in lead time depending upon the particular products and the lot size. The average lead time was 20 days. Its goal was to reduce the lead time to within the "single" period of nine days.

Joking that they would never become single-handicap golfers, MYNAC's managers said that at least they could become single-delivery sewing factory managers. And they succeeded in doing just that. In short, their success lay in developing their production period into three three-day segments:

Cutting and parts coordination:	3 days
Sewing (assembly):	3 days
Finishing, inspection, and shipment:	3 days
Total	9 days

Figures 13-1 shows the flow of work under this three-segment arrangement.

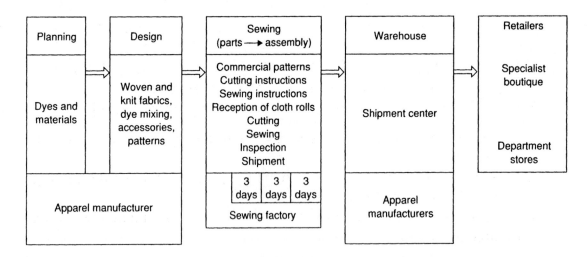

Figure 13-1. Three Production Segments: Orders, Production, and Delivery

The left part of Figure 13-1 shows the apparel manufacturer's production preparation operations, the center part shows MYNAC's production (sewing) operations, and the right part shows the product distribution channels.

Obviously, MYNAC's delivery timing depends upon the punctuality of the apparel manufacturer's production preparation operations. Lacking any guarantees of such punctuality, however, MYNAC decided it was worthwhile to proceed with its improvement plan, even though it might result in only partial success.

IMPROVED FACTORY LAYOUT

The Toyota Production System (TPS) seeks to establish a single flow of work through the entire factory. Therefore, we cannot say that we have adopted TPS if the work flow is established only for a certain set of processes, such as the sewing processes. Toyota manages to assemble an entire car within 20 days of receiving the order for it. I have heard that of those 20 days, the actual production (main assembly) processes take up only ten hours.

This is only possible when the entire factory has an integrated flow. MYNAC's goal was to establish a factorywide flow for itself and thereby achieve "single" (nine-day) delivery.

Figure 13-2 shows the overall layout of MYNAC's factory. The broken lines indicate the U-shaped design of the factory, in which the same person (a quality control manager) handles both the entry and exit processes. Although this layout produces a flow system, it contains four retention points (indicated by star symbols) before and after the sewing lines. If these four retention points can be eliminated, the factory will be able to achieve "single delivery."

The factory's improvement group took on three improvement projects:

1. Integrate the cutting line to reduce the cutting segment's lead time to three days.
2. Establish successive changeover in sewing lines to reduce the sewing segment's lead time to three days.
3. Integrate the finishing line to reduce the finishing segment's lead time to three days.

BASIC MEASURES FOR SINGLE DELIVERY

The improvement group leader announced that they would simply assume their ability to establish single delivery. He told managers who were likely to argue to the contrary that, without a better proposal, they should keep their pessimism to themselves.

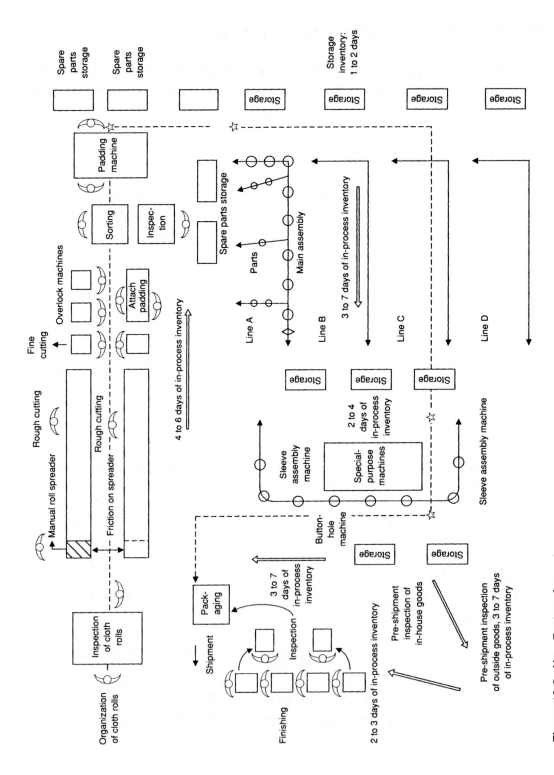

Figure 13-2. New Factory Layout

Measure to Establish Three-day Cutting Segment

Past P-Q analyses had shown them that the cutting line had to be changed each season to adapt to the different seasonal demands. With that in mind, they decided to begin with a plan for the spring apparel.

Organize cutting processes into three lines.

They set up three cutting lines; one for pattern cuts, one for no pattern cuts, and one for lining cuts. The three flow patterns kept the workers occupied even when one of the lines was not busy. Figure 13-3 shows how the cutting processes were organized after improvement. While it may not be apparent at first glance, the processes were organized into three lines.

Organize kit carts by manufacture numbers.

Next, they improved the production flow in the cutting processes by using assembly process withdrawal kanban (based on the weekly production schedule for the sewing lines). Downstream from the cutting processes, they set up separate kit-loaded carts for each manufacture number (see Figure 13-4).

This improvement brought the following results:

1. Organizing the rolls and accessories into kits prevented errors during the preparation of assembly parts.
2. Organizing cut parts into kits and limiting the number of carts reduced all in-process inventory to between a half day and a full day (because the carts took on a full-work function).
3. The roll inspection, spreading, and cutting processes could now flow within the cycle time.
4. The cutting segment was able to flow within the overall cycle time of three days.

Receive rolls ⟶ inspect ⟶ spread ⟶ cut ⟶ process parts = 3 days

5. They were able to reduce manpower in the segment from 15 workers to between nine and ten. (The manpower reduction came as a result of adopting an automatic roll spreader using air tables and improved linking of cutting processes.)

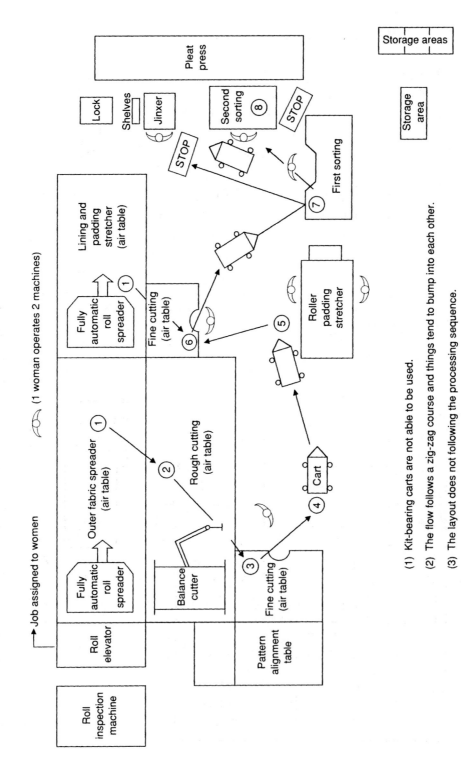

Figure 13-3. First Improvement (Centered on Equipment Improvement and Introduction of Automation Devices)

(1) Kit-bearing carts are not able to be used.

(2) The flow follows a zig-zag course and things tend to bump into each other.

(3) The layout does not following the processing sequence.

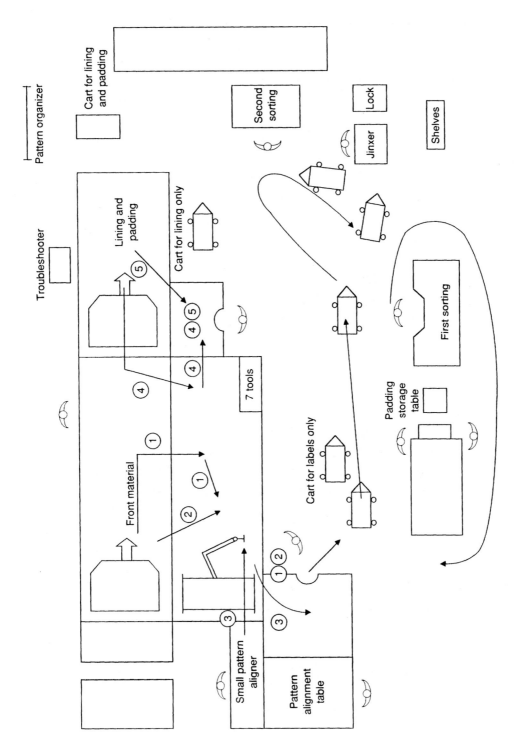

Figure 13-4. Second Improvement (Centered on Improving the Processing Route)

Measure for Achieving Three-day Period in Sewing Processes

Using the principle of the learning curve, they figured that the best time schedule for the sewing processes was a three-day schedule. It so happened that a three-day sewing schedule was also best from the perspective of reducing changeover loss. Using the following formulas to calculate the cycle time, SPH, and SPD, they organized a weekly schedule for the three lines that would put the whole set of lines on a three-day schedule. This weekly schedule is shown in Table 13-1. The diagonal lines in the table indicate the required setup times. The changeover frequency has been averaged out in the table.

$$\text{Required amount per day} = \frac{\text{Required amount per month}}{\text{Working days per month}}$$

$$\text{Cycle time} = \frac{\text{Working hours per day}}{\text{Required amount per day}}$$

$$\text{Added value target per person per day} = \frac{\text{Working hours per day}}{\text{Required amount per day}}$$

Reduction of changeover loss.

They began performing successive changeovers to average out the number of changeovers and to reduce changeover loss to zero. Naturally, any kind of changeover is bound to produce some loss. To make successive changeover easier, they first reorganized the assembly lines into a U-shaped cell with nine lines, of which seven are kept operating at a time (see Figure 13-5). Although this means that some lines will be left idle for certain periods of time, the workers are not idle.

For example, when line E in Figure 13-5 is idle due to a changeover that takes some time, such as switching from production of skirts to coats, line E can be set up beforehand so that the production staff needs only to switch over from another line.

Basic Steps for Model Changeovers

While assigning jobs to changeover specialists, the group also drew up a set of basic steps for changeover (shown in Table 13-2) and practiced them to avoid mistakes and omissions.

Table 13-1. Weekly Schedule

Day and date	1/30 MON	1/31 TUE	2/1 WED	2/2 THU	2/3 FRI	2/4 SAT	2/6 MON	2/7 TUE	2/8 WED
Line K, 6 workers, $613	M112, 86 pieces	76 \ 10	M113 86	86	13 \ 73	M114 86	86	86	53
Line S, 5 workers, $513	26 pieces	M221 26	26	1 \ 25	M223 26	26	26	26	25
Line 0, 5 workers, $513	28 pieces	M301 28	28	16 \ 12	28	M302 28	28	12	
Line T, 5 workers, $513	32 pieces	32	M812 32	32	32	72	M822 72	72	72
Line H, 5 workers, $924	M910, 48 pieces	48	30 \ 14	M922 36	36	36	28		
Changeover frequency	2 times	3	2	3	2	2	1	3	1

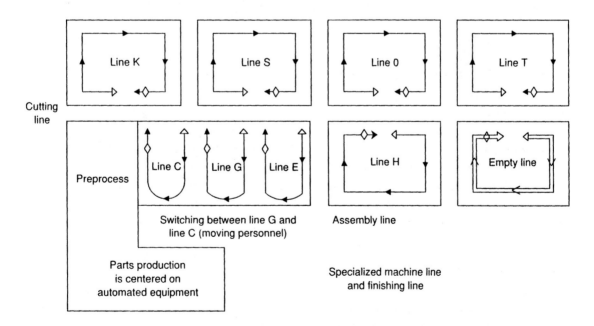

Cutting line

Line K   Line S   Line 0   Line T

Preprocess

Line C   Line G   Line E

Switching between line G and line C (moving personnel)

Parts production is centered on automated equipment

Line H

Assembly line

Empty line

Specialized machine line and finishing line

Figure 13-5. Assembly U-shaped Cell with Nine Lines (Seven Operating)

Table 13-2. Basic Steps (Checkpoints) for Model Changeover

Preparatory waste removal	Organize, consider, remove waste	

1. Prepare order kanban for cutting processes.
2. Send out withdrawal kanban.
3. Take the kit carts around.
4. Use changeover andon.
5. Standardize value analysis (VA).
6. Prepare all needed items and load them onto kit carts.
  a. Thread (upper and lower)
  b. Work clothes
  c. Gauges
  d. Weights
  e. Process charts
  f. Layout diagrams
  g. Accessories
  h. Materials
7. Leave the line empty for the next item.
8. Bring over the kit cart an hour before changeover starts.
	1. Display the processing standards.
	2. Find out if the standards are being stretched at any processes.
	  a. Check the corner stitching and square stitching processes.
	  b. Check the lining pleats, patterns, and standard blind stitches.
	  c. Check stitching in places where the fabric thickness varies.
	3. Find ways to sew without stretching the processing standards.
	  a. This is especially important for items that involve a gauge or sewing of aligned materials.
	  b. It is also important for cases where the pattern largely changes the shape of the material.
	  c. And it is important for cases where upper and lowe pleat seams must be aligned.
	4. Display starting, intermediate, and ending standards for sewing operations such as sewing of aligned materials.
	5. Do not move the sewing machines during successive changeover. Set up machines as part of external changeover.
		6. Check for line imbalances using the call-out method following changeover time measurement, then rearrange job duties or establish mutual assistance zones.
		7. When it seems that there is a missing part, contact the line leader right away.
		8. When a defect has been discovered, stop the line after the changeover.
		9. If the difficulty level is C, have the line leader produce a sample product to use as a demonstration of the standards.
		10. During start-up, the first items should go as far as the finishing inspection. The line leader should check all items at that point.
		11. The line leader should be posted as the quality control manager at the first and last processes in the line.

Establishing and keeping processing standards are a crucial part of quality control. In the case of an apparel sewing factory, there are many standards affecting the lining materials, and this has created a need for the development of sewing machines and jigs that can be used as standard-setters for such lining materials.

Building a U-shaped cell.

The most difficult task in this small-lot (100-150 units) sewing factory was creating a process chart that enabled an optimum U-shaped cell to be maintained after every model changeover. After all, the sewing machines must be moved in a precise manner, special jigs must be built and installed, and the proper kit carts must be prepared. In fact, such methodical precision and organization can be even more difficult than making minor improvements. Nonetheless, building effective U-shaped cells is the foundation for achieving zero-defect production.

After implementing the previous measures, the group found that it had achieved the following in its assembly operations:

1. It was able to reduce manpower on the assembly lines by using 13 to 15 workers with assignments made flexible in response to variation in lot size. All work was able to be completed within the three-day target period.
2. The establishment of nine lines and seven shifts enabled it to reach its zero changeover and value analysis (VA) goals.
3. By incorporating accessory work (such as button-hole making, thread tying, and shoulder pad attachment) into the assembly lines, it was able to virtually eliminate previous dirt, defect, and rework problems. This enabled it to stay within the assembly cycle time.
4. No matter what kind of sewing work they had to do, the variable-staffed U-shaped cell members were able to complete the work within the three-day period.

Measures to Establish Three-day Period for Finishing Segment

Having incorporated the accessory work (previously done on the side by in-house staff) into the line, the improvement group's next step was to also incorporate the finishing, inspection, packaging, and shipment processes to bring the whole finishing segment's operations within the three-day target period. (As of this writing, it was still in the process of taking this step.)

Figure 13-6 shows the specialized sewing machine layout before improvement.

The group put together the test line shown in Figure 13-7 in an attempt to implement process razing and create a smooth flow along the processing route.

It has been trying very hard to get this test line to operate within the cycle time. So far, by pooling everybody's wisdom and developing new jigs and mechanisms to eliminate manual work, the group has successfully established

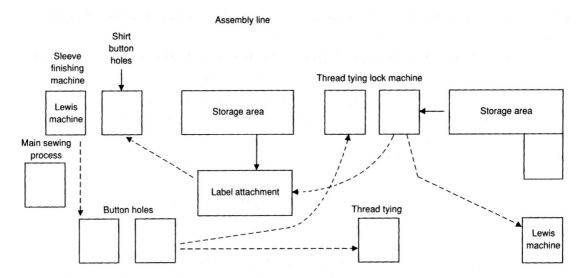

Figure 13-6. Layout of Specialized Machine Processes before Improvement

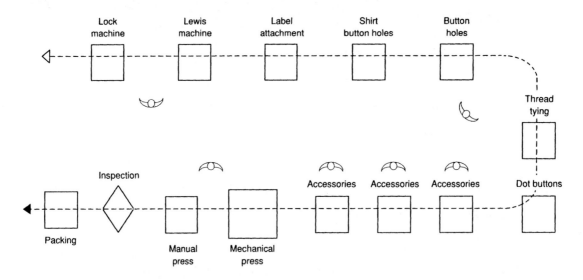

Figure 13-7. Test Line for Finishing Processes (Special Machines, Accessories, Finishing)

one-piece flow and synchronized production. I hope to describe these achievements in another book.

Working in these production system study groups, we all learned how process-razing skills can be used for wide-variety small-lot production in virtually any kind of company or industry. MYNAC's improvement group, encouraged by the results of the U Study Group, is on its way toward achieving its goal of "single delivery for sewing factory operations."

Remembering that improvements are endless, it is still worth noting the following improvements made by the MYNAC group:

- improvement in preparatory operations with customers
- improvement in responses toward products requiring substantially different cycle times
- implementation of VA for production (prior study of manpower reduction measures)
- elimination of manual processes (incorporation of automatic machines in line)
- measures to enable multi-process handling
- training for line leaders in organization and continuity
- preparation for taking on the challenge of one-week delivery periods

I conclude by expressing my gratitude to MYNAC's President Ichinose and Vice President Nenoi.

14

Reducing Waste on Printed Circuit Board Component Assembly Lines: The Case of Kumamoto Electronics

Although the electronics industry works with a wide variety of high-tech materials, components, and products, it is surprising just how "low-tech" some of the factories are that handle these items. Assembly operations in factories that carry out wafer processing, magnetic component assembly, or assembly of VCRs, facsimile machines, and computers are often done using a large number of workers, all seated along the assembly lines. This is true of many printed circuit board (PCB) component assembly lines, which is the main focus of the first part of this chapter.

Companies will not survive long if they continue relying on this labor-intensive approach. Japan and other advanced industrialized countries must take particular heed, since orders for labor-intensive manufacturing will naturally flow toward the newly industrialized economies (NIEs) and other countries where labor costs are substantially lower.

One of the first types of assembly work affected by this shift was the mounting of components on PCBs. This chapter presents methods by which companies can reduce their PCB mounting personnel by half by adopting a new type of production system. Perhaps it is not too late to stop the PCB mounting business from moving overseas.

HOW MUCH MANPOWER REDUCTION DO WE NEED TO REMAIN COMPETITIVE?

Let us consider the case of Company A, which is an electronic parts supplier to Company B. Company A has a video deck assembly plant, where components are mounted on PCBs, then dipped in solder, finished (reworked), and inspected. It employs 100 people, of whom 26 work in PCB mounting, 17 in first-stage finishing, five in second-stage finishing, seven in management, and 45 in assembly. As such, Company A is a typical electronic parts supplier.

Company A bills its labor charges to Company B at ¥0.23 per second, a labor rate low enough to attract Company B's business (and too low to convert into U.S. dollars). Company B's business performance statistics include the following:

Total sales value of production (S):	$200,000/month
Added value (v):	$140,000
Added value rate (v-0):	70 percent
Employees (n):	100 persons
Added value per employee (V):	$1,400/month
Average per-capita personnel cost (w):	$1,093/month
Relative share of wages (R):	71.4 percent

There is no need to include the profit and fixed-cost figures here, since they are result-related figures and we are interested in figures that relate to the month-to-month operation of the factory. The key control statistic for the factory is the added value per employee (V) figure. A simple way of understanding this V figure is to think of it as the amount of money each employee earns for the company. In the above list of figures, the total sales value of the production (S) figure is rather low when divided by 100 employees. This is because the average employee is not earning very much for the company. The prices for the company's main products are determined based on a system of costs versus earnings.

When the rise in the yen's value caused a drop in overseas competitiveness, Company B told Company A that it had to cut its costs by 20 percent if it wanted to remain its supplier. Faced with this situation, Company A's managers looked at their V figures and saw that they could not cut their prices much without losing all their earnings. They found cheaper material suppliers and subcontracted out some orders to a very inexpensive factory, but those moves only brought costs down by 10 percent. They could think of no way to further reduce costs.

They had not considered the kind of manpower reduction plan, shown in Figure 14-1, that could serve as a survival strategy for the company.

We do not need to include the formulas used to calculate the amount of manpower reduction needed to cut costs by 20 percent. Suffice it to say that the

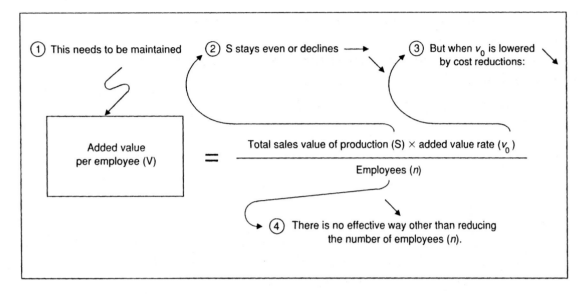

Figure 14-1. Basic Principles of Survival Strategy

result figure was 24.3 percent. Since Company A has 100 employees, this means a reduction of 24 employees was the only road to survival.

Realizing this, management set the following manpower reduction targets:

- mounting process workers: 56 to 42 (a reduction of 14)
- assembly process workers: 45 to 34 (a reduction of 11)
- total targeted reduction: 25 employees

Although small improvements and other small group improvement projects are indeed valuable, they are not enough to achieve the kind of substantial manpower reduction required in this situation. After long study, Company A's president and other managers decided that the only way to ensure the company's survival was to implement full-fledged process razing to cut manpower requirements.

STEPS IN REDUCING MANPOWER ON THE PCB MOUNTING LINE

Level 1.

In Figure 14-2(a), we can see the layout of Company A's factory as it was in 1976. The factory had 27 employees working to turn out 400 PCBs per day using a large lot-style round conveyor.

The employees sat while using just one hand to do the insertion work, as illustrated in Figure 14-3. While this kind of factory layout is becoming rare in Japan, it is still common in the NIEs and other countries where labor costs are lower.

Level 2.

This is Company A's current level as of this writing. It brought in an auto-insertion machine and switched to a split round conveyor system that enables more assembly work to be done by fewer workers. The previous round conveyor system, however, was retained for the solder dip processes.

At level 2, the factory needs 27 workers to maintain a standard production per day (SPD) of 400 PCBs; at level 1 (in 1976), it needed 39 workers. The change from levels 1 to 2 had resulted in a manpower reduction of 31 percent ($[39 - 27]/39) \times 100$), or nearly a one-third cut in manpower requirements. When manpower requirements are cut, however, there should also be a rise in the added value per employee.

Level 3.

The factory layout shown in Figure 14-2(b) is common among large PCB factories. This type of factory is much more automated (the automation rate is usually about 30 percent), and the auto-insertion machines are more specialized. In the figure, there are three types of auto-inserters: jumper, radial, and axial. The manual insert processes have from eight to 20 insert points each, and the solder dip, finishing work, and inspection processes are all in a line.

Compared to level 2, this new level achieves a manpower reduction of 44 percent ($[27 - 15]/27 \times 100$). As long as the company can afford it, this layout would appear to work well. The long, slim layout style is especially popular in North America and Europe. However, it still does nothing to reduce rework and defects.

This factory's major fault is that it is not responsive to the market.

Level 4.

Figure 14-2(c) shows a factory layout in which the auto-inserters are arranged into two equal lines. Thanks to the nine-minute changeover time and the inclusion of an inserter for odd-shaped components, the auto-insertion rate has been raised to over 70 percent, bringing manpower requirements for the PCB mounting processes down to just five workers. The mechanized transfer (MT) rate (i.e., auto-feed and auto-stop mechanisms) has exceeded 20 percent.

This layout is very good for raising the efficiency of the insertion work, but it would be hard to maintain indefinitely a three-shift schedule with solder dipping available only during one shift.

The manpower reduction achieved at level 4 (relative to level 3) was 60 percent ($[15 - 6]/15) \times 100$).

At this level, it becomes easier to use the "5 Why" method to find the underlying causes of defects, and factories are able to cut their rework and defect rates down to just 10 percent of their previous level. Naturally, this enables the factory to reduce the manpower needed for rework.

The line in the figure also includes electronic kanban as part of a "just-in-day" system to prevent missing parts by setting up today all of the components that will be mounted tomorrow.

Level 5.

At this level, shown in Figure 14-2(d), the factory integrates its PCB mounting line with the downstream assembly line. This kind of integrated flow is called the "vertical flow method." Later, the auto-insert machines can be adapted for this layout.

However, this layout does require some tough conditions: The changeover times for the auto-insert machines must be no longer than three minutes, temporary line stops must not exceed 90 PPM, the solder reworking rate must be held to within 2 percent, and the MT rate for the manual insert and mounting lines must be at least 50 percent.

In this vertical flow line, we have full-fledged cycle time production in which the cycle time for each assembled product starts when the PCB is set in

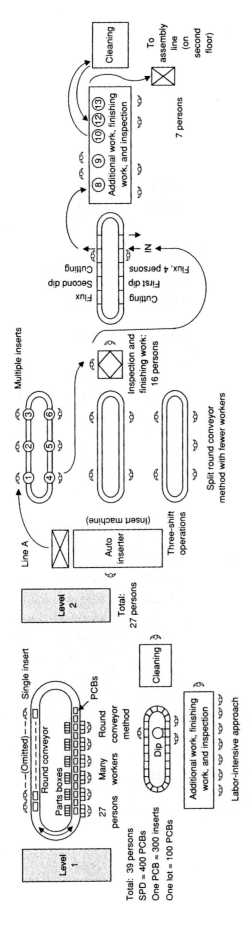

Figure 14-2(a). From Many Single-insert Workers to Few Multi-insert Workers

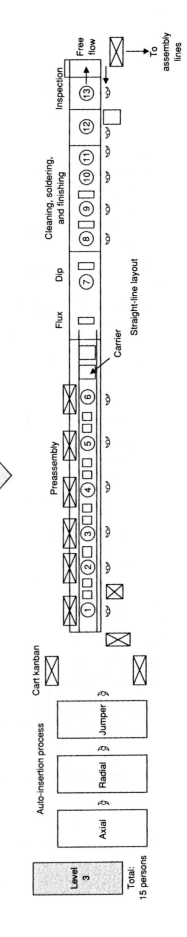

Figure 14-2(b). PCB Mounting Layout for Large-lot Production

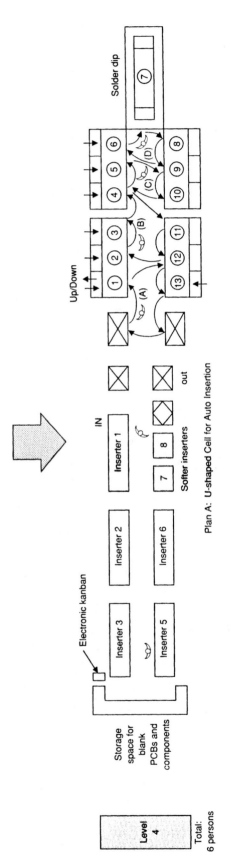

Figure 14-2(c). Plan for Raising Automation Rate

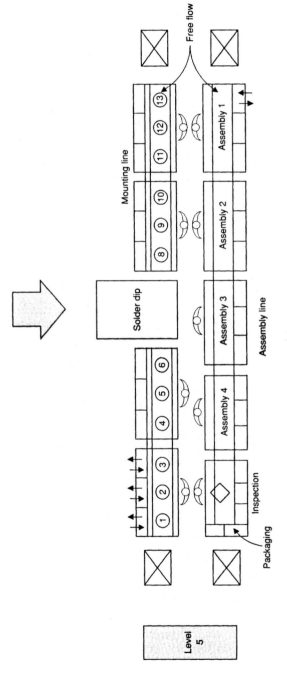

Figure 14-2(d). Vertical Flow System for Integrated Mounting and Assembly Lines

Figure 14-3. Insertion Work at Round Conveyor (1976)

the first auto-inserter. Note that the storage area for blank PCBs and components is located right alongside the product storage area to enable the same person to control the U-shaped cell's entry and exit processes. This is what is needed to ensure zero missing parts.

This level of advancement in process razing has been successfully tested in other industries, and there is no reason why it cannot be achieved in the electronic component assembly industry.

Compared to level 4, the manpower requirement has been reduced by half, thanks to the integration of the assembly line. This dramatic reduction in manpower requirements has been expensive. In fact, in the case just described, the total cost for new equipment is estimated at almost $133,333, which makes this sort of system impractical for factories in NIEs where labor costs are still low. But this type of factory does make sense in countries such as Japan and the United States. Many Japanese companies are eager to boost their scope of production facilities in the United States in order to get closer to the main market, boost America's international competitiveness, and promote a stronger dollar and a weaker yen.

In terms of productivity, level 5 has 8.7 times the productivity of level 1 and 6 times that of level 2. As of this writing, Company A is working to advance from level 2 to level 4. If Company A successfully completes this five-level survival strategy, it can be confident of keeping its business in the country. If it fails, over half of its business could go to other countries before long.

After all, as of this writing, the average labor rate in this industry is $0.11 per minute in Japan but only $0.02 per minute in South Korea and Taiwan.

ELIMINATING WASTE IN PCB MOUNTING LINES

Many of the PCB mounting lines at Company A's supplier company are at level 2 because they have already made changes to meet the wide-variety small-lot production trend.

Step 1: Conduct a P-Q analysis.

Company A first conducted a P-Q analysis to better understand their current wide-variety small-lot production system. Figure 14-4 shows the results of this P-Q analysis. This analysis was done as a graphic representation of the output quantities listed in quantitative order in Table 14-1. This is also the method used to make a quantitative Pareto analysis or an ABC analysis for inventory management.

Step 2: Make a processing route analysis of manual insertion processes.

Next, they did a processing route analysis of manual-insert processes. They indicated the manual-insert processes on the chart's horizontal axis and the PCB model numbers on the vertical axis. They also entered the names, quantities, and insert times of the manually inserted components.

Naming processes is much easier in large-lot production systems than in small-lot ones, so they simply used numbers to indicate processes. Table 14-2 shows the processing route analysis chart.

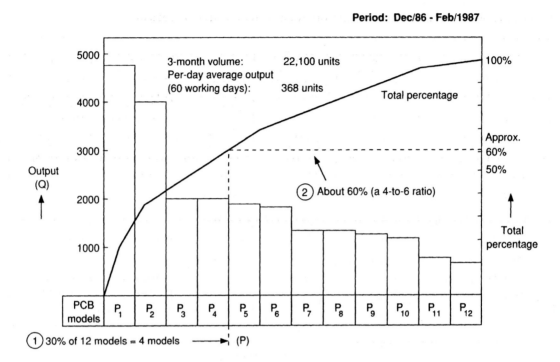

Figure 14-4. P-Q Analysis of Line A at Company A

Table 14-1. Quantitative List of PCB Models

No.	Model No.	Lot Size	Quantity	Average Quantity	Total Percentage
1	P_1	4	4,600	1,150	20.8
2	P_2	3	4,000	1,333	38.9
3	P_3	3	2,000	667	48.8
4	P_4	2	2,000	1,000	57.8
5	P_5	4	1,950	488	66.6
6	P_6	6	1,900	317	75.2
7	P_7	3	1,200	400	80.6
8	P_8	4	1,200	300	86.0
9	P_9	2	1,100	550	91.0
10	P_{10}	4	1,050	263	95.8
11	P_{11}	4	600	150	98.3
12	P_{12}	3	500	167	100.0
	Total		22,100		

Table 14-2. Processing Route Analysis Chart for Manual-insert Processes

Manual-insert Processes on Line A						
Process	1	2	3	4	5	6
PCB A (2 units)	Connectors (× 1) ICs (× 1) (Rest omitted)	Resistors (× 6) Capacitors (× 1) (Rest omitted)	Resistors (× 6) Connectors (× 1)	Resistors (× 3) Connectors (× 1) Transistors (× 1)	Coils (× 2) Connectors (× 1) Resistors (× 4) (Rest omitted)	Leads (× 1) Resistors (× 1) Capacitors (× 1) ICs (× 2)
Seconds	20	34	31	24	39	32
PCB B (1 unit)	LED molds (× 1) Switch levers (× 6) (Rest omitted)	Resistors (× 4) (Rest omitted)	Connectors (× 2) ICs (× 2)	Connectors (× 3) Leads (× 2) ICs (× 1) Resistors (× 3) (Rest omitted)	Connectors (× 1) Parallel (× 3)	Parallel (× 5) Connectors (× 2) ICs (× 1)
Seconds	56	48	30	48	43	47
Seconds	51	59	17	50	50	36
PCB C (3 units)	Foot wires (× 6) (Rest omitted)	Resistors (× 6) (Rest omitted)	VRs (× 6) Push switches (× 3) (Rest omitted)	Parallel (× 6) Mold	VRs (× 6) Parallel (× 3)	Parallel (× 9) (Rest omitted)
Seconds	34	21	114	50	31	67

* Note: Boards have auto-insert rate of 80% $\left(\dfrac{6 \text{ processes} \times 10 \text{ insert points}}{300 \text{ insert points}} \right) \times 100$

Step 3: Implement process-specific waste removal.

The improvement group next studied each process to discover waste. They defined waste as any operation, method, or action that did not add value to the product.

On Line A, they used small round conveyors and assigned six workers to handle a large number of manual insert points. As shown in Table 14-2, this worked out to an average of eight insert points per worker. Sometimes, they would make adjustments in the allocation of work on the line. For example, the third process for PCB type B is a process that has a generally fair amount of work but that gets too busy under certain model-change conditions.

Looking at the P-Q analysis shown in Figure 14-4, we can see that Company A's line A is not what is properly called a wide-variety small-lot line. Its P-Q ratio of 4-to-6, while definitely an improvement over the 2-to-8 that existed six years earlier, is still not high enough to qualify it as a wide-variety small-lot production line. (For a detailed explanation, see *Kaizen for Quick Changeover* (Cambridge, Mass., Productivity Press, 1992.)

Principles for Removing Waste from Conveyor Processes

The main advantage of conveyor-based operations is that they eliminate the need for on-site supervision. Assembly workers who do not share the same cultural and linguistic background can sit down at conveyors and work together without having to communicate much. Such work conditions remind me of the old slave ships, however, in which slaves were chained together and worked to the beat of a drum. In conveyor lines, the pitch time is the drum beat with which the assembly workers must keep pace.

The conveyor line is a child of the industrial revolution and has been a key tool facilitating continuous mass production of standardized goods. It enables factory managers to hire unskilled workers and teach them how to repeat a few simple operations all day long. The managers thus avoid having to deal with the more difficult tasks of training workers in a wider range of valuable skills, providing work incentives, and launching campaigns to improve the workplace.

Surprisingly, even in today's wide-variety small-lot production era, many small-lot factories continue to use the same mass production-style conveyor lines. For example, companies in industries ranging from household electrical products to electronic components, motors, furniture, telecommunications equipment, and auto equipment tend to still use conveyor assembly lines. The long-held notion that "conveyors are the best method for assembly work" does not die easily.

We can extend the process-razing technique to conveyors to carry out "conveyor razing" as a method to eliminate waste and to reduce manpower on conveyor operations. Experience reveals the following seven types of waste most often found in conveyor operations:

1. standby waste (caused by line imbalances)
2. pick-up/set-down waste (caused by conveyor operations)
3. in-process inventory waste (caused by line imbalances)
4. rework and defect waste (caused by overdivision of labor)
5. changeover waste (caused by all-at-once changeover)
6. waste from lack of mutual assistance (caused by sitting while working)

7. waste from 100 percent manual handling (caused by sitting while working)

Let us examine these seven types of waste one by one.

1. Standby waste.

Standby waste is mainly caused by line imbalances. It may happen that the line's fastest worker works twice as fast as its slowest worker. Since conveyor lines can only function as fast as the slowest worker, the faster workers naturally experience a lot of standby time, which means standby waste. Such standby waste is not easy to spot in outward appearances. In order to avoid embarrassing the slower workers, the faster workers tend to look busier than they are and the supervisors tend to turn a blind eye toward the productivity gap between faster and slower workers.

2. Pick-up/set-down waste.

The main cause of this kind of waste is the use of the conveyor operations method itself. The workpieces have to be picked up from the conveyor to be worked on and then set down on the conveyor again to be moved to the next process.

The shorter the pitch time is, the more important it is to eliminate this kind of waste. If we have a pitch time of ten seconds and it takes four seconds just to pick up and set down each workpiece, then 40 percent of the pitch time is being taken up by wasteful activity. Therefore, whenever conveyor operations have a pitch time of 15 seconds or less, we should look first toward eliminating this kind of waste.

3. In-process inventory waste.

Strictly speaking, this type of waste should be divided into waste in in-process inventory on the conveyor and waste in in-process inventory off the conveyor.

The former is caused by line imbalances. The proper line balance (division of work) is usually calculated by making time measurements under the work-factor or method time management method. Such calculated line balances, however, rarely hold out much longer than 30 minutes or so in practice. When the line balance breaks down, the usual response is to redo the time measurements and set a line efficiency rate of no more than 70 percent of the original rate.

One reason for this is that pitch times change with each product model change, so it is not possible to set a standard pitch time for each process. Another reason is that even when provisional standard pitch times are set for certain product models, they are not easily maintained. This is because (1) they are susceptible to differences in the work method of individual workers and (2) such standards tend to lose authority over time.

Consequently, we would be wise to view line imbalances as normal characteristics of conveyor operations, and regard efforts to eliminate them as a waste of time and effort. We are better off admitting that line imbalances are normal and apply our wits toward building better types of lines.

The mass-production method is the main cause of in-process inventory waste related to in-process inventory outside of the conveyor line.

4. Rework and defect waste.

In the strict sense, defects are waste within large-lot production. They are caused by the flow of large-lot production. They are also caused by the division of labor in conveyor lines, in which a sort of invisible curtain exists between workers who are seated next to one another. There are various psychological factors at work on conveyor lines. For instance, the line workers actually look forward to delays at upstream processes, since this gives them an unexpected rest. If the delay is due to a defect that requires a line stop, everyone on the line gets an extra break. Line workers are also generally unwilling to "rock the boat" by checking up on their upstream neighbor's work, and this is especially true when the downstream worker is a temporary employee and the upstream worker is a permanent employee.

Consequently, line workers are tempted to pretend that they do not see the defects in the products they receive. They just keep them moving along. They leave it up to the inspectors and final inspection process to find the defect and hope the line supervisor will discover the cause.

5. Changeover waste.

Changeover waste occurs when the entire line undergoes changeover all at once. Such all-at-once changeover is particularly wasteful when the conveyor line is long and includes a lot of workers. The answer is to implement successive changeover or to reduce conveyor line manpower to just two persons.

6. Waste from lack of mutual assistance.

When the line workers sit while working, they are intent on doing their own tasks and do not get involved in what their neighbors are doing.

No matter how much support and cooperation they give each other when they meet before or after work in small group activities, the workplace will not see much improvement until conveyor line workers learn to help each other out during their work. Conveyor lines should be improved to become small group activities in their own right.

7. Waste from 100 percent manual handling.

This type of waste occurs in lines that are completely devoid of auto-feed devices. The main cause of this kind of waste is also sitting while working. When workers sit in the same position all of the time, they tend to do manual work that could easily be simplified by using auto-feed devices.

After looking into these common types of waste in conveyor operations, we begin to understand that conveyor operations are not even that well suited for mass-production systems, let alone small-lot production systems. So why do so many electrical product companies still use conveyor assembly lines? It is probably because they are not aware of their inherent waste and are only aware of their apparent advantages. These apparent advantages are:

- People remain in fixed positions while the workpieces are moved to them. This is especially helpful when the workpieces are large and/or heavy.
- Conveyors tend to force workers to keep up a certain pace.
- It is easier to learn how to operate one assembly process instead of several processes.

- Productivity can be raised simply by speeding up the conveyor.
- Conveyors eliminate the need for close supervision.
- Conveyor operations encourage people to take action to prevent line stops.

Types of Waste Found on the PCB Mounting Line

Before considering the addition of auto-insertion mechanisms, Company A's improvement group sought to remove waste from the entire PCB mounting line (including the manual insertion, solder dip, finishing, rework, and inspection processes). It based its efforts on the waste elimination table shown in Table 14-3. It also found several common types of waste as it looked for ways to help Company A and its supplier companies reduce manpower.

The largest amount of waste was found in the 100 percent defect rate (rework rate) after the solder dip process. This was because the solder dip conditions were not suitable for the PCB models. In wide-variety production, the solder dip conditions must be adjusted frequently to maintain their suitability for different PCB models. Failure to make such adjustments may be due to laziness on the part of the factory supervisors. In Company A, the PCB mounting line used 16 workers, but the finishing and rework processes used 22 workers (17 for the first finishing process and five for the second finishing process). These 22 workers were mostly kept busy doing rework on solder dip defects and other defects from upstream processes.

Consequently, while recognizing the importance of reducing manpower from manual insertion processes on round conveyors, the prime concern should be to eliminate "defect production waste" from the PCB mounting and solder dip processes. The second largest amount of waste was in the manual insertion that was being done despite the availability of an auto-insertion device. One cause for this was the changeover time for the auto-insert mechanism. When the changeover time approached 30 minutes, the auto-insert mechanism's operation time began to drop. The improvement group decided to launch an improvement project to see if the changeover time could be reduced to within nine minutes.

A second cause was the technological sophistication of the auto-insert mechanism. The mechanism had to be operated by a well-trained permanent employee whereas manual-insert work could be done by ordinary part-time workers. The horizontal-handling approach would have part-time workers

Table 14-3. Process-specific Waste Elimination Table

Process No.	Process name	Discovered waste	Cause(s)	Waste removal plan
(1)	Heat sink	(1) Inadequate use of auto-insert mechanisms	(1) Horizontal handling	(1) Link auto-insert mechanism with mounting process
(2)	Shield	(2) In-process inventory waste	(2) Line imbalance	(2) Organize processes into families based on the cycle time
(3)	Attach LEDs	(1) Standby waste	(1) Line imbalance	(1) Reduce manpower by creating U-shaped cell
		(2) Attach to carrier	(2) Hard to attach	(2) Make notch in PCB to facilitate attachment
(4)	Resistors	(4) Standby waste	(4) Line imbalance	(4) Create and study detailed process analysis chart
(5)	VR (variable resistor)	(5) Manual insertion of connectors	(5) Auto-insert mechanisms unable to handle irregular shapes	(5) Develop auto-insert mechanisms that handle irregular shapes
(12)	Checker	(12) Changing switch positions	(12) Overdivision of labor	(12) Assign one operator for every 2 machines and lengthen the cycle time
(13)	"	(13) Waste in division of labor	(13) Too many operators	(13) Use a jig to change switch positions
		(14) Recycle pallets	(14) Use of conveyor	(14) Remove conveyor and create U-shaped cell

doing manual-insert work while managers worked separately. But removing waste requires a vertical-handling approach, such as seen at level 4 in the steps for reducing manpower described previously. There only needs to be one manager assigned to the line. The purpose of using the auto-insertion devices is to reduce manpower requirements and to eliminate defects.

The third largest amount of waste was found in having two solder dip processes. The improvement group looked into why the PCBs had to be dipped in solder twice. They found that the cutter was unable to make a clean cut and cracks developed where the solder was attached. To make up for the inadequate cutter, the PCBs were given a second dip, which caused another defect problem: Solder bridges formed in places where too much solder had adhered.

These defects were fixed at the finishing and rework processes. Thus, the line was kept very busy producing and dealing with waste.

To solve this problem, they first returned to the source of the problem and established optimal soldering conditions for each type of PCB. Next, they decided to have a short insert with a single dip and to use an electric nipper to remove impurities. They also introduced a free-shape inserter to bring the auto-insert rate close to 90 percent. All remaining components were to have short inserts and were to be given just one solder dip; an electric device was to be used for mechanized transfer during the impurity removal stage. One small improvement was to perform a cutter blade changeover after every two hours of use, an operation that they recognized would have to be done within the cycle time to prevent the production of waste.

The fourth largest amount of waste was found in the use of round conveyors for manual-insert operations. This was probably caused by an unbalanced allotment of work among the line workers, a problem exacerbated by the fact that the most proficient workers can work about twice as fast as the least proficient ones.

When one of the more proficient workers is absent, this proficiency gap becomes quite obvious, as was the case for the type C PCB at process 3, where the processing time rose to 114 seconds (see Table 14-2). At level 4, we address the fact that such proficiency gaps among workers result in standby waste.

The fifth largest amount of waste was found in defects caused by careless mistakes during manual insertion. These defects show up as "missing components," "backward polarity," "incorrectly inserted components," and so on.

However, the true underlying cause for such defects is the forced flow of the conveyor line. When people working at different speeds are forced to keep the same pitch time at the same conveyor, such defects will arise. The waste-removing solutions for this are made at level 4.

The sixth largest amount of waste was standby waste due to missing items. The apparent cause is a failure on the part of the company that supplies the items. The true cause, however, is Company A's inadequate preliminary checking and stock-keeping.

There are three approaches for removing this type of waste.

1. Use a tickler system. All components that are to be assembled tomorrow should be checked over this morning so that any missing items can be ordered for express delivery from the supplier. A meeting to report on missing items could be held at 11:00 AM, for example.

2. Use a "just-in-day" system, in which we divide the parts transaction cycle into a 1-1-1 system. The supplier delivers parts once a day, at which time it receives the order for the next day's parts. The order forms use a 1-1-1 type of code worked out by the people concerned at the supplier company. This code is shown on plates that are similar to kanban but, to avoid confusion, should not be described as kanban.

3. Use electronic kanban.

The seventh largest amount of waste was motion waste. This waste was identified when the process-specific waste elimination table was created and made it clear how wasteful motions, such as the following, were (see Table 14-3).

1. Waste in masking.

    During the finishing processes, it is wasteful to manually apply tape to the PCBs and later remove it. Mechanized transfer machines that handle such solder removal automatically are commercially available.

2. Bending insert wires on manually inserted components to prevent them from coming loose is wasteful.
    - Free-shape insert machines are commercially available.
    - A jig could be used to prevent loosening of components, or other techniques (such as short inserts) can be used for the same purpose.
    - Automatic insert wire-bending machines are commercially available.

3. Manual operations for different types of PCBs.

    Different small presses that are commercially available can be used to remove waste through mechanization.

4. Waste in positioning components during manual insertion.

    It is particularly difficult for the less proficient workers to position components for insertion when the PCB is moving in pace with the forced flow of the conveyor line. This problem requires a level-4 solution. There are always ways to avoid having to insert components into moving PCBs.

5. Waste in changing several connectors.

    This happens often at inspection processes. Although it requires some investment, it is worthwhile to have a switch for the connectors. An auto tester is also advised.

6. Waste in picking up and setting down parts and in returning containers.

    The cause is horizontal handling. The approach toward its removal is to find ways to eliminate these manual tasks.

To remove wasteful motions, we can apply the following ten rules.

Rule 1: First identify the standby waste.

Standby is to motion what retention is to the flow of goods. The fastest workers might have twice as much standby as the slowest workers. This kind of waste will always arise unless we keep a close eye on how the work gets divided up. This is especially true in the case of manual insertion work.

Even when auto-insert mechanisms are being used, we should watch for standby waste in the form of workers who spend a lot of time walking around, who work slowly or intermittently, or who merely supervise the auto-insert devices or other machinery.

Rule 2: Remove variation so that actual time stays within (+ or −) 5 percent of the cycle time.

To establish cycle time-based production, we need to establish standard operations in processes that have wide variation in operation times. After our standard operations combination chart shows that we have removed standby waste, our next task is to establish cycle time-based production.

When the actual time (measured time) is within (+ or −) 5 percent of the cycle time, we still need to be on the lookout for variation and eliminate its causes whenever it arises. Most variation has external causes, such as variation in supplied components. The rework needed for such components, such as defective parallel leads, also causes variation in timing that makes cycle-time production more difficult.

Rule 3: Set up the worktables at elbow height.

In golf or baseball, the correct swing is one that does not overextend or overbend the elbows. The same goes for the worker's position relative to the work table.

It is especially important that PCB mounting tables be set up at the proper height. If they are too high, the workers' shoulders get tired; if they are too low, their backs get tired.

Rule 4: Lay out tools and parts so that they can be picked up using a "breast stroke" type of arm movements. Also train workers in using both hands to do insert work.

It has long been known that the most efficient way of working is to use both hands at once. (See the pattern shown in Figure 14-5.) The workers should be so trained when mounting components on PCBs. This does not mean that using two hands is twice as efficient as using just one. The brief positioning judgment must be made for each hand independently. Because the timing in using both hands slows the manual-insert operation down by about 0.6 seconds from its one-handed speed, the overall efficiency gain in using both hands is only about 40 percent.

This substantial reduction in motion waste can be reached gradually as the workers get accustomed to using both hands at once.

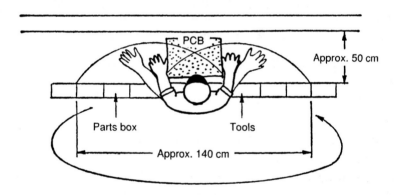

Figure 14-5. Range of Motions in Standing While Working Position

Rule 5: In cases of standing operations, let workers move around.

I suspect that many of you have read a lot of improvement case studies describing new production systems in which assembly conveyor workers are moved from sitting to standing positions while working. However, it is easy to get the wrong impression from these case studies.

As an example of what I mean, let's ask ourselves which is the most comfortable position on a long and crowded train ride: (1) remaining seated the entire time, (2) standing in one place the entire time, or (3) moving about, as does the conductor or snack vendor. Most people would agree that moving about is the most comfortable position.

Earlier we saw a photo of some workers who were standing while working at a free-flow conveyor line. The workers really did not enjoy having to stand in one place while working, but they did not want to be branded as "rebels" against the new production system. Putting their weight on one leg at a time to give the other leg a rest, they tried their best to make the situation tolerable.

When planning new methods of operation, IE experts need to pay attention to how well those methods serve their objectives. They also must have a good grasp of what standing while working really means — and that workers prefer to move around rather than stand or sit in one place.

Rule 6: Reduce the number of motions.

The most commonly found unnecessary motions are searching, finding, selecting, reaching, carrying, and positioning motions. We can see this just by observing the worker's eye movements. Such unnecessary motions each take about 0.6 seconds and add up quickly to create surplus work-hours.

Rule 7: Maintain a steady rhythm.

Assembly operations should proceed as smoothly as a waltz. Things go easier that way. If we can maintain a steady rhythm, we can keep the operation time to within (+ or −) 5 percent of the cycle time and can eliminate careless mistakes.

Careless mistakes are difficult to eliminate, however, and often destroy the rhythm. We must be particularly careful to use checklists for assembly line operations and to note any operations that seem strange, since they are likely to contain the causes of breaks in the production rhythm.

Rule 8: Set the top surface standards to make difficult insertions easier.

Long inserts need only meet the top surface standards and thus take less time to position. Even though short inserts must approximate the rear surface standards as well, they are better overall because they require less finishing work.

Rule 9: Leave workpieces so that they are easy for the next person to pick up.

When we make a motion study of setting up and putting back waste, we find that these operations consist of about ten different motions. These include searching, finding, reaching, picking up, carrying, positioning, and putting down.

Some of this waste is due to the person at the previous process not leaving the object in an easy position for the next person to pick up. For example, it makes more sense to have the object passed manually to the next person's work table rather than having it set down on the conveyor, from where the next person will have to reach to get it.

Rule 10: Do not repeat the same motion several times.

We know there is waste if the same motion is repeated two or more times in the same cycle. Ways to eliminate such wasteful motions include the use of mechanized transfer devices (such as auto-feed or auto-stop mechanisms) or the linkage of processes. For example, if a two-person operation can be condensed into a one-person operation, we can reduce the amount of picking up and setting down waste by half.

The key to finding this type of waste is to cultivate a skillful eye for studying motion. Unless we can break down manual operations into motion elements, we will find it very difficult to remove this type of waste.

Eighth on the list of the most common types of waste is changeover waste. When round conveyors are used, changeover waste is greatest when changeover is done all at once for the entire line. We can reduce waste by changing to successive changeover. We should reorganize the assembly line into families of processes, and then create a U-shaped cell for each family. This will enable us to achieve zero changeover.

Ninth on the list is in-process inventory waste, the primary cause of which is a long conveyor. A second cause is the division of processes.

Tenth and last on the list is conveyance waste. The causes for this are the same causes noted previously for in-process inventory waste.

At this point, we have reached level 4. I encourage all electronic component assembly plants to attempt reaching level 5. This highest level ensures the highest profitability and will help stem the outflow of manufacturing to other countries.

REDUCING PERSONNEL REQUIREMENTS BY HALF ON A PCB MOUNTING LINE

In the first part of this chapter, we discussed the ten most common types of waste in PCB mounting operations. The top seven were:

1. a 100 percent defect rate (rework rate) following the solder dip process
2. unnecessary use of manual insertion (overstaffing)
3. having two solder dip processes
4. use of round conveyors for manual-insert operations (standby waste)
5. defects caused by careless mistakes during manual insertion
6. standby waste due to missing items
7. motion waste

The factors leading most toward higher costs are an unnecessary use of manual insertion (overstaffing) and a 100 percent defect rate (rework rate) after the solder dip process. Accordingly, our first two priorities for reducing costs should be (1) to reduce the number of people performing manual insert work and (2) to reduce solder dip defects.

We can see proof of this by looking at the personnel organization at Company A. Twenty-six people are employed as manual insertion (PCB mounting) workers, 17 as first-stage finishers, and five as second-stage finishers, for a total of 48 people in the PCB mounting line. Although the term "finisher" has a nice ring to it, the fact is that these two stages of finishing processes are really just rework processes for fixing defects that occur at the PCB mounting and soldering processes. In this part of the chapter, we will discuss how the personnel requirements on this PCB mounting line can be reduced by half by removing the major obstacle of the defects that are always produced in the solder dip processes.

Behind the 100 Percent Solder Dip Defects Is Production Engineering's Failure to Keep Up with Design Engineering

The designer's art in today's electronics industry is the pursuit of increasingly complex designs on increasingly smaller surfaces. This pursuit combines advances in surface mounting technology with advances in performance characteristics.

The stage for many of these advances is the printed circuit board (PCB). Sophisticated PCBs are finding their way into a wide range of applications, including automotive electronics, engines, pumps, and motors. Although I do not have an engineer's expertise, I have observed two tendencies:

First, it seems that there is a shift away from inserting components to merely laying them down on the PCB. Figure 14-6 illustrates the difficult positioning work involved in manually inserting PCB components. When each component has several pins (n) that must be positioned over their respective holes (P), the potential for positioning defects is P to the nth power.

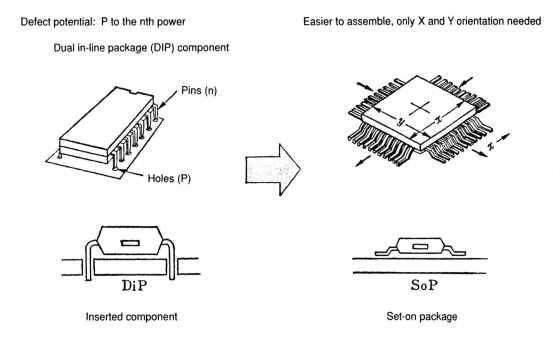

Figure 14-6. **From Inserted Components to Set Components**

Setting down components also involves surface positioning standards and the key to both types of PCB mounting work is accurate positioning. Nonetheless, set-on packages are easier to position than dual in-line packages (DIPs) (see Figure 14-6). As the PCBs grow more crowded with components, new ways must be found to speed up the chip-mounting process.

Secondly, I have noticed that the density (a value we call "β") of components on PCBs is increasing from about 20 percent to about 50 percent. This has led to PCB designs that have components mounted on both sides of the board or in layers. PCB designers are beginning to think like high-rise architects who design buildings that contain many layers of offices, restaurants, recreation facilities, medical clinics, underground garages, and so on.

The battle for survival in the electronics industry is being waged in part in the arena of PCBs, where set-on components compete for PCB real estate with dual-in line components. As long as PCB manufacturers must perform rework on 100 percent of its solder-dipped PCBs, they stand in risk of losing this battle to whoever first substantially reduces or eliminates these solder dip defects.

The March 30, 1987 edition of Japan's *Asahi Shimbun* newspaper contained the following information:

> In June 1986, Kazuo Fukano, 48, head of the labor union at Fukushima Sansui Co., Ltd., a subsidiary of Sansui Electric, reported that his company had just sent off a Taiwan-bound truckload of automatic soldering machines and auto-insert machines used for PCB production.
>
> These machines had been brought into Fukushima Sansui in the early 1980s to boost the company's competitiveness. However, last year, parent company Sansui asked for the voluntary early retirement of 380 Fukushima Sansui employees and announced that it was moving some of its production facilities to an affiliated company in Taiwan. As a result, Fukushima Sansui has laid off 216 employees, most of whom are women, and will use part-time workers to fill future needs.

Not mentioned in the article is the main reason why Sansui decided to move PCB production to Taiwan: The automatic soldering machines have a 100 percent defect rate, which raises personnel costs for all the manual rework. I think it would be safe to bet that, if the company had somehow been able to cut the number of PCB production personnel in half, it could have kept its PCB production in Japan. This is clearly a defeat suffered by production engineering.

Steps in Determining Optimal Solder Dip Conditions

In the era when single product models were turned out in large lots, it was easy to establish and maintain optimal solder dip conditions. Since then, however, many advances have been made in PCB design.

Figure 14-7 illustrates how, over the years, the density β of components on PCBs has evolved from what we might call a "rural" stage to an "urban high-rise" stage. Since the automatic soldering machines still use the same conditions for all PCB types as it did when PCBs were at the rural stage, it is no surprise that all of the solder-dipped PCBs require rework. In fact, it would be a surprise if a single nondefective PCB were produced.

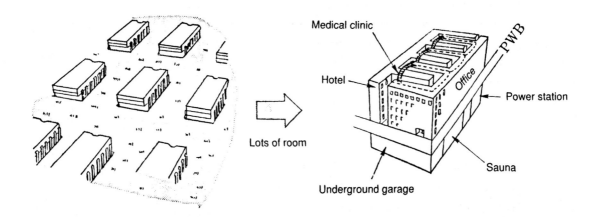

Rural stage of component density on PCBs   **Urban high-rise stage of component density on PCBs**

Figure 14-7. The Same Solder Dip Conditions No Longer Apply

So, what can be done about this situation? The following steps will tell.

Step 1: Form a U-shaped cell study group to study zero-defect production systems.

This study group does not need a large membership, but it does need imaginative and methodical people who are interested in production engineering challenges.

Step 2: Create a table that lists where defects occur in different PCB models, locations, and components. Find ways to eliminate the causes of each type of defect.

Use this table to find out in which PCB models and in which patterns the defects occur most frequently under common dip conditions. Table 14-4 illustrates such a table, although the contents will vary from company to company.

Table 14-4. Defects Listed by PCB Type and Location

Model	PCB	Location	Bridge Con-stant	Bridge Vari-able	Tunnel Con-stant	Tunnel Vari-able	Loose (floating) Con-stant	Loose (floating) Vari-able	Dirty flux Con-stant	Dirty flux Vari-able	Other	Total Con-stant	Total Vari-able
A	P_1 (top)	Top left											
		Top right											
		Bottom right											
		Bottom left											
	P_2 (mid-dle)	Top left											
		Top right											
		Bottom right											
		Bottom left											
	P_3 (bot-tom)	Top left											
		Top right											
		Bottom right											
		Bottom left											
B	P_1	Top left											
		Top right											
		Bottom right											
		Bottom left											
	P_2	Top left											
		Top right											
		Bottom right											
		Bottom left											

Next, the study group compares the data in the table and checks this against the factory floor operations. When addressing each problem, members should ask the question "why" at least five times.

The group should then study the differences in the defect occurrence patterns. For example, it could ask why Type A PCBs have more bridge defects and why Type B PCBs have more loose solder defects. This is another way to use the "5 Why" approach to find the causes of problems. Ironically, older models of production equipment tend to produce fewer defects than do newer models. This is because people have learned through long experience how to establish optimal conditions in the older equipment.

When many different types of PCBs are being dipped, solder dip machine operators are loath to reset the solder dip conditions for each different PCB type and would rather find a condition setting that can be used for all PCB types.

The result, of course, is 100 percent defective PCBs in need of rework. However, if we take the trouble to determine exactly the exact optimal conditions for each types of PCB, we will find it worth the trouble to frequently change the conditions in order to eliminate the need for rework.

Step 3: Create families of PCBs.

Create families of PCBs based on the density α of set-on components and the overall density β. Table 14-5 shows a list of PCB families.

Table 14-5. PCB Families

Chip (component) / Density		Inserted (dual in-line) type		
		β_1	β_2	β_3
Set-on type	a_1	F_1	F_2	F_3
	a_2	F_4	F_5	F_6
	a_3	F_7	F_8	F_9

In the table, we have three Alpha categories and three Beta categories:

α_1: few PCBs (up to 10 percent)
α_2: some PCBs (11 to 20 percent)
α_3: many PCBs (31 percent or more)
β_1: few PCBs (as few as 30 percent)
β_2: some PCBs (30 to 40 percent)
β_3: many PCBs (41 percent or more)

These categories make the vertical and horizontal axes of the table, producing nine PCB families, each with its own optimal conditions.

Step 4: Study the key factors in the solder dip process.

To discover the key factors in the solder dip process, we must identify the causes of solder dip defects. The factors we are looking for must be conditions that can be controlled in the factory. No matter how strong an influence any particular factor has on the occurrence of defects in this process, there is no point in considering that factor unless it is something that can be controlled in the factory.

For example, let us consider the factor of chip intervals (see Figure 14-8).

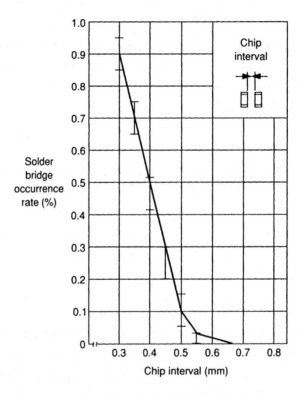

Figure 14-8. Relation between Rectangular Chip Intervals and Solder Bridges

In considering this factor, we cannot think of design factors such as the presence or absence of solder resist layers. We must look at the problem strictly from the factory floor perspective and ask what factors are controllable. Of course, if the same company also designed the product, certain things can be done at the design level. Otherwise, we must go with factors and characteristic levels that can be controlled only in the factory. Table 14-6 lists some of these.

Some factors were not included in Table 14-6 due to lack of space. The study group, however, should be sure to make complete listings. Their objective is to find methods, processing conditions, and characteristic levels that are

Table 14-6. Controllable Factors

Symbol	Factor	Level
A	Flux brand	Current brand A_1 or A_2 brand
B	Flux amount (time)	Current amount B_1 or B_2 amount
C	Flux thickness	Current thickness C_1 or C_2 thickness
D	Flux temperature	Current temperature D_1 or D_2 temperature
E	Solder brand	Current brand E_1 or E_2 brand
F	Solder amount (time)	Current amount F_1 or F_2 amount
G	Solder temperature	Current temperature G_1 or G_2 temperature
H	Soldering method	Single-layer H_1 or double-layer H_2 method
	In the double-layer method, a second layer of solder is laid on to avoid the accumulation of air toward the back of the first layer.	
J	No. of solder replace-ments	Once daily J_1 or twice daily J_2
K	PCB attachment method	Random-flow attachment K_1 or pattern-flow attachment K_2
	This factor may be a block factor. For some PCBs, the PCB attachment method determines whether the solder flows onto the PCB randomly or in a pattern in relation to the process direction.	
L	Preheater temperature	Current temperature L_1 or new temperature L_2

in any way more effective in preventing solder dip defects and that can be controlled in the factory.

When considering characteristic levels, they should always make comparisons with the current levels. In one case, a study group considered two levels and 11 factors. This adds up to 2^{11} in possible combinations. The goal is to select the optimal processing conditions from among these many possible combinations of levels and factors. However, 2^{11} is 4,096, and we can hardly expect any study group to carry out over 4,000 tests to find the best combination. Instead, the group can plan to have eight-round units of tests repeated N times.

- Plan A: Repeat an orthogonal table for L_8 N times (two or more times).
- Plan B: Use the process of elimination to gradually narrow the focus on possible factors.

The disadvantage of using an orthogonal table (plan A) is that confusion arises in the factory whenever a characteristic level is changed. It is possible to do factory tests using small orthogonal tables, but these still often cause confusion. Such tests can be done without causing confusion (1) if the factory has the proper test equipment so that the actual process can be bypassed, and (2) if a manager or someone other than a line worker is available to help. Such is not always possible in smaller companies.

Plan B's gradual elimination of factors is better for factories that do not have separate test equipment or extra staff available for testing. However, the factories do need the following:

1. The process of elimination has to be done using the production facilities and the staff that are turning out the current products. For example, these people must be organized as a team to carry out the process together. They must also plan the tests together and execute them together in the factory. In addition, the condition settings must be double-checked each time.
2. The test should occur whenever a changeover has been made for a different product model.
3. To prevent defects, variation in levels must be kept to within 0.5 Sigma.
4. The repetition of tests should be kept to a minimum.

Table 14-7 shows how factors and levels can be listed, and Table 14-8 shows how the elimination table can be organized.

Table 14-7. List of Solder Dip Factors and Levels for Elimination Process

Symbol	Factor	Current level	Level under consideration
A	Flux brand	A_1	A_2
B	Flux amount (time)	B_1	B_2
C	Flux thickness	C_1	C_2
D	Flux temperature	D_1	D_2

To begin with, we test only for the optimal flux condition and for only the F_5 family of PCBs. Using the current solder dip conditions as our reference level, we set what we think may be a slightly better level and then check it to eliminate factors in a step-by-step approach:

Step 1: Table 14-8 shows the results when test 1 is done for PCB changeover using the current method.

Step 2: Using the test results, we divide the nondefective PCBs from the defective ones and take the number of defectives as our result data.

Table 14-8. Factor Elimination Table

Factor	Brand	Amount	Thick-ness	Temp-erature	Defect data					(P$_2$)
					Location (P$_1$)					
Symbol No.	A	B	C	D	Bridge	Tunnel	Loose	Other	Total	
1	1	1	1	1	y_{11}	y_{12}	y_{13}	y_{14}	Y_1	
2	2	1	1	1	y_{21}	y_{22}	y_{23}	y_{24}	Y_2	P$_1$ P$_2$
3	2	2	1	1	y_{31}	y_{32}	y_{33}	y_{34}	Y_3	P$_3$ P$_4$
4	2	2	2	1	y_{41}	y_{42}	y_{43}	y_{44}	Y_4	
5	2	2	2	2	y_{51}	y_{52}	y_{53}	y_{54}	Y_5	
				Total	Σy_1	Σy_2	Σy_3	Σy_4	ΣY	

Note: "–1" indicates the current method; "–2" a new method.

We then analyze these data in terms of the location of the defects (P$_1$, P$_2$, P$_3$, or P$_4$) and the number of defects per defective PCB. We also must measure the time required for rework, since this time measurement will be used as supplemental data. We must check the number of defects this way for each of the defect locations (P-1, P-2, P-3, and P-4). At least ten of the same type of PCB should be tested, so that we can see how consistent the defects are and map their distribution on a PCB mounting chart.

Step 3: We carry out test 2 on the next PCB model changeover day. We also check the results and the various defect data for each PCB to obtain a y_{21}, y_{22}.....Y_2 value. We then continue with these tests so that we gradually accumulate more and more data on optimal conditions.

Step 4: Once we have gathered all the required data, we can see the results for each factor and can select the optimal processing conditions for the solder dip process via the following successive subtractions:
- Results for factor A (brand)   = $Y_2 - Y_1$
- Results for factor B (amount)   = $Y_3 - Y_2$
- Results for factor C (thickness)   = $Y_4 - Y_3$
- Results for factor D (temperature) = $Y_5 - Y_4$

This combination shows the optimal processing conditions. One tends to think of PCB mounting as purely an electronics technology. We see now that its solder dip process involves some chemistry as well.

Chemical processes tend to use rather large and complex machinery. Figure 14-9 shows the equipment used in a PCB mounting line that includes a solder dip process, finishing process, and inspection process, all laid out in a straight line. In this kind of line, it is very difficult to switch among optimal solder dip processing conditions for different PCB families.

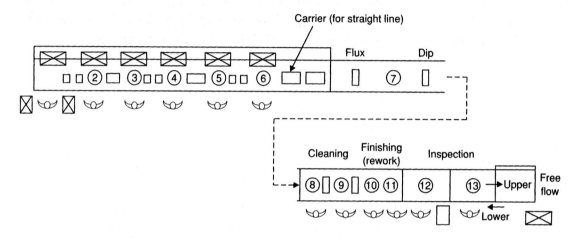

Figure 14-9. Large-lot Type of Solder Dip and 100 Percent Rework Line

Companies must be prepared to manufacture their own solder dip vats for small-lot production, since all the commercially available types are for large-lot production.

This part of the chapter may have been difficult for less experienced readers to follow. Our main concern here is not skill or experience level but rather the solder dip process itself. I would also like to remind readers that eliminating solder dip defects is the key to staying ahead of the competition and preventing a drain of manufacturing industry to other countries, such as the NIEs. I invite any reader who is seriously interested in reducing solder dip defects at his or her own company to write me via my publisher and include a schematic diagram, layout chart, solder dip condition list, and other pertinent data about the solder dip process under study.

Remember — reducing solder dip defects by half translates to a 50 percent reduction in PCB mounting line personnel requirements.

TEST YOUR SKILLS

Table 14-9 shows the test data for determining the optimal solder dip conditions based on an eight-series test (L_8). There are five factors listed (A, B, C, D, and E) as well as two levels. The data are divided into nine locations along the vertical and horizontal axes of the table. The defect points are from 50 PCBs, and the defects are categories (S [short], M [unsoldered], or H [undersoldered]). Find which factors have the best results and determine the optimal conditions.

Table 14-9. Test Data for Determining Optimal Solder Dip Conditions

Test No.	A Soldering method	B Flux density	C Relative speed	D Preheater temperature	E Solder temperature	P1 K1 S	P1 K1 M	P1 K1 H	P1 K2 S	P1 K2 M	P1 K2 H	P1 K3 S	P1 K3 M	P1 K3 H	P2 K1 S	P2 K1 M	P2 K1 H	P2 K2 S	P2 K2 M	P2 K2 H	P2 K3 S	P2 K3 M	P2 K3 H	P3 K1 S	P3 K1 M	P3 K1 H	P3 K2 S	P3 K2 M	P3 K2 H	P3 K3 S	P3 K3 M	P3 K3 H	Total
1	New	Current (−1)	Current (−1)	Current (−1)	Current (−1)																18									8			26
2	"	Current	−α	+V	+α					22											17	32					14						85
3	"	+α	−α	Current	+α																25						7						32
4	"	+α	Current	+V	Current								6								16									10			32
5	Old	Current (−1)	Current	Current	+α				5			8									23									12			48
6	"	Current	−α	+α	Current				7			24						6	28		19	22			18		4		21	14	25		188
7	"	+α	−α	Current	Current																21			28									49
8	"	+α	Current	+α	+α							6						7			23		9				6			7			58
Total									12	22		38	6					13	28		162	54	9	28	18		31		21	51	25		518

Defect items: S = short, M = unsoldered, H = undersoldered

Defect location (PCB diagram)

About the Author

Kenichi Sekine was a 1944 graduate of the Navy Air Force Academy and attended Kurume Industrial Special School in 1948. He joined Bridgestone in 1948 and remained until 1972. At Bridgestone, as chief QC inspector, he introduced TQC and promoted activity for the company's application for the Deming Prize. From 1968 to 1972, he worked for an affiliate of Toyota Motors where he promoted the Toyota Production System (TPS).

In 1973, he left and founded the TPS Consulting Group. Under his direction, the group:

- provided consulting on worksite IE to Toyota-affiliated companies
- built U-shaped lines in an assembly department at Oriental Motors
- built U-shaped line at Nuinac
- built load-load lines in an assembly department at T Company
- minimized automatic assembly personnel at Uni Charm and provided consulting on the JIT production system
- built assembly lines with minimal personnel at TDK
- provided consulting on the high-diversified small-lot production systems in Nagano Prefecture
- provided consulting on worksite IE to Komatsu
- provided consulting to TPS to Danden
- improved the assembly lines at Japan Marantz
- provided consulting to Ishida
- provided consulting on setup improvement to Tateishi Electric
- provided consulting on inventory reduction and setup improvement to Kunimitsu Paper

- provided consulting on worksite to a Komatsu affiliate
- provided consulting on setup improvement of the packaging line at Ajinomoto
- provided consulting on TPS to a Yanma Diesel affiliate
- improved processing lines at Fuyo Industry
- introduced and promoted TPS to Facom (France)

In 1985, he founded the Added Value Management Institute (TPS Consulting Company, Ltd.). Among its achievements, the company:

- built U-shaped lines in a motor department at Mitsubishi Electric in Korea (productivity improved by 50 percent)
- built U-shaped lines in a electronics assembly department at Toyo Precision Industry (OPC) in Korea (productivity improved by 30 percent)
- built U-shaped lines in an electronics assembly department at Modern Electronics in Korea (productivity improved by 30 percent)
- converted conveyor lines into U-shaped lines in an air conditioner plant at Daiu Career in Korea (productivity improved 30 percent). Cut setup time in half. Cut shaft processing personnel from eleven to five.
- built U-shaped line in an assembly department at Mikuni Industry (productivity improved by 100 percent)

Sekine's expertise lies in the specific areas of implementing TPS, zero setup, cutting assembly/processing personnel in half, cutting the designing period and personnel in half, innovative Total Productive Maintenance (TPM), and inventory reduction. He has produced numerous books and videos in Japanese. This is his first book available in English.

Index

Printed in the United States
38236LVS00002B/1-24

9 781563 273254